Heinz A. Richter

Cyprus in the 19th & 20th Century
Collected Articles

PELEUS

STUDIEN ZUR

GESCHICHTE GRIECHENLANDS UND ZYPERNS

HERAUSGEGEBEN VON HEINZ A. RICHTER

BAND 108

HARRASSOWITZ VERLAG WIESBADEN
IN KOMMISSION

VORMALS VERLAG FRANZ PHILIPP RUTZEN
WWW.RUTZEN-VERLAG.DE

Heinz A. Richter

Cyprus in the 19th & 20th Century
Collected Articles

Translated and modified

2021

HARRASSOWITZ VERLAG • WIESBADEN
IN KOMMISSION

PELEUS
Studien zur Archäologie und Geschichte Griechenlands und Zyperns
Herausgegeben von Heinz A. Richter
Band 108

Umschlagvignetten:
Umschlagbild: Wikipedia NASA Zypern
Gegenüber Titelblatt: Innenbild einer Schale des Peithinosmalers, Berlin, Pergamonmuseum (CVA Berlin 2, Taf. 61).

Bibliografische Information der Deutschen Nationalbibliothek
Die Deutsche Nationalbibliothek verzeichnet diese Publikation in der Deutschen Nationalbibliografie; detaillierte bibliografische Daten sind im Internet über http://dnb.d-nb.de abrufbar.

Bibliographic information published by the Deutsche Nationalbibliothek
The Deutsche Nationalbibliothek lists this publication in the Deutsche Nationalbibliografie; detailed bibliographic data are available in the internet at http://dnb.d-nb.de

Printed in Germany on fade resistant and archival quality paper (PH 7 neutral).
Gesamtherstellung: Beltz Bad Langensalza GmbH, Bad Langensalza

www.harrassowitz-verlag.de

ISBN 978-3-447-11629-9
ISSN 1868-1476

CONTENT

I dedicate this book to my old friend

Hans Hummel

in gratitude for his life-long friendship

INTRODUCTION

The history of Cyprus is one of my research fields, the other is Greece. I wrote four volumes on Cypriot history[1] and numerous comprehensive studies on Greek history. Many of these deal with Greek history in depth, e.g. WWI, the Greek Turkish War, the Metaxas Dictatorship, WWII, the Dekemvriana, the Civil War, and the Military Junta. In my four volumes of the history of Cyprus I touched upon all topics dealt with in the present study. In spite of the length of these four volumes the single aspects were dealt with rather sketchily. Yet there are historical events that demand more detailed descriptions.

There are events in the history of both countries which deserve special attention and demand a more detailed analysis. In my functin as coeditor of the interdisciplinary journal THETIS which exclusively dealt with Greece and Cyprus I found the possibility to publish on those topics that needed an in-depth treatment. All of these contributions were all written in German. In addition to these studies I had the opportunity to publish several articles in other German language periodicals. Sine German is no longer a leading scholarly language among historians, only few scholars took note of them. When I realized several years ago, I decided to translate those of my studies into English that might be of interest for international scholars.

The English editions of these studies reached afar larger audience. I therefore decided to also translate those of my articles which I consider to be of major interest.

The first article contains a description how Cyprus became British in the 19th century.The second article described how Cyprus left the Ottoman world and became a European country, While all other states which had been parts of the Ottoman Empire retained the political culture of clientelism through today. Cyprus abandoned this Ottoman tradition as early as the 1920s. This is the reason why the Soviets considered the Cypriot comrades as Western Europeans and sent them for training to the academy of Western European commuist parties. All other CPs from former Ottoman states were sent to KUTV the university of the eastern peoples.

Similarly the Communist Party of Cyprus (KKK) and later the AKEL were not orthodox communist parties but rather left leaning social democratic parties. This was one reason why later the General Secretary of AKEL Christofias was eleccted president and no one in Western Europe was surprised.

The Constitution of Cyprus is one of the most complicated in Europe. It was designed to enable the two peoples on Cyprus to live peacefully together. This could have worked without the interference of the so-called mother countries. This interference, however, caused not only a division between thee two peoples but also divisions within those two groups as well. The assassination attempt on Makarios and the murder of the interior minister Georkatzis were the results of this rift.

The coup of 1974 by the Greek junta and the ensuing Turkish invasion is one of the most horrific events in Cypriot history. This article analyzes Henry Kissinger's attitude vis-à-vis this event and it is plausibly showb that he might have stopped the horrible developmebts, however, he did not do this forreasons that remain incomprehensible, as the article argues in detail.

The High Level Agreement might have led to a reconciliation of the two ethnic groups of Cyprus, but Turkey intervened and prohibited it. The Varoşa versus Nicosia airport deal would have been positive for both groups but it was torpedoed by Denktash for incomprehensible reasons.

---

1 Heinz A. Richter, *Geschichte der Insel Zypern 1878-1977* Band 1-4 (Möhnesee: Bibliopolis, 2004-2009)

While all articles go into details the last article is an overview of all the events until the end of the 20th century; it is a kind of resume of the entire period.

All articles deal with important events in the 19th and 20th century and were published in German in the 1990s. Chronologically they end with the imminent entry into the EU. Membership in the EU became a kind of live insurance for the Cypriot state. Turkey presumably will not dare attack an EU member state. Because of its attitude towards Cyprus it preventing its own entry into the union.

Recently the conflict deepened. Some time ago Prime Minister Erdoğan announced that he planned to annex the North of the island. When recently gas was found in the sea floor he violated the international sea law by claiming parts of the sea shelf that clearly belongs to Cyprus. He even sent exploration vessels there. In this way the Cyprus conflict is continuing and there is no end in sight.

THE GRAND GAME

the Balkans, the Congress of Berlin and Cyprus

In 1878 Great Britain and the Ottoman Empire concluded a Convention by which Cyprus was leased to the British until that distant day in the future agreement, when the Russians would move out of Batum, Ardahan and Kars in Armenia. This Convention, the *Cyprus Convention* as it was soon called, was the result of highly complex developments far away from the island, which had begun half a century earlier. In my following exposition I will try to give an outline of the main strands of the story and their interdependence

There were two main causes which led to the Cyprus Convention: the growing unrest among the peoples in the Balkans and the global rivalry of Great Britain and Russia known as the *Grand Game*. But these conflicts were well known all through the nineteenth century and until 1878 had not had any influence on Cyprus. This time, however, it was different.

The event, which in 1875 triggered the new development, was one of those periodical peasant revolts against merciless tax farmers in the Ottoman provinces of Herzegovina and Bosnia. In the past the Turks had crushed such revolts easily, but this time there were three new factors which gave this local rebellion an international dimension,[2] namely the pan-Serbian and pan-Slav movements, and Austro-Hungarian expansionism. The Pan-Serbs in Beograd dreamed of a Greater Serbia including all south Slavs. The Russian Pan-Slavists wanted to unite all Slavs under the lead of Russia. The Austrians abhorred the idea of a Greater Serbia and therefore aimed at the annexation of Bosnia-Herzegovina. Both, the Russians and the Austrians agreed that the Ottoman Empire had to be dissolved, however, they disagreed about the method to achieve dissolution and even more so about the share each of them should get; consequently war was threatening.

The situation was further complicated by two additional facts: The rivalling Austrians and Russians were allies of Germany in the *Dreikaiserbund* and the latter wanted to preserve this alliance. Furthermore there was Great Britain who wanted to keep the Russians away from the Mediterranean at almost any cost.

In order to avoid a general conflagration as in the Crimean War twenty years earlier, the Austrians and the Russians together with Bismarck worked out a compromise solution, the so-called *Berlin Memorandum*, which was accepted by the French and Italians as well. But the British refused to approve the compromise.[3]

Until 1874 Britain under Prime Minister Gladstone had followed a policy which was known as 'splendid isolation'. His successor, Disraeli, was an imperialist, i.e. he wanted to expand the British Empire and secure its maritime ways of communications. In his eyes the old European concert of powers controlled by British balance of power politics had been ruined by the creation of Germany. He wrongly distrusted Bismarck's assurances that Germany was *saturiert* [saturated] and rightly suspected the Russians and Austrians wishing to carve up the Ottoman Empire. In order to cope with this threatening situation he did his best to sow the seeds of discord among the members of the *Dreikaiserbund* and took measures to keep the Russians away from the Mediterranean and to strengthen the life line of the British Empire through the Mediterranean to India.[4] In 1875 he brought the Suez Canal under

---

2 Winfried Baumgart, *Europäisches Konzert und Nationale Bewegung. Internationale Beziehungen 1830-1878* (Paderborn: Schöningh, 1999), p. 420; Leften S Stavrianos, *The Balkans since 1453* (New York: Holt, Rinehart and Winston, 1965), p. 397.

3 Baumgart, *op. cit.*, p. 420; Stavrianos, *op. cit.*, p. 400.

4 Dwight E Lee, *Great Britain and the Cyprus Convention Policy of 1878* (Cambridge: Harvard UP, 1934), p.

British control by buying shares of the Egyptian Khedive and detached navy units to the Dardanelles.

In the meantime the revolt in Bosnia and Herzegovina had escalated into a war between Turkey and Serbia. In the spring of 1876 an upheaval of the Bulgarians was crushed by the Turks in such a brutal way that the *Dreikaiserbund* intervened and forced Turkey to conclude an armistice. In December 1876, an international conference was held in Constantinople. Though the three powers exerted considerable pressure on Turkey to initiate reforms, the British secretly backed the Turks enabling them to continue their intransigent policy. Thus, the conference of Constantinople failed.

This meant war. In order to avoid a direct confrontation with the British the Russians made a last diplomatic effort. In March 1877, Russia, Austria, Germany and Britain signed a protocol asking the Turks to introduce those reforms they themselves had proposed at the Conference of Constantinople three months earlier. The Turks, however, believed themselves to be in a position of strength and rejected the Russian proposal. Thereupon Russia declared war on the Ottoman Empire on 24 April 1877.

The Russians attacked in two directions: in the Balkans and in Trans-Caucasia. Romania consenting, they crossed the Danube and marched towards Sofia. A strong Turkish attack from the fortress of Plevna on the western flank stopped the thrust until December. But in January the fortress surrendered and the Russians advanced rapidly towards the Straits. At the end of January an armistice was signed which allowed the Russians to proceed to Agios Stefanos (today Yesilköy), a suburb of Istanbul; and on 3 March 1878 the peace treaty of San Stefano was signed.[1]

For British interests this peace treaty was a catastrophe. Among the many territorial changes was the creation of a Greater Bulgaria. The mere extension of this new state, from Lake Ochrida in the West, the Danube in the North, the Black Sea in the East, almost to Adrianople (today Edirne) in the Southeast and the Aegean in the South, was a provocation to all its neighbours. It was clear that this 'monster' state could only survive as a Russian satellite, and thus indirectly Russia would have become a littoral state of the Mediterranean, a nightmare for the British.

To make things worse, the Russians gained the Black Sea harbour of Batoum and the strategically important towns of Kars, Ardahan and Bajesid in Armenia. Obviously Russia was moving towards Mesopotamia and an advance towards Alexandretta (today Iskenderun) could no longer be excluded. At the same time the Straits were at the mercy of the Russians. In London the alarm bells rang: this peace treaty threatened Britain's route to India, the Life Line of the Empire. In Disraeli's eyes this treaty had to be revised thoroughly.

Ways to minimise the damage for Britain began to be considered when the possibility of a Russian-Turkish war had loomed on the horizon in late 1876. Recollections of the horrible Crimean War excluded any direct armed intervention. Another option had to be found. After intensive discussions among the military Colonel Robert Home reported: *England might maintain Turkey at the expense of enormous blood and treasure, but what good would that do? She had better leave Turkey to her fate and seize upon some place that would be of use to her such as the Dardanelles and Cyprus.* Alternatively, Crete, Egypt, or Rhodes or all three might be occupied.[2] The latter was a radical concept and Disraeli did not like it. He

---

19.

1 Adolf V. Horsetzky, "Der Russisch-Türkische Krieg 1877-1878", in: Hermann Franke (ed.), *Handbuch der Neuzeitlichen Wehrwissenschaften* (Berlin: Walter de Gruyter, 1936), pp. 367-371.

2 Lee, *op. cit.*, pp. 36, 38.

and his ambassador in Constantinople, Austen Henry Layard, *believed that England should support Turkey, aid her by diplomatic pressure to reform in the interests of both Christians and Mussulmans alike and thus continue to guard the route to India by maintaining the Sultan's rule over Constantinople, the Straits, and Armenia.*[1] But how this could be achieved was unclear.

In early 1877, London demanded Russian guarantees of British interests in the Suez Canal, Egypt, Constantinople, the Straits and the Persian Gulf, but the Russians refused to guarantee Constantinople and the Straits. During the Russian advance in Bulgaria, London fearing the occupation of Constantinople toyed with the idea of entering the war, but when the Russian advance was slowed down, the British politicians calmed down again and started exploring alternatives.[2]

In view of British interests in Asia Minor and Armenia and the safeguarding of the route to India the best solution seemed to be the acquisition of a *Place d'Armes* in the eastern Mediterranean. The Straits were dismissed quickly since there were no suitable harbours. After intensive studies of maps, Rhodes and Cyprus were found inapt for the purpose and Crete was disposed of because of the rebellious character of its inhabitants. The discussion procrastinated but when in November 1877 the Russians took Kars, London got nervous again.

The Press called for the occupation of Egypt and the conversion of Cyprus into a Gibraltar of the East from where the British Navy could control the Syrian coast, the Suez Canal and the Straits. Additionally, an old idea resurfaced: the project of building a railway from Alexandretta to the valleys of Euphrat and Tigris to Basra and from there to India. The starting point of this second route to India could be protected from Cyprus.[3]

When the British learned that the Russians had reached the Straits they despatched parts of the Navy there. Ambassador Layard successfully got the Sultan interested in the railway concept and offered a permanent alliance with Great Britain. In London the new Foreign Minister Salisbury liked the idea of an alliance with the Ottoman Empire and the acquisition of a *Place d'Armes* in the region. The question was whether this place would be situated in the Persian Gulf or in the Mediterranean. After analysing all political, geographic, military and commercial aspects, Colonel Home suggested that Cyprus was the most suitable place.

Thus, Britain had returned to a vision which had been formulated sixty years earlier: *The possession of Cyprus would give England a preponderating influence in the Mediterranean, and place at her disposal the future destinies of the Levant. Egypt and Syria would soon become her tributaries, and she would acquire an overawing position in respect to Asia Minor, by which the Porte might at all times be kept in check, and the encroachments of Russia, in this quarter, retarded, if not prevented. It would increase her commerce in a very considerable degree; ... It is of easy defence; and under a liberal government would in a very short space of time, amply repay the charge of its own establishment, and afford the most abundant supplies to our fleets at a trifling expense.*[4]

In the meantime diplomatic haggling about the revision of the San Stefano Treaty had begun. Towards the end of May 1878 the Russians signalled that they were ready to withdraw from the Balkans and accept a reduction of Bulgaria's size but that they would remain in Armenia. This was used as a pretext by the British to put pressure on the Sultan to con-

---

1 Ibid., p. 45.

2 *Ibid.*, p. 52f.

3 *Ibid.*, p. 67f.

4 John MacDonald Kinneir, *Journey through Asia Minor, Armenia, and Koordistan, in the Years of 1813 and 1814* (London, 1818), p. 185f, quoted by Lee, *op. cit.*, p. 80. In a similar way Disraeli in 1848: Benjamin Disraeli, *Tankred or the New Crusade* (London, 1848) *passim*.

clude the alliance. On 4 June 1878 a secret Defence Alliance, which became known as the Cyprus Convention, was signed. Its central provision was: As long as the Russians occupied those towns in Armenia, Great Britain promised to help the Sultan militarily in case of further Russian advances in Asia. In return the Sultan promised certain reforms in favour of his Christian subjects *"and in order to enable England to make necessary provision for executing her engagement, ... the Sultan further consents to assign the Island of Cyprus to be occupied and administered by England."*[1]

Thus, even before the Congress of Berlin redrew the boundaries of the Balkan countries, Cyprus had *de facto* changed its proprietor and since the Russians would hardly move out of Armenia this change was for good. The Cypriots had been no party in this development which had begun as a peasant revolt and led to a big oriental crisis; they were objects of this process and – ended as British subjects.

At the Congress of Berlin which lasted from 13 June to 13 July 1878 all statesmen of Europe met. The results were frustrating for all participants but one: Britain. The big power interests had prevailed; the freedom dreams of the enslaved peoples of the Ottoman Empire were sacrificed for reasons of state. Not one of the Balkan problems was solved; they were only covered up superficially to resurface again in the explosion of September 1914. Bismarck allegedly played the honest broker, in reality he had done his best to keep the oriental wound open secretly encouraging the other statesmen to carve up the Ottoman Empire, playing off one state against the other.

Britain succeeded in pushing the Russians back from the Mediterranean and halting their advance in Armenia. Thus, strictly speaking, the reason for the acquisition of Cyprus had become void. And as the Cyprus Convention had up to this point been kept secret, it could have been invalidated rather noiselessly. But diplomatic processes cannot be stopped abruptly without those involved fearing political damage and loss of prestige. So the final negotiations for the signature of the Sultan under the Cyprus Convention dragged on during the sessions of the Berlin Congress.

On 7 July 1878, the Sultan finally signed the *Firman* ratifying the Cyprus Convention. In the House of Commons Disraeli justified the acquisition of Cyprus on 18 July: *"In taking Cyprus the movement is not Mediterranean; it is Indian. We have taken a step there which we think necessary for the maintenance of our Empire and for its preservation in peace."*[2] The British Press reacted in a mixed way: The London *Times* considered Cyprus *"an admirable naval station, whether for the purpose of protecting the Suez Canal, securing a second road to India, or giving this country the requisite authority in its relations with the Porte."* The *Daily News* was afraid of *"limitless cost, unceasing stress, strain, and danger"* as never before in English history. The Commentator of the *Fortnightly Review* was even more pessimistic: *An island, two hundred miles long, ravaged by famine, a nest of malaria, with a fatal fever of which it enjoys a monopoly, without harbours, and possessed of a growing population of lepers, is held by Englishmen adequate consideration for an obligation to spend scores or hundreds of millions in defending an empire which either cannot or will not defend itself.* There were even doubts about the military value of Cyprus. Ambassador Layard believed that the acquisition of a *Place d'Armes* in the Persian Gulf might have been better.[3]

1 C W J Orr, *Cyprus under British Rule* [London, 1918], reprint (London: Zeno, 1978), p. 36.

2 Lee, *op. cit.*, p. 113.

3 *Ibid.*, pp. 117-122.

However that may have been, for the time being Disraeli had won a point in that perpetual Russian-British competition known as the Grand Game. For the Cypriots the 300 gloomy years of *Tourkokratia* had ended. It was said that Cyprus was the *best* administered Ottoman province of the time. This may be so but whoever knows the facts will agree that if we want to be precise, of all Ottoman provinces Cyprus was the *least badly* administered one. In other words, at the end of Turkish domination, Cyprus had been run down as never before in its history. With the change to Britain there seemed to be a bright future for the island, as a British naval base. A lot of investment capital would flow into Cyprus in the wake of the British building their *Place d'Armes*. Under the benevolent administration of the British, Cypriots would become well-to-do British subjects. If this bright picture did not become true this was due to yet another turn of the wheel of fortune of international politics.

Since the construction of the Suez Canal the Egyptian Khedive was heavily indebted to the British and the French. When he could no longer repay his debts, Egypt's debt-service was put under the supervision of an Anglo-French Commission. In 1879 this Commission replaced the disobedient Khedive with a more compliant one. This triggered a rebellion of the Egyptian army under the lead of Colonel Arabi. Soon he controlled most of the country but when he refused to repay his country's loan, the creditors became restive. As the French parliament refused to intervene militarily the British acted alone in 1881. They landed troops in Egypt and beat Colonel Arabi's forces. From now on they were the masters of Egypt. The ensuing Madhi rebellion in Sudan led to a permanent military occupation of Egypt and the Suez Canal.[1]

This development changed the situation of Cyprus radically. Having direct control of the Suez Canal and the harbour of Alexandria the British no longer needed Cyprus as a *Place d'Armes*. If they had considered their own interests alone, they would certainly have come to the conclusion to cancel the Cyprus Convention and hand the island back to Turkey. But apart from the loss of prestige which such a move would have entailed and the difficulties involved in the uprooting of an administration just planted in the island, there would have been undoubtedly a strong feeling in Britain and in Europe against handing back to Turkey a country containing a population more than three-quarters of which were Christians.[2] But there was another aspect strongly advocating the permanent occupation of Cyprus: The Ottoman loan of 1855.

In 1855, during the Crimean War, the Ottoman Empire had secured a loan from England and France guaranteed by the two Governments. In the following years the Turks had continued to borrow heavily and in 1875 the Ottoman debt had reached £200 million. £12 million, half of the annual Ottoman revenues were used to pay the interests of the various loans. In 1877 Turkey had to declare bankruptcy.[3] The British Chancellor of the Exchequer was alarmed because the 1855 loan had been guaranteed by the Government: if Turkey could not pay, the British taxpayer had to take over. The British Minister of Finance began searching for a solution which would not lessen his revenue.

And precisely during this period the discussion about the acquisition of Cyprus began. As early as July the Chancellor of the Exchequer signalled that he would use the revenues

1 David K Fieldhouse, *Die Kolonialreiche seit dem 18. Jahrhundert* (Frankfurt: Fischer, 1965), p. 146.

2 Orr, *op. cit.*, p. 44f.

3 Nicolae Jorga, *Geschichte des Osmanischen Reiches nach den Quellen dargestellt,* V, (Gotha: Perthes, 1913), pp. 540f.

of Cyprus to redeem the 1855 loan.[1] Later voices asserted that the Turkish debt had been the main reason for the acquisition of Cyprus.[2] This seems a little exaggerated, but not too much, if we look at the development of the so called Cyprus Tribute. Indeed, Cyprus paid the annual interest of that Turkish debt to the British bondholders until the First World War and continued to pay even when the island was annexed and made a Crown Colony, until 1927.[3] The Turks had squeezed the Cypriot taxpayer but oriental inefficiency had left enough on the Island; British administrative effectiveness squeezed the last drop out of the island. But this is a different story.

---

1 George Hill, *A History of Cyprus. The Ottoman Province, The British Colony 1571-1948,* IV (Cambridge: Cambridge University Press, 1952), p. 466.

2 Lord Hailey, *The Future of Colonial Peoples* (Oxford, 1943), p. 9 stated that "Cyprus was ceded by Turkey in 1874 (sic) in payment of a debt to Great Britain", quoted by Hill, *ibid.*

3 George Georgallides, "Churchill's 1907 Visit to Cyprus: A Political Analysis," *Yearbook of the Cyprus Research ter*, 3 (1969) *passim.*

THE POLITICAL CULTURE OF CYPRUS

In this paper I am going to describe and comment on the political culture of Cyprus. At a first glance such a topic seems superfluous: Looking from Western Europe it seems to be pretty clear that the Cypriot political culture must be rather the same as that of Greece since it is a Greek island. But this is a prejudice as will be proved. But in order to get a clear picture I suggest that as a first step we define what is typically European. As a second step we will take a close look at Greek political culture and note the differences. In a third and final step we will describe the Cypriot counterpart. And this will have astonishing results.

In 1930 the Spanish cultural philosopher Ortega y Gasset wrote in his famous essay *Revolt of the Masses* that though Spaniards, Germans, English, French are as different as you like and will remain so, they have the same mental structure. If one analyses their theories and norms, their wishes and suppositions one comes to the conclusion that most of them do not stem from our various fatherlands but from our common European heritage. The European by far outweighs the German, Spaniard, French and the English. In the light of present state of politics in Europe this view seems rather exaggerated and idealistic but was Ortega y Gasset totally wrong? What are these common elements which characterise a European?

The basis is the unique blend of Greek-Roman philosophy and Christian religious teaching. This influence was felt again in the age of renaissance which led to the reformation. On the one hand this lead to a confessionalisation of politics on the other hand it promoted the individualisation of human life. New ethic standards influenced by Calvinism lead to the ascent of a new class i.e. the bourgeoisie. The decentralised feudal order of the middle ages could not cope with the new requirements of big economic units thus a revolution from above took place: monarchical absolutism. The result was a kind of rationalisation of politics and a rather efficient administrative apparatus. Enlightenment and the French Revolution proclaimed the universal human rights. Rousseau's concept of the sovereign autonomous national state and the idea of individual liberty as well as the right of participation in the running of the state took firm roots. At the same time new liberal, democratic, socialist, conservative and nationalist ideas developed which ideologized politics. Since then this right-left pattern has become an accepted European feature. Political pluralism is an integral part of the common European political culture. It remains to be seen whether we will succeed in adding multiculturalism to this concept.[1]

The process which led to these results began around 1500 and it took about 300 years until its main features were developed. But this process was confined to Western and Central Europe though it was exported to North America. Eastern Europe beyond the borders of the Hapsburg Empire participated in this process in a very limited way. In Southeastern Europe only the countries of the Hapsburg monarchy took part. But what about the other countries of the Balkans? And what about Greece? It is precisely in this region of our continent where the difficulties begin.

In the Balkans outside Hapsburgian control we encounter a totally different development. The European Middle Ages had not taken place there. During that period large parts of the Balkans had belonged to the Byzantine Empire. Thus these countries never went through the vitriolic conflict between *regnum* and *sacerdotium*, between the Emperor and the Pope which poisoned the West. But right when the West began his process of rebirth, Byzantium was conquered by the Ottomans in 1453 and the Byzantine Empire disappeared.

1 Peter Reichel, (ed.), *Politische Kultur in Westeuropa. Bürger und Staaten in der Europäischen Gemeinschaft* (Frankfurt: Campus, 1984), pp. 10-3.

The Ottoman occupation was to last for three hundred years, and in some parts of the Balkans even for four hundred years. Thus Greece and the other Balkan countries did not experience Renaissance, Reformation and Counterreformation, Absolutism, Rationalism, Enlightenment and Bourgois Revolution. Greece and the other Balkan countries were cut off from Europe. For 300 years time stood still.[1]

When the Ottomans conquered a country they usually exterminated the ruling oligarchy in order to render the people leaderless and thus prevent potential upheavals. What remained were local notables who often acquired a double function: They became the leaders of local population and the target for repression of the Ottoman authorities if something went wrong in their village. They interceded with the authorities on behalf of their fellow citizens which gave them prestige, power and wealth. In return they could expect loyalty of those for whom they did the favours. And there was another less impressive aspect: They were rich enough to lend money to their fellow villagers thus increasing dependency.[2] This patron-client structure was omnipresent in the Ottoman Empire and it is the source where Clientelism stems from.

The Greek War of Liberation was fought on the basis of this structure. Clientèle chiefs cooperated locally and created small horizontal clientelistic nets which grew into large vertical networks. When independence was achieved Greece did not know any other political mechanism or organisation by which the country could be administered. Clientelism thus became a means to run the country. But by doing so the basic structure of a mutual relationship based on free will was changed radically: from now on it became the means to integrate forcefully the individual into society. The up to then protectors began to mingle in politics and quickly found out that their patron-client relationships could be used for political purposes as well. The patrons used their new power to attribute favours to their clients and in turn expected their clients to vote for them in elections. In the course of the 19th Century Greece was covered with rivalling clientelistic networks. A highly refined system of favouritism, nepotism and *rousfetia* emerged. The state became an object of exploitation for the chiefs of the networks: job haggling, patronage, a spoils system, and corruption of the state machinery, the judicial system and the military were normal. Buying of votes and falsifying of election results were common features. Towards the end of the 19th century a member of the Greek Parliament characterized this system as political procuring.[3]

The resulting political parties shared only the denomination "party" with their European counterparts. Things like party programms, organisations or congresses let alone internal democratic structures or expression of will by the members were unknown to them. The party was the clientel of the party leader and he alone decided on the course to follow. Conflicts within a party led to the separation of sub-networks. Party allegiance became a function of the success of the leader i.e. of the rousfetia he could distribute. Change of power was achieved by change of allegiance of sub-networks. In general elections Greeks did not vote for a party but against that party which had not procured the expected rousfeti.

---

1 Heinz A. Richter, "Zwischen Tradition und Moderne: Die politische Kultur Griechenlands", in: Reichel, *op. cit.*, p. 147.

2 Keith R. Legg, *Politics in Modern Greece* (Stanford: Stanford University Press, 1969), p. 34.

3 Hariton Korisis, *Die politischen Parteien Griechenlands. Ein neuer Staat auf dem Weg zur Demokratie* (Hersbruck, Nürnberg: Karl Pfeifer, 1966), p. 105. The MP was A. Diamantopoulos.

To make things worse this system was not confined to internal politics. The first Greek parties considered themselves the clients of Russia, France and England and accordingly called themselves the Russian, French and English party. The three protecting powers used their respective parties to influence Greek politics and the leaders of these parties tried to exploit the powers for their aims. When in the 1860s the British became the only protecting power the other two parties disappeared and the English party gave birth to a conservative and a liberal party which continued the traditional game.

The monarchy was a part of the system, too. Otto was a Bavarian import and the Glücksburg dynasty was of German-Danish origin. On the one hand the Monarch was able to distribute favours and to do *rousfetia* for his henchmen. On the other hand he was the lieutenant, the agent, the viceroy of the Powers and later of Britain. He was a king by the grace of the powers. But this fate he shared with his colleagues all over the Balkans with the exception of the Serbian king. As the monarchy never took real roots in the country it became the head of the Greek Right in order to secure its position. Thus the king became part of the clientelistic system. The Foreign Office considered Greece as a British protectorate and the British ambassador was a kind of high commissioner. Even after the protecting power changed in 1947 when the Americans took over under the Truman doctrine nothing changed.[1]

This system survived the great changes and crises of the 20th century. It survived the urbanisation process in the 50s and 60s. It proved to be so strong that it could even adapt fascism to its needs. A modified version of fascism came into being, clientelistic fascism. In other Balkan countries the same thing happened. Later the northern neighbours of Greece encountered a similar phenomenon in regard to communism i.e. clientelistic communism. The Ceaucescu régime was a typical example. In the case of Greece the external clientelistic dependence ended in 1974; Cyprus had to pay the price. But the internal clientelistic system survived even this shock. And the entry of Greece into the European Union has made only little difference. The patrons still handout the expected favours to their clients and supply them with jobs. Thus Greece has more than 600,000 civil servants; the ministry of economics alone has over 20,000.[2]

Greece is the only country within the European Union which does not share the common past of Western and Central Europe. West Europeans who were confronted with Greek reality were totally irritated. The comment by the first commander of the British Military Mission to Greece, Brigadier Myers, may serve as an example, when he wrote in 1943: *"The Greeks are Asiatic. One cannot judge them by European standards."* Myers as professional soldier obviously sensed the difference but found the wrong explanation, as beyond any doubt the Greeks are Europeans. West Europeans, however, do not know much about the southeast of our continent. But this is true for the central Europeans as well. Only the Austrians have some ideas about the Balkans due to their past imperial experience. But even for them the fact that the Balkan countries share a common Ottoman heritage i.e. clientelism is not fully understood. If the Europeans knew the present mess in former Yugo-

1 On the British protectorate see Heinz A. Richter, *British Intervention in Greece. From Varkiza to Civil War, February 1945 to August 1946* (London: Merlin Press, 1985). The American version is ably described by Lawrence S. Wittner, *American Intervention in Greece 1943-49* (New York: Columbia University Press, 1982).

2 So the Minister to the Prime Minister G. Pottakis in May 1995. *Athener Zeitung* (26. Mai 1995), p. 2.

slavia would not have occurred. Even less are they conscious of the fact that clientelism is a common feature of all countries of the former Ottoman Empire, including Turkey; though the Arab version of clientelism is a modified one since elements of clan and tribalism entered the game.

The mildest form of Western European reaction to the phenomenon of clientelism is bewilderment. In most cases the reaction is negative. Europeans judge Greek political phenomena by projecting European standards and ethical principles on Greece though these are totally alien to modern Greek society and the Greek political culture. In European eyes the outward signs of clientelism such as favouritism or rousfetia are reduced to corruption. Another typical example of misunderstanding is the Macedonian problem. Europeans do not understand why the Greeks reacted in the way they did and do. Europeans know nothing of the different sense of time the Greeks have. For the Greeks the Empire of Alexander is not a far away past but is a living heritage which is still present in the head of each Greek. The events of the Second World War are still present politics. Many more examples could be found. Europeans do not know much about the way Greeks think and vice versa. There is a barrier of misunderstanding between Greece and Europe. The result is known: For the last few years the image of Greece has steadily deteriorated in the public opinion of Europe, especially, however, in Germany and Britain. The language is not the barrier, this can be overcome. What Greece needs is a kind of intercultural interpreter who explains to Europeans how the Greeks think and how their political culture functions.

As this intercultural interpretation is missing the rift between the West and Central Europeans and Greece has been growing. In NATO the Greek Turkish conflict has been poisoning the atmosphere between the allies for many years. Greek fears have not been taken seriously and their insistence on guarantees have been dismissed as querulous. In the European Union Greek actions and reactions provoked similar sensations. European frustration and anger has assumed such proportions that one wonders whether Greece would today be accepted as a member of the Union. I guess all Eastern Europeans would have priority. But thus Europe would be reduced to only those parts which in the Middle Ages were Catholic.

In Europe we talk about a multicultural society but we experience difficulties in understanding that within Europe we have two basically different pasts which produced two fundamentally different political cultures. Only if we understand and accept this fact there is a chance that Europe can be truly united. It is within this context that the present Balkan trouble can be solved i.e. by integrating these parts of Europe into the European Union in the long run. In order to help people there to find a way out of the maze of hate and violence the Europeans should show them a humane perspective.

This readiness, however, is not very well developed as the Greek case has shown and the case of Cyprus proves. Europeans project the prejudices they developed towards Greece on Cyprus. It is for this reason that I have made this lengthy excursion into the political culture of one of Cyprus' mother countries. In the eyes of the European decision makers Cyprus is just another Greece and they fear the idea of duplicating the Greek trouble. And European public opinion agrees since the information at hand seems to corroborate this opinion. Moreover Cyprus is tied up in a conflict with Turkey and the European Union does not want to add to its already existing troubles. Thus there are voices within the European Union which want to postpone the admission of Cyprus *ad calendas Graecas* i.e. to the day when the perennial Cyprus conflict will be solved. But is Cyprus just a second Greece? A simple carbon copy?

From my own experience I would deny this suggestion. Cypriots are as different from Greeks and Turks as are Austrians or Swiss from Germans. Culturally they certainly belong to the Greek and Turkish *Kulturnation* as that phenomenon was called in the 19th century, but at the same time they identify themselves with Western European culture. Their political culture, however, is totally different from that of the mother countries. It demonstrates all features of a Western European country and almost no visible sign of the Ottoman heritage, i.e. clientelism. The absence of clientelism in this part of the world is indeed astounding and needs explaining.

The Ottoman rule of Cyprus began later but lasted longer - nevertheless its duration was a little shorter than in Greece. When Cyprus came into the British orbit in 1878 the social structures were roughly the same as they had been in Greece at the beginning of the fight for independence in 1821. But as there was no fight for independence there was no need for broader organisation for the time being. Thus the petty local patron-client relations did not develop into vertical hierarchical and horizontal networks. In 1882 the British introduced a kind of parliament, the Legislative Council, which could have developed into a machine distributing *rousfetia.* But the British controlled the governmental expenditures and thus there was no chance of distributing *rousfetia* on a broad scale. And when the island's agriculture needed capital investment, the British ruined the money lenders' business by encouraging the agricultural cooperative movement in 1914 and by founding the agricultural bank in 1925. Thus clientelism died before it had the chance to grow.

Almost 20 years ago the Center for Mediterranean Studies of the American Universities Field Staff organised a conference in Rome on the topic of clientelism in the countries around the Mediterranean basin. Though Greece itself was not analysed the results of all the other countries are applicable because of the shared Ottoman: clientelism. But there was one notable exception: Cyprus. The contributions written by two Cypriot scholars were an effort to trace some clientelistic vestiges in Cyprus. They described the local patron-client relationship which we mentioned and came to the conclusion that in Cyprus clientelism did not exist.[1] Apparently the 80 years of British colonial rule have had this positive result. In many discussions with Greek and Turkish Cypriots it struck me that they have difficulties in understanding the political culture of their motherlands. The underlying thinking structures are alien to them. In order to understand the clientelistic system in Greece or Turkey they must undergo the same learning process as western Europeans are obliged to. Clientelism is not a part of the Cypriot socialisation process.

Indeed Cypriot parties resemble their European, i.e. mostly British, equivalents, though they are more numerous than in Britain. They are parties based on programs and practice internal democracy. Members of Parliament are not distributors and managers of rousfetia. Protectionism exists of course but it does not go beyond the standard practised in Europe. Corruption is not only a legal offense as it is in Europe but it is considered a violation of the moral code aswell. Public opinion reacts very sensitively and negatively to such transgres-

---

1 Peter Loizos, "Politics and patronage in a Cypriot village" and Michael Attalides, "Forms of peasant incorporation in Cyprus during the last century", in: Ernest Gellner, John Waterbury, *Patrons and Clients* (London: Duckworth, 1977).

sions. And the Auditor General enjoys respect in a degree which must make Germans, at least, jealous. Though there are still prejudices against the former colonial masters the basic values of British society have been taken over and are being practised. Punctuality, efficiency, honesty, politeness, fairness, tolerance, reliability, and sensibility are among those virtues which characterize Cypriot society in both parts of the island. Cypriot society is a highly civic society.

Religion used to play a central role in Cypriot society. Thus the archbishop of the autocephalous church was not only the spiritual head of the Greek Cypriots but also leader of the ethnic group i.e. *ethnarch.* After the death of the towering figure of Makarios religion lost much of its traditional weight. In both Cypriot societies religion is a private matter as it is in Western Europe. Islamic fundamentalism has no chance in the enlightened Turkish Cypriot community.

The educational system is efficient. The languages are taught so well that pupils are able to speak them. Graduates of Cypriot secondary schools can continue their studies at European universities without encountering any kind of cultural shock. Cypriot students are rather successful at European universities and the resulting number of academics is so high that many of them must look for suitable jobs in Europe. The new university of Cyprus was set up in close cooperation with European and American universities and looks very promising. There is only one flaw: The provision in its charter that the teaching languages are Greek and Turkish should be updated by including the new *lingua franca* of scholarship namely English.

There are many more features which show how close Cyprus is to Western Europe. Cypriot planners develop strategic concepts to be realised over a longer period. I do not want to enter the field of economics but let me make one statement: I do not have any difficulty seeing Cyprus developing into a second Luxemburg in the Mediterranean. The role Lebanon used to play has been taken over by Cyprus. And there is no shadow economy worth mentioning. But inspite of economic successes ecology plays an important part in Cypriot thinking. Violations of the environment provoke immediate protests. Cypriot efficiency produced an economic miracle after the catastrophe of 1974 which parallels or perhaps surpasses the German *Wirtschaftswunder* of the 1950s. Efficiency is found everywhere. In state offices the civil servants work and do so efficiently. The acceptance of computers is astounding: there is almost no office whithout one, and - they are being used, too.

The move away from clientelism became visible already in the 1920ies. When Cypriot communists went to Moscow for training the Soviets did not send them to the KUTV school where the Greeks were sent to. KUTV was the school for the eastern people. Cypriot communists became students of the school training the western European comrades. Unfortunately this was not noticed in Western Europe nor in Greece.

In Cypriot history there was only one event which reminded of clientelism. I am talking of the period immediately after independence when a new administration of trustworthy people had to be built and many fighters of EOKA found their way into highly qualified positions. Fortunately for Cyprus only few proved unsuitable. Since 1974, however, another experiment in clientelism has been going on which might become dangerous for the Turkish Cypriot society. I am talking of the immigration policy in the north of Cyprus.

The Turkish Cypriot society used to function much in the way as its Greek counterpart. The invasion of 1974, however, triggered off a development which might cause many difficulties. The settlers from Turkey did not only change the demographic balance on the island but they brought with them the traditional political culture of Turkey, i.e. clientelism. On the basis of confiscated Greek Cypriot property Denktash's National Union Party was able to distribute favours and the Turkish equivalent of rousfetia. But not only Turks from Turkey were the beneficiaries of such transactions, it is well known that Denktash rewarded influential foreigners from Western Europe with such gifts, too. Denktash's attempt to make the leadership of this clientelistic network hereditary by trying to appoint his son secretary general he encountered a strong opposition from the subnetworks around Eroglou. Denktash thereupon broke with Eroglou and founded the Democratic Party which again is a clientelistic network. And in this party his son plays the expected role. The other Turkish Cypriot parties of Özgür, Akinci or Durduran are based on European principles and concepts.

Let me conclude. European anxieties that Cyprus will cause problems are baseless. The integration of Cyprus into the European Union will be an economic asset for European economy. Cyprus might even become a net payer. At least it will not be constantly connected to the drip. The political culture of Cyprus resembles that of western Europe. Thus Cyprus will fit smoothly into the concept of the European Union. The European Union on the other hand should live up to its obligation by accepting its most eastern outpost into its political organisation. The Cyprus conflict has been going on for over 30 years; for the last 21 years the island has been occupied by Turkey. Despite many efforts made by the United Nations no solution has been found. Entry into the European Union could solve the problem. The necessary prerequisites are there: a highly efficient economy and a compatible political culture, and this in both parts of the island. Greek Cypriots and Turkish Cypriots can live together peacefully as is proved in this country. The hardliners on both sides must understand that their ideas no longer fit into the Europe of today.

THE CYPRIOT COMMUNIST PARTY
AND THE COMINTERN

Research Situation

The story of the first Communist Party of Cyprus (KKK - *Kommounistiko Komma Kyprou*) is still waiting for its historian. The only accounts so far published are a British government paper and two articles.[1] The historian[2] of the second CP of Cyprus AKEL (*Anorthotiko Komma tou Ergazomenou Laou* - Progressive Party of Working People) used that British paper extensively[3] and almost exclusively as the basic source for the early years of the party.

The source situation on KKK is indeed desperate. The party has not published any collection of documents except an album[4] which contains a few reproductions. An accessible party archive does not exist. Only very few of the former protagonists have written any memoirs.[5] Until very recently there was not even a major quarrel in the party which might have induced some of the purged comrades to wash the party's dirty linen in public. AKEL has for quite some time been promising to publish an official history of the party but so far has apparently found no historian able to cope with the problem to present a party history which will not need a constant rewriting according of the oscillations of the party line.[6] Though in the early years the Greek Communist Party (KKE) and KKE/AKEL often cooperated and had close personal links, not even the Greek communist documentary collections contain noteworthy information on KKK. The same is true of the reminiscences of former KKE protagonists. Apparently the early story of Cypriot communism was considered an embarrassing affair better skipped in the family saga.

Faced with that predicament, the author of this study can only supply the reader with an overview of the party's history containing sporadic pieces of research, point to certain special problems the Cypriot communists have been confronted with and show where future researchers could do spade work.

The history of KKK is rather short: The party was founded in 1926. Right from the beginning it was under the tutelage of the Greek CP (KKE) which often obliged the Cypriot party to steer a disadvantageous course. In 1931 the colonial authorities suppressed KKK and forced it underground. During the Second World War the British lifted the ban and a new party, AKEL, was founded. Right from the start AKEL's character was very close to

---

1 Colonial Government of Cyprus, Communism in Cyprus (Nicosia, 1955); This paper was prepared by the Cyprus Intelligence Committee; Heinz A. Richter, "Die Kommunistische Partei Zyperns 1926 - 1944" THETIS 3 (1996), pp. 207-216; Yiorghos Leventis, "The Politics of the Cypriot Left in the Inter-War Period," Synthesis: Review of Modern Greek Studies, 2:1 (1997), pp. 1-15.

2 T. W. Adams, *AKEL: The Communist Party of Cyprus* (Stanford: Hoover Institution Press, 1971).

3 Actually the first forty pages are scarcely more than a paraphrase of *Communism in Cyprus*. See as well George C. Fidas, "The Evolution of Cypriot Communism", *Studies in Comparative Communism*, 6:1/2 (Spring/Summer 1973), p. 438f.

4 AKEL, *AKEL, To Komma tou Ergazomenou Laou* (Nicosia, 1976); a shorter English edition which appeared in the same year has the title *AKEL, The Party of the Working People*.

5 Giannis Lefkis, *Oi Rizes. Istoriki Meleti* (Lemesos:1984) and the memoirs of Ploutis Servas which will be quoted later in this paper.

6 According to G. Leventis, *op. cit.*, p. 3 footnote 10 AKEL asked the CC member Minos Perdios in the 1960s to write a story of the party. Perdios wrote a 340 pages long piece with the working title *Dokimio Istorias tou KKK kai tou AKEL* [Essay on the History of KKK-AKEL]. In 1968 the CC discussed the manuscript but no decision for its publication was taken. With the exception of Leventis no one outside AKEL ever obtained the permission to study the manuscript.

what we call today democratic socialism. Within a rather short period AKEL absorbed the remnants of KKK.

Economic and social conditions in a colonial society and the founding of the Communist Party of Cyprus (KKK)

If Greece in British eyes was considered a kind of protectorate,[1] Cyprus since the mid-twenties was a crown colony. Though both countries had been parts of the Ottoman Empire, only Greece inherited the specific political culture which was described in my paper on KKE.[2] In Cyprus British influence since 1878 reduced the Ottoman heritage to such a degree that one might come to the conclusion that at least today Cyprus' political culture more closely resembles European than oriental structures.[3] But on the other hand, Cyprus was a colony. The struggle of the Cypriot communists was therefore twofold: primarily a struggle for social change and only some time later a fight for national liberation from the colonial yoke.

At the turn of the century Cyprus was an agrarian society.[4] Less than 20 % of the population lived in the various small towns of which Limassol was the most prosperous. There were a few oil mills, cheese dairies, small plants drying fruit and vegetables and wine and cigarette producing units, but all this could scarcely be characterised as industry. There were mainly two factors which obstructed any industrial development: the heavy tax burden and the depredatory character of the Cypriot usurer capital.

When the Ottoman Empire leased Cyprus to Britain England had promised to *"pay to the Porte whatever is the present excess of the revenue over the expenditure in the Island; this excess to be calculated upon and determined by the average of the last five years."*[5] The Turkish diplomats apparently managed to inflate the alleged net tax revenue so that London committed herself to pay £ 93.000 annually.[6] In reality the average gross revenue before the cessation had scarcely exceeded £ 130.000 *per annum*. When London took over the island it soon found out the truth. However, as London was not ready to spend the British tax payer's money for this purpose there remained only one solution: squeeze more tax out of the island and do not spend much there. Very soon the efficient new British tax collecting system managed to collect revenues which amounted to £ 160.000 and £ 180.000 annually. However, not one pound was paid to the Porte; the money collected was used to

1 See Heinz Richter, *British Intervention in Greece. From Varkiza to Civil War, February 1945 to August 1946* (London: Merlin Press, 1986), p. 91.

2 Heinz A. Richter, "The Greek Communist Party and the Communist International" *Jahrbuch für Historische Kommunismusforschung 2002*, (Berlin: Aufbau-Verlag, 2002), pp. 111-140

3 Heinz A. Richter, "Gehört Zypern überhaupt zu Europa? Anmerkungen zur politischen Kultur Zyperns" *POLIS* 5 (September 1996), pp. 8-10: Idem, *Gedanken zur Politischen Kultur in Griechenland und der Türkei unter Berücksichtigung Zyperns* (München: Hans Seidel Stiftung, 1999); Hubert Faustmann, "Klientelismus in der griechisch-zypriotischen Volksgruppe während der britischen Kolonialherrschaft", *Thetis* 4 (1997), pp. 211-231.

4 In the following I follow mainly Nearchos Ioannou, *Die Akkumulation des Kapitals auf Zypern. Eine historisch-ökonomische Studie über den Prozeß der sogenannten "ursprünglichen" Kapitalakkumulation während der Kolonialzeit und der kapitalistischen Kapitalakkumulation in der Periode zwischen 1950 und 1987* (Frankfurt, Bern, New York: Peter Lang, 1989)

5 Harry Luke, *Cyprus Under the Turks 1571-1878* (London: Hurst, 1989), p. 260f.

6 Freiherr v. Lichtenberg-Gotha, *Cypern und die Engländer. Ein Beispiel britischer kolonialer Willkür* (Leipzig: Veit, 1915), p. 7 The real net tax revenue was a little over 66,000 £

pay the interest of an earlier Ottoman loan which had been guaranteed by the British government and with the rest the British administration was kept running. No wonder that the investment in the infrastructure and the cost for education remained below 3 % of the gross income. The main burden of this system was carried by the peasantry since taxes on income or profit were unknown.[1]

Due to the lack of any banking system the peasants' need for credit was met by usurers. As the colonial administration and the usurers were competitors in the exploitation of the peasantry the latter did not have the chance to accumulate enough capital to invest in any industrial enterprises before 1914.[2]

The First World War, however, changed the situation. The price increase for agricultural products induced the Cypriot peasants to increase their production. This, however, necessitated investment capital which was again supplied by the usurers. Thus by the end of World War I the Cypriot peasants were more in debt than before and the usurers who were traders at the same time had absorbed all profits. When the war was over prices for agricultural products fell again and many of the indebted peasants lost their properties to the usurers.[3]

The dispossessed peasants moved to the towns and to the mines to find work. Mining had started in 1914 when copper pyrite was discovered and foreign companies (Canadian and American) invested in the island. The mining companies found ideal conditions in Cyprus. The British administration granted to them extraterritorial rights so that they had a free hand to exploit their workers at random. As there were many more workers than jobs the entrepreneurs in the towns and the mines exploited them pitilessly. Though in the meantime Great Britain had annexed Cyprus and made it a crown colony the tax burden was not reduced at least not the indirect taxes. 63 % of the islands revenue came from indirect only 12 % from direct taxation, i. e. the rich were almost taxfree. The mining companies' profits were enormous: In 1922 the Amiantos paid 40 % dividend.

During those early years a few intellectuals apparently influenced by Christian social thinking published a journal called *Nazoraios* which, however, did not gain any importance. Soon after the Russian revolution news about this went round the island. Thus in 1919 the first signs of opposition of the working class against this exploitative system became visible: The construction workers of Limassol founded a first union. Cigarette makers and tobacco workers followed a little later. In 1920 the shoemakers organized. A parallel process was initiated in the countryside by the foundation of a credit society movement which tried to free the peasants from the claws of the usurers.[4] The main center of the beginning union movement became Limassol. Indeed, for long years this town on the south coast was not only the most important harbor of Cyprus but the most progressive township of the island. It was through this inlet that the first socialist ideas found their way into Cyprus and that the first moves to organism the communist party of Cyprus took place.

---

1 On the Tribute see George Georghallides, "Cyprus and Winston Churchill's 1907 Visit, Part 1" *Thetis* 2 (1995), p. 149-159.

2 A description of the system is found in C. W. Orr, *Cyprus under British Rule* (London: Zeno, 1972), p. 149.

3 G. S. Georghallides, *A Political and Administrative History of Cyprus 1918 - 1926, with a Survey of the Foundations of British Rule* (Nicosia: Cyprus Research Centre, 1979), p. 317.

4 *Ibidem*, p. 332-334.

But besides these special economic conditions of an exploited colony the situation in Cyprus differed radically from the circumstances in Greece in another respect. Whereas the Greek party was confronted with a relatively homogenous ethnic population except for the slavophone and moslem minorities in Northern Greece, in Cyprus there were a Greek majority, a strong Turkish minority as well as small Armenian and Maronite groups.

Since Greek independence the Cypriot bourgeois establishment under the leadership of the Orthodox Church had propagated union (*enosis*) with Greece. Though in schools the teachers taught Greek history out of books printed in Greece and thus promoted the case of union with Greece the early workers' movement was by far more interested in improving everyday life than in dreaming of *enosis*. But very soon after the foundation of the party the Cypriot Left was confronted with the ethnic problem.

The Cypriot Communists in principle wanted *enosis* too, but there were the minorities whose rights had to be taken into consideration as well, though the Turkish Cypriots during the interwar years were still indifferent on this question. Thus KKK was confronted with a dilemma. On the one hand it had the chance to bridge the gap between the majority and minority on the basis of the struggle for social change. But on the other hand any move for *enosis* might alienate supporters KKK had won on the other battlefield. Thus KKK was obliged to steer a cautious oscillating course on this question. It could propagate an anti-colonial struggle but could not come out with the *enosis* slogan because this would repel the Turkish Cypriots. In face of this dilemma KKK came out with the ambiguous autonomy slogan which could imply *enosis* but also the creation of an independent state. With this slogan it could hope to become the vanguard of the anti-colonial struggle and not to offend the feelings of the Cypriot minorities. Had KKK been left alone on this course it might have succeeded but there were forces (KKE, Comintern) which at times obliged KKK to take a clearer stand and landed the party in a major imbroglio. Only during the Second World War, when these foreign factors lost their influence, could the Cypriot communist develop an identity of their own.

The story[1] of Cypriot communism began in the early 1920s in Limassol. There was a book store called *I Ellas* where books from Greece could be found. It was there that a few young idealistic intellectuals (about 10) found the first news about the October Revolution and began to study Marxism/Leninism to find answers to the social problems of this British colony. Among them was a young retail clerk, Leonidas Stringos, a bank employee, Christodoulos Christodoulidis and Dimitrios Christotominis an accountant. The first two soon left Cyprus for Moscow to be trained there and became members of KKE where their careers led them in the 1940s into the Politbureau of KKE.[2] Another member of the group who became famous later on was Aimilios Chourmouzios from Limassol. He left Cyprus to study law in Athens but soon took up journalism.[3] Other members of the group were the mail line company employee Giannis Papangelou (Lefkis), the carpenter Kostas Christodoulou (Skeleas), the barber Charalambos Solomonidis and the merchant tailor Christos

1 In describing the development of the Cypriot party I mainly follow *Communism in Cyprus*.

2 Christodoulos Christodoulidis became known under his party pseudonym Alexis.

3 In 1945 Chourmouzios became editor of the Athens conservative daily *Kathimerini*. In the 1950s he won some fame as an author.

Savvidis.[1] In October-November 1922 they decided to organize themselves into a party, called *Kypriako Ergatiko Komma*. They got in contact with the socialist P. Fasoulidis and together they began publishing a bimonthly small newspaper, *Pyrsos* (Torch).[2] Its first number called for the political organization of the workers and peasants. It attacked the colonial government and accused the British as responsible for the calamity of the Cypriot people. At the same time it praised the British Labour Party as a a shining example to be emulated, i.e. the character of the party was not yet committed.

This wavering course continued in 1923 and in June the party changed its name into *Kypriako Ergatiko kai Agrotiko Komma* but in November it changed again, calling itself now Kommounistiko Komma Kyprou. This provoked first governmental countermeasures: Pyrsos was sued for libeling and Fasoulidis was jailed for three months. During the trial in March 1924 Fasoulidis dissociated himself from his comrades' communist leanings, broke with party and ended the publication of *Pyrsos*.[3]

But soon the Limassol communists found a new leader: Dr Nikolas Othon Gianopoulos. Giavopoulos was born in Limassol in 1898 from Greek parents. During his studies at Athens University from 1919 to 1924, Giavopoulos had become a member of KKE. When he returned to his native Limassol he established a Labourers' Club which quickly became a center for the more class conscious workers. But soon this club attracted members of peasant unions from the area which had been set up by peasants dispossessed of their land by the usurers. At the same time he took over the lead of the communist group which by now counted about thirty-five members.

Gianopoulos was assisted by his brother in law[4] the opthalmologist Dr. Vasos Vassiliou (the father Georgios Vassiliou, later President of Cyprus, born in Famagousta in 1931).[5] In January 1925 the group began to published a fortnightly *Neos Anthropos* (New Man) which declared itself the organ of the communist party of Cyprus. In the following months the journal attacked all kinds of social problems and the authorities retaliated by fines and terms of imprisonment for libeling. On 1 May Gianopoulos dared to invite the District Commissioner of Limassol to the May Day celebrations at the Labourers' club. The Commissioner showed up but warned those present that the authorities would tolerate only their labour, not their communist, activities. This warning led to the withdrawal of many union members from the club.[6]

---

1 Leventis, *op. cit.*, p. 2.

2 Georghallides, *op. cit.*, p. 309

3 *Ibidem*, p. 309

4 Adams, *op. cit*, p. 13 erroneously made him a son-in-law.

5 After the disturbances in October 1931 the family left for Athens because the situation was rather difficult in Cyprus for left wing people In 1936 Dr.Vassos left Athens and settled in Mytilini due to difficulties he was facing with the Diktatorship of Metaxas. In 1941 before the occupation of Greece by Germany he was tipped by the local Police Head to flee the country since he was to be arrested. The family left for Aivali, Turkey and then for Smyrna (Izmir) were it stayed for a month before returning to Cyprus. Dr, Vassos remained in Famagusta for a month before proceeding to Cambos tis Tsakistras his native village. There he helped the foresters to set up their Union (*Syntechnia ton Ergaton tou Dasous*). In September 1941 the family settled in Paphos. I am quoting on this an interview by G. Vassiliou " I Zoi Mou Se Proto Prosopo" in *Selides* Magazine (19 May 2002), p. 24. I am indebted to Ambassador Nicolas Macris who was kind enough to send me this information.

6 *Ibidem*, p. 347 footnote 3.

The whole time through Giavopoulos kept contact with KKE and Moscow. In July 1925 when the colonial authorities deported Dr. Giavopoulos to Greece because he was "threatening the island's peace", the conservative newspaper Alitheia hailed this repressive act of the colonial government. The doctor later was expelled from the party and became a non-person.[1] His place in the Limassol group was taken over first by Kostas Christodoulidis (Skeleas) and then by the Moscow-(KUTV)[2]-trained Charalambos Vatiliotis (Vatis) after his return to Cyprus.

During the following months KKK and its newspaper war under strain. In November 1925 the police raided the the Labourers' Club and the homes of the leading members confiscating their books and papers. The Colonial Secretary Reginald Popham Lobb did his best to unleash anticommunist energies of the police and private citizens who sued *Neos Anthropos* for libeling. Its editor Charalambos Solomonidis was sentenced to two months' imprisonment. It was a kind of private war against the communists of which the Colonial Office in London knew little.[3]

Despite of these persecutions the communists continued and learned to work clandestinely. In August 1926 20 Cypriot Communists (all Greek Cypriots) held their First Congress in Limassol in absolute secrecy during a public holiday. The organizer was the Cypriot Charalambos Vatiliotis who was a member of the Central Committee of KKE and had come over from Greece to guide the Cypriot comrades through their congress.[4] His presence showed the interest of the Greek party in its Cypriot offspring. Kostas Skeleas was elected Secretary General of KKK.

According to the Congress' manifesto the problem of the poor peasants was the most pressing. The were preyed upon by the usurers who expropriated them. Their ordeal could only be ended through the island's independence. The manifesto then denounced the petty politicians (politikanides) who were propagating enosis ("harp on the string of enosis") but did not care abut the poverty of the peasants and workers and called on all workers and peasants to join the ranks of the party in order to exact some concessions. The manifesto listed some concrete reforms leading to improved living conditions and added two main political demands: extensive self-administration (aftodioikisis) and accountable government based on universal suffrage. The final aim, however, was independence.[5]

Additionally the Congress adopted a charter of KKK. According to this document published in Neos Anthropos on 24 December 1926 the party struggled for three aims:

"(i) the struggle for the organisation and the economic improvement of the circumstances of the classes fettered by the present day capitalists of Cyprus;

---

1 He is not included in the album published by AKEL in 1984. AKEL, *AKEL. The Party of the Working Class* (Nicosia, 1984).

2 Communist University of the Workers of the East (*Kommunisticheskij Universitet Trudyashchaya Vostoka*; KUTV; 1921 -1952). At the end of the 1920s Cypriot communists were sent to the Communist University of the Workers of the West. Apparently the Soviets considered the Cypriot Communists more European than their Greek counterparts who continued to be sent to KUTV.

3 Georghallides, *op. cit.*, p. 353 footnote 1.

4 George S. Georghallides, *Cyprus and the Governorship of Sir Ronald Stors: The Causes of the 1931 Crisis.* (Nicosia: Cyprus Research Centre, 1985), p. 106 footnote 2; Leventis, *op. cit.*, p. 6.

5 *Ibidem*, p. 7 on the basis of *Dokimio Istorias*, pp. 29-44.

(ii) the struggle for the political independence of Cyprus from the imperialistic yoke of the United Kingdom;

(iii) the development in Cyprus of the international solidarity of the labour movement and the unification of the struggle of the labourers and peasants of Cyprus with that of their colleagues in other countries."[1]

The first aim was the traditional aim of organizing unions among workers and peasants. The formulation of the second aim was a little vague when it called for political independence from Britain but obviously excluded enosis. The third aim, however, contained besides the formula "development of international solidarity" an explicit call for solidarity between the various ethnic groups in Cyprus. was another.

All this was pretty conventional and not breathtaking. George Leventis, however, found the handwritten original of the charter in the Cypriot State Archive in Nicosia. In this document there is another paragraph between (ii) and (iii) which reads: *"The struggle for the establishment of a Soviet Republic of workers and peasants in Cyprus."* The explanation why the leadership of KKK preferred not to print this paragraph may be found in the field of communist tactics, as was admitted by Fifis Ioannou (Secretary General of AKEL from 1945 to 1949) self-critically in 1976 when he wrote: *"The slogan for a 'Cyprus Soviet Republic' in conditions of an underdeveloped economy and a social formation in which traces of the 'proletariat' barely made their appearance for the first time or the atheist preachings of historical materialism in an atmosphere of deeply religious, feudal or be it petty bourgeois but above all peasant society, could not but lead to isolationism.*"[2] In his eyes the course of the could be characterized as sectarian, displaying leftist extremism, the typical childhood illness of a newborn communist party.

On the horns of a dilemma: autonomy or enosis

This ambitious program obliged the party to fight on various fronts. In comparison with the second and third, the first aim was a relatively simple task. In the ensuing three years KKK succeeded in organizing unions and strikes. In 1927 a strike of 1,000 asbestos miners ended successfully: Their working hours were reduced from ten to nine hours per day. In 1929 6,000 miners went on strike. The British mining company invoked the help of the colonial authorities which crushed the strike by force. Though many workers were fired and their communist leaders were jailed or exiled this strike strengthened KKK. It had proved to be a political factor which had to be taken seriously

The other two aims brought KKK into conflict with the Church and the nationalist leaders who were dreaming of union with Greece (*Enosis*). The congress had stated: *"In the present phase of the political situation in Cyprus the right practical and tactical line for KKK is the united anti-British front for obtaining self-government and self-determination."*[3] The

1 A brief account of the founding congress may be found in "To idrytiko Synedrio tou KKK-AKEL", *Neos Dimokratis*, 74 (July/August 1983), p. 57f

2 Fifis Ioannou, "St'achnaria mias dekaeatias 1940-1950: Etsi archise to Kypriako" *Apogevmatini*, Part 2 (March 1976) quoted after Leventis *op. cit*, p. 8. Why the British did not publish this paragraph in their paper is less easy to explain A possible explanation could be that the original was handwritten in Greek and the civil servant who prepared the report "Communism in Cyprus" could not read Greek handwriting.

3 Andreas Fantis, "To KKK - AKEL Symaioforos ston Antiimperialistiko Agona", *Neos Dimokratis*, 91 (1986), p. 14.

unpublished party history evaluated the anti-imperialist course rather critically: *"Though it saw so clearly the anti-imperialist liberation struggle and armed it with the irresistible and effective weapon of the united front, the KKK could not see with clarity the end of this struggle. It supported the liberation of Cyprus, the self-determination of the Cypriot people and was fighting consistently for this aim, but it had as a final aim the full independence through the establishment of a worker-peasant republic in Cyprus and its accession to the Balkan Federation and not enosis of the island with Greece."*[1]

In other words, KKK was following a popular-front-from-below-course by propagating the fight for autonomy but it did not define the ultimate meaning of autonomy. It is not fully clear whether it was at this time or later in 1928 that the Comintern-slogan for the integration of an autonomous Cyprus into the Socialist Balkan Federation was taken over by KKK.[2] However, this may have been, the Cypriot communist leadership apparently understood that the propagation of this slogan in public would have similar disastrous consequences for KKK as the slogan for Macedonian autonomy had had for KKE[3] and therefore did not launch the slogan but in January 1927 come out with a cautiously worded anti-colonial program: *"Not until we obtain our freedom and cease to be the slaves of British imperialism shall we be able to breathe economically. All parties that recognize the need for saving Cyprus from the foreign yoke as the first condition for economic and national restoration should direct their endeavors in that direction. But, in order that such endeavors should bear fruit, they should be united. All the anti-British elements, whether they be townspeople or of the proletariat, whether they be Greeks or Turks, and whether they want Greece or autonomy, must cooperate in the struggle against foreign rule. All views meet on this point. The Communist Party which was the first to suggest the idea of a united front calls everybody to battle against British Imperialism at this critical moment when the British threat looms as a dark cloud over the Cyprian horizon. [...] The united anti-British front must be our answer to the British threat. This front must include all Cypriots, all classes and all parties which, for one reason or another, do not want British rule."*[4]

Obviously KKK tried to include Greek, Turkish, Armenian and Maronite Cypriots alike in the struggle for self-determination thus making an effort to overcome the incipient ethnic split of the island. This precluded, of course, the solution aimed at by the Church and the Greek nationalists: *Enosis*. Though during this period KKK never took a stand against *Enosis* in public, it was clear that union with Greece was not its course.

The main aims of KKK's internal policy were similar to those of its bourgeois competitors: Universal suffrage to all men and women above the age of eighteen; transformation of the Legislative Council into a real parliament with proportional representation of the ethnic minorities; accountability of the government to parliament; abolition of the Tribut and an according reduction of taxes; reinvestment of the surplus Tribute payment in Cyprus; removal of the British armed forces and their replacement by a local civil guard. All this was to be put before the British Government by a representative Delegation elected by a bi-com-

1 Dokimio Istorias quoted after Leventis, *op. cit*, p. 8
2 Ploutis Servas, "Kypriaki Aristera", *Anti*, 40 (11 January 1975), p. 26; Ploutis Servas, *Kypriako. Efthines* [2](Athens: Grammi, 1985), p.116.
3 Literature on this topic can found in Richter, *Communist Party*, p. 122f footnotes 39-42.
4 *Neos Anthropos*, 8 January 1927 quoted in *Communism in Cyprus*, p. 4.

munal congress and sent to London to lobby for grant of self-determination.[1] This concept differed only in one point from the recipes applied by the bourgeois politicians: Their delegations used to ask for *enosis*.

Under the tutelage of KKE

In 1928 when the British celebrated the 50th anniversary of their rule over Cyprus KKK published a manifesto which bitterly attacked the colonial administration and ended: *"Forward then to a united anti-British front. Onward with the struggle against the occupiers and the struggle for autonomy.*[2] In the same year the Comintern apparently established its first contacts with KKK but at the same time directed the Cypriot party to report its activities to KKE. Obviously the Comintern considered KKK a section of KKE. To what degree this subordination went and in which form control was exercised at that time is unclear. There is not the slightest documentary clue how the internal quarrels in KKE during this period influenced KKK's course. But from events in the ensuing two years it may be concluded that KKE was probably authorized to give directives to KKK. Whatever the details, the KKK-KKE connection linked the Cypriot party to the political line followed by the Greek party. Thus KKK became an object of the political game played in Athens and the KKE players did not pay much attention to the specific interests of their Cypriot counterpart as long as it served their aims. This relationship reminds one of the notorious relationship of the mother-country and Cyprus which is characterized by submission under the "national centre".

In 1929 Prime Minister Venizelos enacted the *idionymo* law which threatened agitation against the existing social order with imprisonment. Venizelos' anti-communist measure triggered a mechanism which became a consistent feature of the policy of the Cypriot communists: KKK's interest in *enosis* cooled considerably, since *enosis* would have brought the anti-communist repression practised in Greece to Cyprus as well. This reaction became a constant in KKK/AKEL's policy from now on. Whenever anti-communism was predominant in Greece the Cypriot communists' interest in *enosis* dwindled. But for the time being KKK did not come out openly against *enosis*.

The developments of the following two years are rather obscure and there is an almost total lack of sources. Thus we can only reconstruct the outlines of the development.

In 1929 Venizelos, who wanted to have good relations with the protective power of Greece, Great Britain, advised the Cypriots in an interview with the newspaper *Eleftheria* to refrain from provocations, and the leader of the Anti-Venizelists, Panagiotis Tsaldaris told the Cypriots the same thing. The Cypriots, however, did not heed the advice and in September 1929 they sent a delegation headed by the Bishop Nikodimos of Kition to London.

Bishop Nikodimos knew that enosis was excluded but he hoped that he might achieve a greater degree of autonomy. The communists quickly grasped their chance and came out publicly for autonomy and against enosis.[3] And when the bishop's delegation returned rather frustrated by British intransigence the communists saw a chance to unite their forces

1 *Dokimio Istorias* quoted by Leventis, *op. cit.*, p. 10.

2 AKEL, *AKEL. To Komma tou Ergazomenou Laou* (Nicosia, 1976), p. 61; according to Internationale-Presse-Korrespondenz the manifesto appealed to the workers and peasants to boycott the festivities, to rise against the imperialist oppressors and against the local betrayers of their classes and to fight for a workers' and peasants' government. *Inprekorr*, Nr.93 (1928), p. 1736.

3 Georghallides, *Storrs*, p. 201.

with those of the bourgeois camp and create a united front against British imperialism. But soon quarreling started between these two strange bedfellows so strongly that the British authorities feared that this might "result in serious disorder involving loss of life".[1]

The Greek consul in Nicosia, Alexis Kyrou, disobeying his instructions, furthered the Cypriot *enosis* movement. Thus in Athens the impression was created that Venizelos was actively promoting *enosis*. This impression triggered KKE, which since 1929 had been looking for a chance for revenge, into action. They instructed KKK to follow an opposite course. KKK was to start a propaganda campaign against the Church and the Cypriot capitalists (middle-class traders, usurers) who under the leadership of the Church propagated *enosis*, insinuating that the Cypriot nationalist leaders were only aiming at replacing the British capitalists so that they themselves could exploit the workers. Cypriot communists should work for the liberation of the island from imperialism and for the establishment of a free Soviet Democracy of workers and peasants in Cyprus.[2]

In June 1931 Governor Storrs reported about their activities: *"The first overt action of the communist party, composed almost entirely of Greeks, was to inaugurate counter demonstrations on the 25th of March, the "National Independence Day". At Limassol they tore down the Greek and substituted a Bolshevik flag; both there and at Nicosia they endeavoured to break up meetings for union. They presumably looked for Government indifference, but a number were arrested by the police and sentenced to imprisonment for terms up to two months. As one of the main subjects of their attacks is the Church, the Synod is doing what lies in its power to suppress the movement. On the whole their attacks are far more bitter against their fellow-countrymen than against the Government at present. The movement has spread rapidly; the number of communists registered by the police having increased from 181 to 365 in the last six months: the meetings held are well attended by potential supporters. The effect of their activities is to increase the general unrest and to render still more imperative the necessity for strengthening the position of the Legislature."*[3]

To what extent these instructions were obeyed and propagated by KKK has not been researched. But ensuing developments suggest that KKK reacted reservedly. Indeed, in the October 1931 unrests KKK followed an opposite course: After some initial hesitation the Party joined the 1931 anti-British pro-*enosis*-riots after they had been launched by the Church and the nationalists on 20 October 1931. Obviously KKK did not want to leave the anti-colonial struggle to the nationalists and the Church. Vatiliotis was arrested in Nicosia on 25 October when he was delivering a pro-*enosis* speech and Skeleas one day later in Limassol with pamphlets demanding autonomy. Obviously KKK-leaders had their own thoughts about the right course. The colonial authorities deported the two KKK leaders to Britain.

After the disturbances the colonial government suspended the civil liberties of all Cypriots but the communists were hit mercilessly. Trade unions and associations of whatever kind were prohibited. In August 1933 the Criminal Code was amended so that the authori-

---

1 *Communism in Cyprus*, p. 5.
2 *Ibidem*, p. 5
3 Storrs to Passfield, 4 June 1931 quoted by Georghallides, *Storrs*, p. 651; the Synod excommunicated members of KKK.

ties could "deal effectively with the communist menace". On 16 August 1933 KKK and seven sub-organizations were proscribed. Proudly the British report stated in 1955: *"During 1933-1934, after years of patient work, twenty-eight of the leading Cypriot communists were convicted on charges of seditious conspiracy and received sentences ranging up to 4 years' imprisonment. The movement had by that time suffered a severe blow."*[1] For the next 10 years Cypriot communists had to work in illegality. Only a handful of them remained free in illegality. Many left Cyprus and took refuge in London. After the outbreak of the Spanish Civil War in 1936 sixty joined the International Brigades and fought in the ranks of the British Battalion. Among them was the later Secretary General of AKEL, Ezekias Papaioannou. Fourteen Cypriot communists paid for their participation with their lives.

Comintern intervention and illegality

This unauthorized move in October 1931 brought about an intervention by the Comintern. At the beginning of the year 1931 the 11th Plenum of the Executive Committee of the Comintern had accepted KKK as a member.[2] It is not clear if KKK's subordination to KKE was abrogated at that point, but later developments suggest that this was not so. Whether the Comintern intervention after the October events took place in connection with its intervention during the 4th Plenum of KKE in December 1931 or whether there was a parallel intervention in Cyprus is unknown.[3] The fact is that from then on KKK was placed under the supervision of the Communist Party of Great Britain and on 17 December 1931 the Comintern organ *Internationale Pressekorrespondenz* (Imprekorr) published the following statement by Vatiliotis and Skeleas in London: *"The Communist Party will struggle for the fulfillment of the immediate economic demands of the workers and peasants, for the exposure of the betrayal of the 'National-Unionist' leaders and their counter-revolutionary slogan [enosis], for the united front against imperialism of the toiling Turks and Greeks, for the Free Workers' and Peasants' Soviet Republic of Cyprus."*[4] In other words: The Comintern and the CP of Great Britain forced a course upon KKK which would have been ruinous for the party if it had become known to the public since it obliged KKK to steer a course which was against Cypriot public opinion. Fortunately for KKK the British had suppressed the party and thus spared it self-destruction.

In 1935 KKK which at that time counted less than 60 members came under the energetic leadership of Ploutis Servas. Servas (really Ploutarchos Loizou Savvidis, brother of Christos Savvidis) was born in Limassol in 1907. During his grammar school days he got in contact with communist ideas and in 1924 at the age of 17 he organized the first communist pupils' group of Cyprus at the Limassol grammar school. At the First Party Congress he took part as one of the representatives of the party's youth movement. In 1928 he was amongst the leading figures of the party. One year later he went to Greece and from there to Moscow to study social sciences. Between 1931 and 1934 he was editor of a Greek newspaper in Marioupolis [Mariupol; after 1948 Shdanov] in Ukrainia. In 1934 he returned to

1 *Ibidem*, p. 5f.
2 *Imprekorr* Nr. 38 (1931), p. 955.
3 *Inprekorr* which contains substantial information about KKE is rather silent about KKK. On the Comintern intervention in KKE affairs see Richter, *Greek Communist Party*, p. 129
4 *Inprekorr*, Nr. 118 (December 1931), p. 2.712.

Greece to do illegal work in Kokkinia in Athens. In September 1935 the right-wing Greek government deported him to Cyprus. The colonial authorities allowed him to return despite the fact that under the 1931 Defense Regulations he had been banned from Cyprus, but they made him sign an undertaking that from then on he would refrain from communistic and political propaganda and activities. Servas signed and went to work.[1]

In 1936 the colonial government of Cyprus reduced the repression and allowed the formation of unions. Servas used this chance and ordered his comrades to organise crypto-communist unions. He told them to keep a low political profile but make every effort to promote the union movement. Up to the beginning of the Second World War he managed to organize almost 4,000 workers in various unions. Following the British example the unions were according to trades. In August 1939 the unions held their first Pan-Cypriot Union Congress.[2] In 1940 the unions united in the Pan-Cypriot Trades Union Committee (*Pankypria Syntechniaki Epitropi* -PSE). Typically for the time, the unions struggled for an eight-hours work day, higher wages, improvement of working conditions, social security, etc. In 1943 the entrepreneurs and the British reacted and sponsored the formation of conservative unions which united in SEK (Synomospondia Ergaton Kyprou - Federation of Cypriot Workers). In 1946 the British prohibited PSE because of alleged anti-British propaganda and jailed some of its leaders. The unions reorganized themselves under the name PEO (Pankypria Ergatiki Omospondia. The story of the left unions is well documented.[3]

During the same period the Cypriot communists managed to build up a peasant organisation in the villages. Towards the end of the 1930s districts organizations were set up and after WWII, in summer 1946 first demostrations against the miserable life of the peasants were organized and in October of that year EAK (Enosis Agroton Kyprou - Organization of Cypriot Peasants) was founded. But let us return to the development before the war.

Though the union movement progressed the party remained an outlawed sectarian group. In June 1937 the colonial authorities got hold of the first issue of a clandestine bulletin of KKK which contained information about efforts to revive the party. In 1938 the Communist Party of Great Britain claimed that KKK had been reorganized and was given every assistance. Later in the same year Servas was prosecuted and convicted for having in his possession a printing machine without official permit. Shortly before the war KKK counted sixty members. Servas understood that KKK could not be revitalized. The British would not allow its legalization and since 1931 its image was simply too bad. This became even worse when KKK slavishly followed the swaying Comintern course in 1939 and 1940 (Hitler-Stalin Pact).

---

1 This undertaking should not be confused with the *diloseis* the Greek communists were forced to sign under the Metaxas dictatorship whereby they had to denounce communism. Servas at first refused to sign but when he was kept aboard the ship which continued its journey for twenty days he contacted KKK. It was under the explicit advice of the CC that he signed the undertaking.

2 "Diakiryxi tis K. E. gia ta 60 Chronia tou KKK-AKEL", *Neos Dimokratis*, 91 (1986), p. 6f.

3 PEO (ed.), *Istoria PSE-PEO 1941-1991* (Nikosia, 1991); *PEO 50 Chronia* (Nikosia, 1991); personal reminiscences of union members may be found in: PEO (ed.), *Ta emmistha stelechi tis PSE-PEO kai ton syntechnion tis (1940-19749* (Nikosia, 1995).

Towards democratic socialism: the founding of AKEL

When World War II began the British repression relaxed. The colonial authorities announced municipal elections for the year 1943 which implicitly meant that political parties would be recognized. The message was understood immediately in all political directions of Cypriot society. In a conversation between Ploutis Servas and Georgios Vasiliadis, a lawyer who was close to the Church/Ethnarchy, the latter developed the idea to create a new party of the left. It was pretty clear that such a party could not fight for the independence of Cyprus or for *enosis* but it could contend for the improvement of the life of the people of the island.

This disclosure caused Servas to act. Since he had become Secretary General of KKK in 1935 it had been his task to fight for the legalization of the Communist Party, an assignment which under the prevailing conditions was simply illusionary. But even after the British announcement it was fairly clear that the colonial authorities would not accept parties which would follow a course contrary to British aims let alone a communist party. Thus any idea of legalization of KKK had to be dropped. Servas understood this and appreciated the Vasiliadis' proposal and merged it with his own concepts.

For some time he had endorsed the opinion that only a new party with broad a popular basis but secretly under communist control had the chance to play a leading role in the future and to compete with the Church/Ethnarchy in the anti-colonial struggle. It is not known when Servas brought his ideas before the CC of KKK but as he had previously assured himself of the consent of KKE and CPGB he succeeded in extracting a CC-resolution to found a new party.

This decision, of course, provoked the hardliners in KKK who had watched Servas' union policy with misgivings. Now they suspected Servas of right-wing deviationism and wanted to keep the new party under their control from the beginning. The more liberal-minded wing of KKK, mostly intellectuals, appreciated Servas' ideas and were of the opinion that the known hard core members should not participate at all in the launching congress. Despite the fact that Servas was an intellectual himself and sympathized with them he knew that the orthodox wing was too strong and therefore he decided to include some of the hardliners so as not to provoke their total opposition.

On 14 April 1941 with the permission of the colonial authorities he called a meeting in the village of Skarinou. Servas had invited prestigious personalities such as advocates and doctors who had studied abroad. Among those thirty-six persons present twenty-two were communists of both trends. The rest were progressive intellectuals and even former nationalists. Among them were Georgios Vassiliadis, Zenon Rossidis and Lefkios Zenon who later held eminent government posts.[1] But in 1941 they simply hoped to start a political career by joining the new party. After discussions the participants voted the charter (Memorandum of Association) of the new party (AKEL) and elected a Pan-Cypriot Organizing Committee and local committees for the biggest towns. It was decided that the principles governing the new party would be published later. It was regretted that no Turkish Cypriot had been able to attend the meeting and that only a small number of peasants participated. The assembly decided that AKEL as a party should not take part in the next municipal elections. Finally it

1 Vasiliadis became Chief Justice of the Cyprus High Court; Zenon served as a judge; and Rossidis was Cypriot ambassador to Washington.

was stated that AKEL had a democratic, anti-fascist and anti-hitlerite character and that it was in full accord with the ongoing struggle against violence and despotism.[1] By clever manoeuvering Servas succeeded in having the assembly elect only candidates of his liking to the various committees. This, of course, infuriated the KKK veterans. The Cypriot right wing press reacted strongly against the new political force ridiculing or denouncing it. This induced the more cautious bourgeois intellectuals to withdraw from AKEL.

After Hitler's attack on the Soviet Union and the conclusion of the alliance between Great Britain and the USSR Servas decided to exploit the new situation. On 5 October 1941 - again with the permission of the colonial authorities - AKEL held its First Congress in Limassol. Apparently the Congress adopted the statutes and the program of the Party. In the latter it was stated that AKEL believed in democratic centralism, party discipline and unity and detested factionalism and fractionalism.[2] In other words, AKEL became the second Leninist party of Cyprus. Ploutis Servas was elected General Secretary of AKEL as well.

Thus confirmed, he went to work. Years later after he had been ousted from AKEL the orthodox leadership criticized him in a most massive way. According to his critics he had shown respect neither for Politbureau resolutions, nor for the Central Committee nor of Congresses. He allowed the building of factions and had even formed a fraction for himself. The anti-Servas fraction stated: *"Instead of educating the members by his example in the right way, for a whole period he proved to be the bad demon of the party, an example of undiscipline and underminer of the unity of the party."* Finally they denounced Servas for having introduced the so-called democratic revolution into the party, the rebellion of the rank and file against the leadership.[3] Servas obviously practiced a democratic style of leadership which was alien to the veterans. It is unclear, however, which resolutions Servas did not obey, most probably those of the still existing KKK-structures.

How strong Servas' position in AKEL was became visible when in 1942 during the 2nd AKEL Congress he was able to make *enosis* one of the aims of the party. Shortly after the foundation of AKEL the hard-core members tried by a Politbureau resolution to bring the party under their control by ordering the removal of the party's headquarters from Limassol to Nicosia where KKK had its seat. With this step the hard-liners intended to control Servas more closely. Servas refused to yield.

In 1943 he violated even the resolution of the founding congress when he decided that AKEL should participate in the municipal elections. Under his lead the party put up candidates everywhere and he allowed himself to be nominated as candidate for the mayor's seat of Limassol. Servas was elected and so was the AKEL candidate in Famagusta. In other towns AKEL missed election victories by a narrow margin. Servas' enemies in KKK and AKEL fumed.

Later in 1943 he pushed AKEL even further along the national course. Before the Italian attack on Greece KKK had made propaganda against recruitment of Cypriots into the British forces.[4] When the Greek army fought successfully against the invaders the Cypriot pub-

---

1 AKEL, *AKEL*, p. 48.

2 Andreas Fantis, "I Pali tou AKEL gia tin Epikratisi kai ton Sevasmo ton Organotikon Archon tou Kommatos Neou Typou", *Neos Dimokratis*, 80 (July/August 1984), p. 8f.

3 *ibidem*.

4 *Communism in Cyprus*, p. 10.

lic reacted enthusiastically and thousands enlisted in the British army. 6.000 Cypriots are said to have fought in the British expeditionary force to Greece. KKK had had no part in this.

For a variety of reasons Servas considered this abstention as negative for the party. First of all he believed that it was the duty of AKEL to participate in the struggle against Fascism. Secondly, he sought to ingratiate AKEL with the British. If the Cypriots participated in the war Britain would be obliged to make concessions after the war. Third, enlistment in the army might free him from some of his opponents. Fourth, the enlisted AKEL members might indoctrinate their future comrades and win them for the party's case. Fifth, it was intended as a kind of anti-dote against Axis propaganda which was propagating *enosis*. Thus on 16 June 1943 the Central Committee of AKEL published a resolution which asked its members to volunteer for the British army in order to strengthen the struggle for the liberation of Greece, for the liberation of other countries, for the national, political and social future of the island. Indeed, eleven of the seventeen members of the Central Committee and 700 of the rank and file of AKEL volunteered.

During the same time AKEL considerably increased its influence on the workers. By 1943 PSE controlled unions with a total membership of 13,000. In the same year Andreas Ziartidis was elected General Secretary of PSE and AKEL voted him onto its Central Committee. The well-organized unions became the basis of AKEL. Parallel AKEL did its best helping the peasants (EAK) and even managed to attract shop-owners and other middle-class Cypriots. Cultural and sports organisations completed the picture. In 1944 the CYC (Communist Youth of Cyprus) was replaced by AON (Anorthotiko Organosis Neolaias - Progressive Organization of the Youth) and in 1946 the Coop-Organization was added.[1]

The successful development of the resistance movement in Greece seemed to confirm Servas' course. In 1944 Servas considered his position strong enough to reshuffle the Central Committee and to include more moderates and oust some of the hardliners. Then he suggested dissolving KKK. This step brought the old guard to the brink of rage. Grinding their teeth the KKK veterans had to accept the compromise offered by Servas: the admittance of some KKK-Central Committee members to the Central Committee of AKEL and the merging of their party into AKEL. Thus in autumn 1944 AKEL could come to the fore as the communist party of Cyprus.

Towards a mass party

The resolution to dissolve KKK and integrate its members into AKEL proved to be the right decision. It freed the new party from the bonds of orthodoxy within and outside the party. It was precisely the opposite development from Greece. There in 1947 KKE was outlawed and after KKE had lost the Civil War in 1949 its leadership fled to eastern Europe. When it became clear that for long years KKE would not be readmitted to political life, in 1951 it was decided to imitate the Cypriots by setting up EDA (*Enomeni Dimokratiki Aristera*, United Democratic Left). But unlike Ploutis Servas the EDA leadership never managed to get rid of the grip of the communist leadership. The members of KKE joined EDA but did never give up their loyalty to the exiled KKE leadership. The exiled communist leaders,

1 Kypros Kourtellaris, *50 Chronia Synergatikes Epavlis 'Onisia Ltd* (Levkosia: Pankyprioas Synergatikis Synonmospondia, 1996).

however, soon lost contact with the post Civil War reality of Greece. Thus the EDA leadership could never steer a course of their own, a course which corresponded to Greek reality but was obliged to listen to the orders from abroad. The long-standing EDA-leader Ilias Iliou could be heard complaining that the non-Stalinists within EDA had never had the clearsightedness of the Cypriots who absorbed the communist party.

Indeed, under the successful leadership of Ploutis Servas AKEL developed a mass basis in the unions previously unknown to KKK. Despite lip-service to Leninist principles AKEL in reality was steering a reformist course. It was developing rapidly towards a popular democratic socialist party. Obviously AKEL freed from the influence of the Comintern underwent a process similar to what happened with KKE in Greece during the occupation.

During the war years the hard-liners had to give in. But they did not forget. When the Cold War broke out they took revenge. Servas was purged and the mandatory process of bolshevisation which had been interrupted in the early 1930s was carried through. AKEL was led back to the path of orthodoxy and for long years came thereby again under the control of the forces outside Cyprus,[1] but this is another story.

1 On AKEL see Heinz A. Richter, "AKEL - Kommunistische Partei Zyperns" THETIS 9 (2002), pp. 219-238

THE CONSTITUTION OF CYPRUS:
A CRITICAL ANALYSIS

The central problem that had to be regulated by the constitution was the fact that Cyprus was home to two ethnic groups of different sizes and two minorities.[1] According to the 1960 census, the Greeks numbered 442,521 heads, which corresponded to 81.1 per cent of the population. The 104,350 Turks represented 18.9 per cent; there were also 2,708 Maronites and 3,628 Armenians.[2] Another complicating factor was that these ethnic groups were mixed geographically in different ways. In the countryside there were villages with purely Greek and purely Turkish populations, but also mixed villages. Overall, 62.9 per cent of the villages and towns had a purely Greek population, 19.1 per cent a purely Turkish population and 18.0 per cent a mixed population. When converted to the total population of the island, there were 50.3 per cent purely Greek, 6.7 per cent purely Turkish and 43.0 per cent mixed villages and towns. The number of purely Greek and mixed villages was thus almost equal. The population of the cities was also quite diverse.[3]

But the definition of who belonged to which ethnic group was not uncomplicated. For centuries, these ethnic groups had lived together peacefully, but the different religions had prevented assimilation. Culturally, they felt they belonged to the respective mother country. A Cypriot identity had not yet developed, although there had been attempts to do so in the past. At the time we are interested in, the island Turks were of the opinion that the decisive criterion was the mother tongue, with which they ultimately defined the people group affiliation via the ius sanguinis. Those groups that were neither Turks nor Greeks, i.e. the Maronites and the Armenians, were to be free to decide which of the two ethnic groups they felt they belonged to. The Greeks, on the other hand, regarded religion as the decisive criterion, as the first constitution of Cyprus had postulated. The Christian Armenians and Maronites, as well as the British living in Cyprus, would thus have been assigned to the Greek side, which would, however, have moved dangerously close to the old Ottoman Millet system.

In the years of the struggle for independence, however, the British and the two underground organisations EOKA and TMT had deepened the existing differences between the ethnic groups for tactical motives to such an extent that island Greeks and Turks were hostile to each other. The constitution was supposed to bridge these gaps. A federal construction in the form of cantons, as in Switzerland, was ruled out by the settlement character. It could only have been achieved through a resettlement action on the largest scale. This had been considered in the past, but since it would have meant a kind of ethnic land consolidation with a lot of human suffering and could have become the precursor to a partition of the island, it had been officially renounced. Nevertheless, a limited internal migration of Turkish Cypriots from the south of the island to the north had already begun during those years [4] On the other hand, the creation of a central state with a majority and a minority was out of

1 This study is based on Volume 3 of my History of the Island of Cyprus (Geschichte der Insel Zypern) which appeared in 2007.

2 Greek Communal Chamber Cyprus, *Cyprus. A Handbook on the Island's Past and Present* (Nicosia: Greek Communal Chamber, 1964), p. 21f. Offensichtlich wurden bei der Prozentzahl für die Griechen die christlichen Minoritäten mitgerechnet.

3 The ratio of Greeks to Turks in the cities was as follows: Nikosia 7:1; Kyrenia 4:1; Famagousta 4:1, Larnaka 2:1; Limassol 1:1; Paphos 2:1.

4 Heinz A. Richter, *Geschichte der Insel Zypern, II, 1950-1959* (Mannheim & Möhnesee: Bibliopolis, 2006), p. 542.

the question for the Turkish Cypriots and their motherland. The solution was a so-called ethnic group constitution.

Although the Cypriots had participated in the margins of the constitutional negotiations, the result was an octroi, because the representatives of the two Cypriot ethnic groups had hardly had any part in the formulation of the constitutional text and neither the Cypriots nor their government, which had been elected in the meantime, could express their will. The constitution was an octroi of the mother countries and the previous colonial power. The text itself had 198 articles and was about 40,000 words long, plus five pages of annexes. It was (and is) indeed one of the longest and most wordy constitutions in Europe.[1]

The room for manoeuvre for the fathers of the constitution was very narrow due to the requirements of the Zurich and London Agreements, which is why the first drafts from the Greek and Turkish sides, those by the professors Themistoklis Tsatsos and Nihat Erim were very similar in principle. At their first meeting in Geneva in the second week of June 1959, Tsatsos and Erim compared their previous drafts of the constitution. There was much agreement, some of which they had to seek the agreement of their governments on, and some of which they had reservations about. Two articles gave rise to major debates: The Zurich Agreement had stated that the future state of Cyprus would be a presidential republic.[2] Tsatsos now insisted that the term "sovereign" be inserted because this was the only way to ensure UN membership, since only sovereign states were represented there. Implicit in this sovereignty, however, was the possibility of making constitutional changes in the future, but these were more theoretical considerations, for Article 182 severely restricted this, as we shall see. Erim accepted Tsatsos' formulation, and so the first half of Article 1 read: *"The State of Cyprus is an independent and sovereign Republic."*[3]

When Erim tried to replace the term "communities" of the Zurich Agreement with "peoples" in the second part of this article, he met with fierce resistance from Tsatsos. After long discussions, a compromise was reached on this issue: the second part of Article 1 of the Constitution retained the wording of the Zurich Agreement and now spoke of the Greek and Turkish communities, but qualified them by referring to the Constitution ("as hereinafter provided").

The next stumbling block in the July negotiations on the constitution was the voting mode in the future parliament. The Zurich Agreement had stipulated that a simple majority should suffice for the adoption of laws.[4] Erim now tried to push through separate majorities of the ethnic groups or at least qualified majorities, which Tsatsos rejected as it violated the Zurich Agreement. The Greek side proposed a parliament with 50 deputies, the Turkish wanted 80; they finally agreed on 50 mandate holders. Then Erim wanted the 7:3 ratio of the parliament to be applied to the committees as well, whereas Tsatsos wanted to see the

---

1 Stephen G. Xydis, *Cyprus: The Reluctant Republic* (The Hague: Mouton, 1973), p. 507. For comparison, the Basic Law of the FRG has 146 articles and counts 19,582 words, the French Constitution of 1958 has 88 articles and about 9,000 words. The US Constitution consists of 8 articles and about 4,000 words - with amendments.

2 Richter, *op.cit.*, p. 641 *"The State of Cyprus shall be a Republic with a presidential regime, the President being Greek and the Vice-president Turkish elected by universal suffrage by the Greek and Turkish communities of the Island respectively."*

3 Xydis, *op. cit.*, p. 494.

4 Richter, *op. cit.*, p. 642 *"Law and decisions of the House of Representatives shall be adopted by a simple majority of the members present."*

political composition of the parliament reflected. The compromise that was then found proved to be an explosive device, as we shall see.

Another even bigger dispute developed over the relationship between the president and the vice-president. The Turkish side, based on the formulation of the Zurich Agreement, sought to make the two equal constitutional bodies, exercising their power jointly on all issues. Tsatsos, on the other hand, sought to give more power to the office of the president, arguing that in a presidential system the elected president is the head of the executive and the ministers are only executive "secretaries" and responsible to him. Cooperation with the vice-president, he said, was limited to certain areas prescribed by the Zurich Treaty.[1] The *Times of Cyprus* summed up the dispute when its headline on 17 August 1960 read as follows: *"One President - or Two?"*. After a lengthy back and forth, which even involved the governments in Athens and Ankara, it was agreed in early November, after discussions with Makarios and Governor Foot and renewed consultations with the Greek and Turkish governments, to leave it at the Zurich guidelines.[2]

The constitutional text was the work of Tsatsos and Erim, the British had no part in the drafting of the constitution. Quite obviously, the process that had begun in Zurich continued: the British lost more and more influence on developments in Cyprus. Decisions were made between Athens and Ankara. After some hesitation, London resigned itself to its fate and limited its criticism of the constitutional text to semantic and linguistic improvements. After the successful conclusion of the negotiations on the military bases, the representatives of the Cypriots and the mother countries signed the final amendments to the Constitution on 6 July 1960. On 14 July, all texts relevant to Cyprus' statehood were presented to the British Parliament in the form of a White Paper, together with the Cyprus Independence Bill. On 14 July 1960, the second, decisive reading took place. On 29 July, Parliament passed the Bill and on 3 August, Queen Elizabeth decreed by Order-in-Council that the Constitution of the Republic should come into force on 16 August 1960. This was agreed to by Parliament on 12 August. But after this overview of how the Constitution came into being, let us turn to the text itself.

The Constitution

Already Article 1 of the Constitution shows its ethnic character: *The State of Cyprus is an independent and sovereign Republic with a presidential régime, the President being Greek and the Vice-President being Turk elected by the Greek and the Turkish Communities of Cyprus respectively as hereinafter in this Constitution provided."* [3] The president was thus elected by the island Greeks and the vice-president by the island Turks. Article 2 of the constitution defined these two ethnic groups on the basis of descent, mother tongue, cultural tradition and religious affiliation, primarily therefore via the ius sanguinis. Since the Maronites and Armenians did not fall under these categories, they were granted the special status of a religious group. Individuals who did not belong to either of these groups were to

1 Xydis, *op. cit.*, p. 495f.
2 *Ibidem,* pp. 496-502.
3 Great Britain, *Cyprus Cmnd* 1093 (London: HMSO, 1960), p. 91. The then British ambassador in Ankara argues in his memoirs that the Cypriot constitution has a federal character, which is most certainly wrong. Bernard Burrows, *Diplomat in a Changing World* (Spennymoor: The Memoir Club, 2001), p. 124.

choose one of the two ethnic groups for electoral purposes. Article 2 has 7 paragraphs and regulates affiliation in great detail.[1] No attempt was made to define a Cypriot nation.

Article 3 decreed that Greek and Turkish were the official languages of the Republic. Eight paragraphs regulated the application of this provision in every detail. There was obviously no more room for English out of an anti-colonial reflex.[2] Article 4 required the Republic to have its own flag, but explicitly allowed all state agencies to fly the flags of Turkey and Greece together and all citizens to fly the flag of their respective "mother country". Article 5 allowed the two ethnic groups to adopt the national holidays of the "mother countries".

The fundamental rights

Articles 6 to 35 contain a detailed catalogue of fundamental rights on 11 pages, which in its details goes far beyond what is usual in other European constitutions, but in part corresponds word for word with the formulations of the European Convention on Human Rights. Obviously, the attempt was made to do justice to all eventualities and to prevent violations of rights on the basis of the experiences from the time of the struggle for independence. Restrictions on rights should only be possible in precisely described exceptional cases. In addition, the articles contain some noteworthy provisions. Article 9 contains a far-reaching welfare state requirement: *"Every person has the right to a decent existence and to social security. A law shall provide for the protection of the workers, assistance to the poor and for a system of social insurance."* Habeas corpus law, contained in Article 11, seeks to protect the freedom of citizens in 9 paragraphs. Article 12 contains classic legal principles such as sine lege nulla poena, ne bis in idem, presumption of innocence, right of defence and guarantee of legal process, making Cyprus a constitutional state.

Article 23 guaranteed the right to movable and immovable property. However, the Republic reserved the right to underground water resources, minerals and antiquities. The following paragraph is interesting: *"In the event of agricultural reform, lands shall be distributed only to persons belonging to the same Community as the owner from whom such land has been compulsorily acquired."* This implicitly recognised the need for land reform. But the largest landowners in Cyprus, the Orthodox Church and the religious Muslim foundations (Vakfs) were protected from land reform by paragraph 9 of this article: *"No deprivation, restriction or limitation of the right [...] of any removable or immovable property belonging to any See, monastery, church or any other ecclesiastical corporation [...] shall be made except with the written consent of the appropriate ecclesiastical authority."* Expropriation is only possible in the case of state construction measures.

Article 26 regulated working life and recognised the collective bargaining sovereignty of trade unions and employers. A law would prevent the exploitation of persons. Article 27

---

1 *Cmnd 1093*, p. 91. Thus a married woman automatically belonged to her husband's ethnic group, just as children who were not of age were counted as belonging to their father's ethnic group.

2 *Ibidem*, p. 92f. It was not understood that this provision was a huge translation burden, as all official documents had to be in both languages. When the University of Cyprus was established a few years ago, these two languages were consistently stipulated as obligatory for teaching. The consequences are clear: foreign professors may only teach there if they speak one of the two languages and foreign students must learn one of the two languages. Since Cyprus has become an EU member, this constitutional article violates EU law and is in urgent need of revision.

established the right of workers to strike, but provided that the state could intervene in a regulatory way. Article 28 contained a ban on discrimination and a long list of possible violations.[1] The same article abolished the nobility. Article 33 guaranteed fundamental rights even in the case of a state-proclaimed emergency, and Article 35 obliged the legislative, executive and judiciary to respect these rights.

The Executive

The President of the Republic, always a Greek Cypriot, is the Head of State and the Vice-President, always a Turkish Cypriot, is the Vice-Head of State, ranking after the President (Art. 36). Both are elected for five years according to democratic principles in general and secret elections held on the same day, separately for their respective ethnic groups (Art. 39). In the first round of voting, a candidate must receive an absolute majority of votes to be elected; in the second round a week later, a relative majority is sufficient (Art. 39). Candidates must be 35 years old and have no criminal record (Art. 40).

The President and the Vice-President represent the Republic, the former acting and the latter being present (Art. 37, 38). Horizontal and vertical interdependence of powers is prohibited; thus neither the President nor the Vice-President can be a minister, a member of parliament, a member of the National Assembly or the mayor of a city (Art. 41). Article 45, on the one hand, grants immunity to both, and on the other hand, regulates its abrogation in the case of high treason or criminal acts. Paragraph 2 of Article 36 regulates the question of representation: Should the President be out of the country or temporarily unable to exercise his office, he shall be represented by the Speaker of the House of Representatives, or in the case of the Vice-President, by the Vice-President of that House. The President of the House of Representatives is always a Greek and his deputy a Turk; both are elected by members of their respective ethnic groups (Art. 72). This makes the Cypriot presidential system fundamentally different from all other such systems, where the vice is always the deputy of the president. The president and the vice-president are the supreme representatives of their ethnic groups and assuming responsibility for the other ethnic group is thus ruled out; it would break the principle of bicommunality. The same applies if one of the two highest offices of the Republic should become vacant (Art. 44).

The President and Vice-President are not only the dual heads of state, but they are also heads of government, i.e. they exercise executive power, assisted by a Council of Ministers consisting of seven Greek and three Turkish ministers. The respective ministers are chosen by the two heads of state from their respective ethnic groups and appointed by a joint act, i.e. the instrument of appointment must be signed by both. The ministers do not have to be MPs at the same time. One of the following three ministries must be filled by a Turkish Cypriot: Foreign Ministry, Defence Ministry or Finance Ministry. If the President and Vice-President agree, this arrangement can be replaced by rotation of offices. Decisions of the Council of Ministers must be taken by absolute majority (Art. 46). There is no provision for ministers to be accountable to Parliament, but they can be dismissed at any time by the President or Vice-President according to their ethnicity (Art. 59,3).

---

1 *"Discrimination against any person on the ground of his community, race, religion, language, sex, political or other convictions, national or social descent, birth, colour, wealth, social class, or on any ground whatsoever." Ibidem*, p. 103f.

Article 47 lists those policy areas where the two presidents must cooperate, such as the drafting of laws for publication in the Government Gazette. Article 48 describes the specific rights of the President, Article 49 those of the Vice-President. Crucial in both articles is the final right of veto against decisions of the Council of Ministers and the House of Representatives concerning foreign policy, defence and security policy, as mentioned in points (d) and (f). Points (e) and (g) contain a suspensive right of veto in relation to decisions of the Council of Ministers and the House of Representatives. Finally, Article 50 specifies the right of veto of both Presidents, which may be exercised separately or jointly, over decisions of the House of Representatives concerning the same policy areas.

Article 51 contains a suspensive veto right for both presidents over the budget law (budget) passed by the House of Representatives, which can be exercised jointly or separately. The House of Representatives must resubmit the rejected bills within a specified period. If the House of Representatives insists on its decision, the law must be enacted or the case must be brought before the Constitutional Court. The President convenes the Council of Ministers and sets the agenda. The Vice-President has the right to introduce items on the agenda (Art. 56).

Looking at the provisions on the President and the Vice-President, one is inclined to consider them as a kind of co-presidents. Although the ministers administer their ministries independently, Article 58 subjects them to the supremacy of the presidency; at the same time, they are part of the respective ethnic group, and the president or vice-president expects their loyalty. The hierarchy usual in a presidential constitution gives way here to quasi-equality. Both presidents are the guardians of the interests of their ethnic groups. If there is mutual trust, this cooperation can work, but in the opposite case, the two presidents can severely hamper government activity. All in all, one can probably speak of a bicommunal construction of the executive.[1]

The legislature

The legislature also has a bicommunal character. It consists of the House of Representatives and the two Communal Chambers. The House of Representatives has legislative competence in all cases except those expressly reserved for the Communal Chambers (Art. 61). The number of deputies is 50, 70 per cent of whom are elected by the Greek ethnic group and 30 per cent by the Turkish ethnic group (Art. 62). Every citizen over the age of 21 has the right to vote and every citizen over the age of 25 has the right to stand for election. (Art. 63, 64). The legislative period is five years (Art. 65). If a Member of Parliament retires, his or her mandate is filled by by-election (Art. 66). Parliament has the right to dissolve itself by an absolute majority, with at least one-third of Turkish MPs voting in favour (Art. 67); however, it cannot be dissolved by the President. No deputy may be a minister, a member of the People's Chamber or of a city parliament or mayor of a city (Art. 70). The President of Parliament is always a Greek elected by the members of the Greek ethnic group. The same applies to the Vice-President, who must be a Turk. Their representatives are the oldest deputies (Art. 72).

1 Stanley Kyriakides, *Cyprus. Constitutionalism and Crisis Government* (Philadelphia: University of Pennsylvania Press, 1968), p. 63.

Articles 73-79 describe in detail the functioning of the House of Representatives. Normally, laws and resolutions are passed by a simple majority of the deputies present, with at least one third present. However, Article 78 contains restrictions: *"Any modification of the Electoral Law and the adoption of any law relating to the municipalities and of any law imposing duties or taxes shall require a separate simple majority of the Representatives elected by the Greek and the Turkish Communities."* (Art. 78). This provision contains an explosive element, because at least the provision on taxes potentially contains a kind of veto right for the smaller ethnic group with regard to state revenues, which can lead to a blockade of state activities.

In concrete terms, this meant that a law which the Council of Ministers had passed unanimously, i.e. with the approval of the Vice-President and all Turkish ministers, and which had also found a majority of Greek and Turkish votes in the House of Representatives, could be stopped if it did not find a majority in the separate vote of the Turkish members of parliament. An example illustrates the problem: The House of Representatives had 50 members and consisted of 35 Greek and 15 Turkish MPs. If 42 MPs voted in favour of such a bill, it could be blocked by 8 Turkish votes.[1] This provision had been included in the constitution to prevent the majority from overreaching the minority in tax matters. In fact, it acted as an additional veto power for the Turkish Cypriot side, which could be used as political leverage, as was already evident in March 1961.

The legislative initiative lies with both the parliament and the executive. However, this right is curtailed in the case of the budget. *"No Bill relating to an increase in budgetary expenditure can be introduced by any Representative."* Thus, the executive has the sole right of legislative initiative with regard to the budget (Art. 80). However, the debate and adoption of the budget is a matter for parliament. In the case of parliament, bi-communality thus also applies in the form of the 70:30 ratio, both in terms of its composition and in its functioning, right down to the committees, which ultimately amounted to de facto equality.

Article 86 stipulates that both ethnic groups elect the members of the respective ethnic group chamber. These chambers shall exercise legislative power over the following areas: *"(a) all religious matters; (b) all educational, cultural and teaching matters; (c) personal status; (d) the composition and instances of courts dealing with civil disputes relating to personal status and to religious matters; (e) in matters [...] of purely communal nature such as charitable and sporting foundations, bodies and associations created for the purpose of promoting the well-being of their respective Community; (f) imposition of personal taxes and fees on members of their respective Community [...]; (g) [...] subsidiary legislation [...] relating to municipalities [...] (h) in matters [...] of control of producers' and consumers' cooperatives and credit establishments [...] (i) in such matters as are expressly provided by this Constitution."* These provisions further deepened the division between the two ethnic groups. The separation of education was particularly worrying because it perpetuated the division introduced by the British; this was made fatal by Article 108: *"The Greek and the Turkish Communities shall have the right to receive subsidies from th Greek or the Turkish Government respectively for institutions of education, culture, athletics and charity belonging to the Greek or the Turkish Community respectively."* The constitution also provided that both mother countries could send teachers, professors and clergy to Cyprus. Textbooks

1 Glafkos Clerides, *Cyprus: My Deposition. I* (Nicosia: Alithia, 1989), p. 118.

were included in the "Subsidies". The British had introduced this condition in colonial times to save costs and thereby neutralise the ambitions of the two ethnic groups. The school policy had been a part of the divide-and-rule policy of the British and this was now codified. Of course, the new state could not publish its own textbooks for its two ethnic groups for reasons of cost, but anyone familiar with the Greek and Turkish textbooks of those years knows that extreme nationalism was taught in the mother tongue lessons and especially in the history books of both states. The formation of a Cypriot identity would hardly take place in this way, because through the books and the "imported" teaching staff, a Greek and Turkish identity was conveyed with the nationalism and image of the enemy that went with it, with the result that in both societies the dreams of Enosis and Taksim would remain alive in the Republic. The importance of this provision to the fathers of the constitution is shown by the fact that it was enshrined once again in Article 108. Education and culture were matters for the ethnic groups; the overall state of Cyprus had no business in these areas.[1] A Cypriot consciousness and a separate Cypriot identity would naturally not develop in this way.

It was clear to the fathers of the constitution that the tax on the ethnic groups provided for in point (f) could not cover the costs by far, especially not those of the Turkish side, because the Turkish-Cypriot ethnic group was considerably poorer than the wealthy Greek one. Therefore, Article 88 stipulated that the budget of the state as a whole should include subsidies for the ethnic groups, which, however, should not be distributed according to the usual 7:3 ratio, but in the ratio of 8:2. Article 89 granted the chambers political ("direct policy") and administrative leadership ("exercise administrative powers") within the scope of their competences. They were also to control the cooperatives. Article 90 set the limits of the sanctioning powers. The next articles (91-107) set the rules of the game for the work of the chambers, which largely correspond to those of the House of Representatives.

Article 109 stipulated that each recognised religious group was entitled to representation in a chamber. Specifically, this meant that the Maronites and Armenians had representatives in the Greek Chamber. Article 110 recognised the right of self-government of the Autocephalous Church of Cyprus, including in relation to its land holdings, and the Greek Chamber was prohibited from interfering ("shall not act inconsistently with such right"). Accordingly, the Turkish Chamber was forbidden to interfere in the internal affairs of the religious foundations (Vakfs).

The bi-communality already noted was substantially reinforced by the ethnic chambers, on the one hand their connection to the mother countries was made closer, on the other hand the division of Cypriot society was institutionalised down to the grassroots level.

The ensuing articles (Articles 112-121) concern the office of the Attorney-General, the President of the Court of Auditors, the Governor of the Bank of Cyprus and their representatives, who must be from the other ethnic group. Articles 122 to 125 describe the Civil Service. Here too, the 70:30 rule applied, at every level of public administration, as Article 123 (1) emphasises. In cases where 100 per cent of the population belonged to one of the two ethnic groups, this rule could be waived. A Public Service Commission, which is also composed analogously to the 70:30 key, was to decide on the filling of civil servant posi-

1 Polyvios G. Polyviou, *Cyprus. Conflict and Negotiation 1960-1980* (London: Duckworth, 1980), p. 17 *"Education in particular is obviously conceived in a very narrow sense, as simply the transmission of communal cultural and religious values from which the state must strictly abstain."*

tions, whereby the members may only make this decision for members of their respective ethnic group.

A separate section of the Constitution is dedicated to the armed forces. *"The Republic shall have an Army of two thousand men of whom sixty per centum shall be Greeks and forty per centum shall be Turks."* There is no compulsory military service (Art. 129). The security forces consist of the police and the gendarmerie totalling 1,000 men. The 70:30 rule applies to their composition. In order to avoid large-scale dismissals, the percentage of Turkish Cypriots was allowed to be up to 40 per cent in the initial period.[1] One of the commanders of the army and the security forces must be a Turkish Cypriot, their respective deputies must belong to the other ethnic group (Art. 130). Probably to avoid provocation, Article 132 decreed: *"Forces which are stationed in parts of the territory of the Republic inhabited in a proportion approaching one hundred per centum only by members of one Community shall belong to that Community."*

The Judiciary

The judiciary is headed by the Supreme Constitutional Court, which consists of one Greek Cypriot judge, one Turkish Cypriot judge and one neutral, the latter to preside (Art. 133) and must not be from either of the mother countries. The term of office of the judges should be six years. The two Cypriot judges must come from the judicial service of the Republic and the retirement age is 68. The Court takes decisions according to the majority principle. The President and the Vice-President may, alone or together, apply to the Court of Justice to have a law or decision of Parliament reviewed for its constitutionality (Art. 137). This also applies to the Budget Act (Art. 138). The Court also settles organ disputes between the House of Representatives and the ethnic chambers (Art. 139). Articles 152-164 contain provisions on the relations of the Constitutional Court with the subordinate courts.

Final provisions

Article 173 of the Constitution provides that *"Separate municipalities shall be created in the five largest towns of the Republic, that is to say, Nicosia, Limassol, Famagusta, Larnaca and Paphos by the Turkish inhabitants thereof."* After four years, the President and the Vice-President are to examine whether this separation of the municipalities should be maintained. In these cities, separate councils are to be elected by the members of the respective ethnic groups. A coordination body consisting of two members each of the Greek and Turkish municipal councils as well as a president elected by both city parliaments *"shall carry out services entrusted to it by agreement of the councils [...] and shall concern itself with matters which require a degree of co-operation."*. Further coordination bodies, e.g. for urban planning, were foreseen (Art. 175).

Along with Article 78, Article 173 was the most problematic passage in the Constitution. In order to understand the problem of separate municipalities, it is useful to look at the following statistics. With the exception of Nicosia, all the cities in Cyprus at that time were

1 During the EOKA struggle, many Greek Cypriot police officers had resigned and the police force therefore consisted mainly of Turkish Cypriots.

small towns and the smaller of them had financial difficulties to support such a city even without the division of the municipalities.[1]

1960	Number of inhabitants	Turks	Greeks	Turks in %
Nikosia	95515	22134	64207	23
Famagousta	34774	6120	24506	17,5
Larnaka	19824	4058	13101	20
Limassol	43593	6115	31263	14
Paphos	9083	2851	6218	31
Kyrenia	3498	696	2373	19
Total	206287	41668	141668	20

Since the Turkish municipalities existed only de jure, an attempt was made after Cyprus' independence to define the boundaries of the respective municipal areas. Within a short time, it became clear that this was an almost impossible task. The Turkish Cypriot leadership from Nicosia wanted to establish contiguous Turkish districts that would be self-sufficient to a certain extent and therefore possibly have access to a harbour and a connection to a main road. Such neighbourhoods were designed at the green table, but in practice, different ownership of land and buildings prevented the establishment of ethnically homogeneous neighbourhoods. Many Turkish Cypriots wanted to live among themselves and expected the Greeks to leave the future Turkish neighbourhoods, but the Greeks did not think of voluntarily giving up their property. As a result, the Turkish quarters took on bizarre shapes, prompting the Greek press to ridicule them as having the shape of an octopod or even a decapod. Opposition from the Greek side was general and across the political spectrum. On this issue, the AKEL mayors of Famagousta, Larnaca and Limassol cooperated with their conservative counterparts in Nicosia and Paphos and together started a campaign against the establishment of separate Turkish municipalities.[2] Behind this was the fear of many Greek Cypriots that the creation of separate neighbourhoods and municipalities was the first step towards the partition of the island, for just as they themselves had not actually given up enosis, so it was assumed that the Turkish Cypriots had not finally given up on the partition of the island either. Article 173 became the main obstacle to the functioning of the republic.

Article 181 decrees that the Treaty of Guarantee and the Treaty of Alliance are part of the Constitution and have constitutional force as Annexes I and II. Article 1 of the Treaty of Guarantee read: *La République de Chypre s'engage à assurer le maintien de son indépendance, de son intégrité territoriale et sa sécurité, ainsi que le respect de sa Constitution.*

---

1 The figures are taken from the Cyprus Handbook of 1964, p. 22.

2 Diana Weston Markides, *Cyprus 1957-1963 from Colonial Conflict to Constitutional Crisis. The Key Role of the Municiapal Issue* (Minneapolis: Minnesota Mediterranean and East European Monographs, 2001), p. 74. Mayor Pougiouros was reacting to protests from Greek citizens living in the projected Turkish neighbourhoods *"We want a common municipality because they are common interests that we cater for."* *Cyprus Mail* (21 January 1961).

Elle assume l'obligation de ne participer intégralement ou partiellement à aucune union politique ou économique avec quelque Etat que ce soit. Dans ce sens elle déclare interdite toute activité de nature à favoriser directement ou indirectement aussi bien l'union avec autre Etat que le partage de l'Ile."[1] In this way, the republic undertook to actively stand up for its independence and to fight efforts towards Enosis and Taksim. Political or economic affiliation with a state was excluded, meaning of course one of the mother countries. There was no question of an alliance of states such as the EU; the Turkish government's argument, put forward before Cyprus joined the EU in 2004, that the treaty of guarantee forbade annexation, was therefore untenable.[2]

In Article 2, Britain, Greece and Turkey undertook to guarantee the independence, territorial integrity and security of the Republic of Cyprus and the order established by the Constitution. At the same time, they undertook to prohibit any activity that sought Enosis or Taksim. Cyprus, Greece and Turkey assured in Article 3 to respect the sovereignty of the British bases. Since Article 4 of the Treaty of Guarantee formed the basis in international law for Turkey's intervention in 1974, it will again be quoted in full: *"En cas de violation des dispositions du présent Traité, la Grèce, le Royaume-Uni et la Turquie s'engagent à se concerter en vue des démarches ou mesures nécessaires pour en assurer l'observation. Dans la mesure où une action commune ou concertée ne s'avérerait pas possible, chacune des trois Puissances garantes se réserve le droit d'agir dans le but exclusif du rétablissement l'ordre créé par le présent Traité."*[3] The guarantee treaty thus also allows unilateral action, but only to restore the status quo ante.[4] Article 5 stipulated that the Guarantee Treaty would enter into force upon signature.

The Treaty of Guarantee reduced the sovereignty of the Republic of Cyprus, creating conditions reminiscent of the limited sovereignty of the FRG between 1955 and 1990. The status of Cyprus had features of a protectorate of the guarantor powers. As long as Cyprus behaved well in the sense of the guarantor powers, it was sovereign.

This solution was very much in line with Turkish ideas. As late as the summer of 1958, the Turkish side had demanded the partition of the island. When, in view of the collapse of the Baghdad Pact, it realised that this aim was no longer feasible, it accepted what it considered the second-best solution: independence with limited sovereignty in favour of Turkey.

---

1 *"The Republic of Cyprus undertakes to ensure the maintenance of its independence, territorial integrity and security, as well as respect for its Constitution. It assumes the obligation not to participate, in whole or in part, in any political or economic union with any State. In this sense, it declares prohibited any activity likely to promote directly or indirectly either the union with another State or the partition of the Island".*

2 Also Christian Rumpf, "Verfassung und Recht" in: Klaus-Detlev Grothusen (ed.), *Südosteuropahandbuch Band 8* (Göttingen: Vandenhoeck & Ruprecht, 1998), p. 159. In the following article, Rumpf argues even harder: Christian Rumpf, "Die staats- und völkerrechtliche Lage Zyperns," *Europäische Grundrechtszeitung*, 24:21-22 (1997), pp. 533-546: *"Da der Garantievertrag verfassungsrechtlichen Rang hat, stellt die Aufnahme in die EG bzw. EU einen Bruch der Verfassung von 1960 dar."* ("Since the Treaty of Guarantee has constitutional status, admission to the EC or EU constitutes a breach of the 1960 Constitution.")

3 "In the event of a breach of the provisions of this Treaty, Greece, the United Kingdom and Turkey undertake to consult each other with a view to taking the necessary steps or measures to ensure compliance. In so far as joint or concerted action proves impossible, each of the three Guarantor Powers reserves the right to act with the sole aim of restoring the order created by the present Treaty".

4 This article was cited by Turkey in 1974 as justification for its invasion of Cyprus. This may have been true for the first phase of the intervention, but with the continuation of the invasion in August 1974 at the latest, there could be no question of it being about restoring the status quo ante.

Since the Treaty of Guarantee did not define the casus foederis precisely, Turkey could interfere in Cyprus at the slightest disturbance, or if the leadership of the Turkish Cypriots considered it necessary. Finally, the Treaty of Alliance allowed the stationing of 950 Greek and 650 Turkish soldiers on the island.

Article 182 shows the only way in which constitutional amendments can be made, and only in a very limited way: *"The Articles or parts of this Constitution [...] which have been incorporated from the Zurich Agreement [...] are the basic Articles of this Constitution and cannot, in any way, be amended, whether by way of variation, addition or repeal."* If in the Constitution of the Federal Republic of Germany the fundamental rights are largely unchangeable, in the Constitution of Cyprus it is the provisions of the Treaty of Zurich. The will of the mother countries laid down in this treaty thus takes precedence. But the hurdle is also quite high for changes to the articles of the constitution not laid down by Zurich, as they require a two-thirds majority of the representatives of the two ethnic groups in the House of Representatives (Art. 182 para. 3). The constitution can therefore only be interpreted as an exercise of the right to self-determination to a very limited extent.[1]

The constitution set a final point. Nancy Crawshaw put this in the classic formula: *"The Constitution was in reality the legacy of inter-communal strife rather than a model for sound government based on democratic lines."*[2] The British wanted to get rid of the Cyprus problem and any solution was fine with them, as long as it left them their bases. Athens saw it similarly and was therefore prepared to come to an agreement bilaterally with Ankara. Preventing a new conflict was the main concern of the constitution. The way forward was to strengthen bi-communality at all levels, with major concessions made to the Turkish Cypriots that raised their influence far above their real strength (18%). Politically, they were no longer a minority, not yet equal de jure, but de facto. For the Greek Cypriots, this was a hard pill to swallow. On the contrary, they made it clear that they would strive for change. The Turkish Cypriots, on the other hand, were highly satisfied with the result and regarded any attempt at change with the greatest suspicion. Thus, the prerequisite for the functioning of the constitution, namely good understanding, trust and goodwill to cooperate, was not present, and so the constitution and the republic that emerged from it were doomed to failure. Similarly, just as the Weimar Republic failed not because of its admittedly complicated constitution but because of a lack of democrats, so the Republic of Cyprus failed not because of its even more complicated constitution but because of a lack of Cypriots.

Nowhere in the constitution is there a provision that the two Cypriot communities could have understood as an encouragement or invitation to inter-communal cooperation. The speculative question arises whether a different result would not have been achieved if the Cypriots had been more involved in the drafting of the constitution. The attempt to do constitutional justice to all eventualities and to create an "ideal" bi-communal constitution led to institutionalised immobility through exaggerated "checks and balances" and overlooked the fact that this prevented a dynamic development towards the emergence of a Cypriot nation and institutionalised and cemented the division of the ethnic groups provoked by the British.

---

1 Rumpf, *Verfassung und Recht*, p. 160f.

2 Nancy Crawshaw, *The Cyprus Revolt. An Account of the Struggle for Union with Greece* (London: Allen & Unwin, 1978), p. 361.

At the same time, it programmed conflicts because the majority would not accept in the long run that ultimately the minority determined the course. *"As will be shortly seen, the relevant provisions increased rather than reduced tension, did nothing to foster cooperation between the two Communities and, as a result, constituted in their totality a peculiarly structured and difficult to operate constitutional anomaly with no parallel elsewhere."*[1] For Tom Driberg, MP, the constitution was "a manifestation of the rigid pinciple of apartheid", and he was right.[2]

---

1 Polyvios Polyviou, *Cyprus. In Search of a Constitution* (Nicosia,1976), p. 20.
2 Tom Driberg, "Birth of a Nation" *New Statesman* (27 August 1960), p. 271.

THE ASSASSINATION ATTEMPT ON MAKARIOS IN 1970 AND THE MURDER OF POLYKARPOS GEORKATZIS

The emergence of political parties in Cyprus

The independence of Cyprus in the 1960s also changed its political landscape: political parties developed. Until then, only the communist AKEL had existed as a thoroughly organised party. When political restrictions were largely lifted after the Second World War, no political parties emerged nevertheless, as the Church and the Ethnarchy Council took the lead in the anti-colonial struggle that slowly began. Although there were occasional political groupings in the form of temporary associations for the purpose of elections, these were centred on a few personalities and existed only in the cities. In contrast to the political world, the world of labour and agriculture was very well organised. There were two trade union confederations, the strong left-wing PEO (Pankypria Ergatiki Omospondia) and the considerably weaker right-wing SEK (Synomospondia Ergaton Kyprou - Federation of the Workers of Cyprus), and the peasants had united in the left-wing EKA (Enosi Kyprion Agroton - Union of Cypriot Peasants) and the right-wing PEK (Panagrotiki Enosis Kyprou - General Union of the Peasants of Cyprus). In addition, there were professional associations, which were also ideologically divided.

After the end of the liberation struggle, even before the founding of the republic, extremist EOKA members who still wanted Enosis and regarded Grivas as their legitimate leader and Makarios as a traitor, had united in the EDMA (Enomeno Dimokratiko Metopo Anadimiourgias - United Democratic Front of Reconstruction). In July 1959, the EDMA had briefly caused irritation in the context of the conflict between Makarios and Grivas, but had then sunk back down to a sectarian rump.[1] In the first presidential election campaign, Makarios' opponent Themistoklis Dervis and the father of the parliamentary speaker, Ioannis Kliridis, founded a short-lived party, the DEK (Dimokratiki Enosis Kyprou - Democratic Union of Cyprus), which opposed Makarios and AKEL, but soon sank back into insignificance.[2] The second presidential election in February 1968 breathed new life into it and it again supported Makarios' opponent, Takis Evdokas. As is well known, the latter won 3.7 per cent of the vote in the elections.[3]

In the meantime, other politicians also realised that action had to be taken, because new elections had to be held by 1970 at the latest.[4] Kliridis writes in his memoirs that he was also of the opinion that the power of the church and its influence on the political life of the country should be reduced.[5] He certainly meant Makarios, who exercised his paternalistic influence through the Patriotic Front (Ethnikofronon Parataxis).[6] Indeed, Makarios was not too pleased about the existence of political parties. He preferred a network geared to him,

---

1 Heinz A. Richter, *Geschichte der Insel Zypern 1959-1965* (2007) p. 97. 102f

2 *Ibidem* 124 f.

3 Ploutis Servas, *Kypriako. Efthines*, III, (Athen: Grammi, 1985), p. 167.

4 Soula Zavou, *Ta politika kommata tis Kyprou ston 20o aiona* (Athen: Kastaniotis, 2002), *passim.*

5 Glafkos Clerides, *Cyprus: My Deposition*, II, (Nicosia: Althia, 1990), p. 314.

6 The Patriotic Front (Ethnikofronon Parataxis) was founded in 1959 by EOKA supporters loyal to Makarios in order to secure the election of the archbishop as president. It brought together a wide variety of organisations and groups, all of which had one thing in common, loyalty to Makarios. The Front had no political programme of its own and had never attempted to build an organisational structure. It was a clientelistic network of Makarios supporters. After the 1960 presidential election, the Front went into deep sleep, only to be reactivated at the next election. Most of its supporters now joined the Eniaio Comma. Richard A. Patrick, *Political Geography and the Cyprus Conflict 1963-1971* (Waterloo: University of Waterloo, 1976), p. 180.

whose members were dependent on him and did not pursue independent policies. Parliamentarians were, in his eyes, transmission belts of his ideas.[1]

Be that as it may, Kliridis decided to found his own party. He informed Makarios of his intention: *"It was unacceptable that the only political party should be that of the left, while the tremendous majority of the Greeks, who were not left wing, had no political parties, appearing thus politically backward and of medieval political mentality. I do not think Makarios appreciated my last remark about the medieval political mentality. He understood that it was a reference to the dominant political role of the church."*

Nevertheless, Makarios agreed to the plan, but warned him against Interior Minister Georkatzis, who would certainly cause trouble. But then he developed some strange ideas that indicated his reduced understanding of democracy: The foreign minister and the finance minister would have to be non-partisan, because they would have to pursue policies beyond party politics. If the party of another minister held a different opinion from that of the government, the minister in question would either have to resign or leave the party.[2] For Makarios, the government was an executive body of his ideas.

Polykarpos Georkatzis

Interior Minister Polykarpos Georkatzis was a colourful figure. During the EOKA liberation struggle, he had been the intelligence chief of this organisation, successfully infiltrating the police. In contrast to Grivas, Georkatzis was a secretive person who rarely put anything on paper. In May 1955, Grivas still put him in charge of the executions. Georkatzis put together execution teams, but he himself never took part in the actual killing.[3] He was arrested several times and even brought to trial, but since nothing could be proven against him, he had to be released. A spectacular escape from British custody earned him the nickname, the Houdini of the EOKA. After independence, he became the first Minister of the Interior of the Republic of Cyprus at the age of 25. During the struggle, he had developed organisational skills, leadership qualities and a certain charisma, through which he won the loyalty of his comrades-in-arms and later his staff. In the Ministry of the Interior, he gathered around him a circle of closest confidants with whom he built up a kind of precursor organisation to the secret service KYP and who in turn maintained contacts with the CIA. For a few weeks he was supported by Georgios Papadopoulos, later dictator of Greece, and a large number of Greek officers. The latter and his comrades had come to Cyprus in August 1960 as part of the official Greek contingent (ELDYK - Elliniki Dynami Kyprou) provided for in the Alliance Treaty. Close cooperation was agreed upon and indeed, from then on, leading cadres of the Cypriot KYP were trained in Athens.

In parallel, he built up a private network of informants, whose members provided him with information from every ministry, town and village. With the support of the CIA, he hired agents to observe the activities of the PEO and AKEL. In the process, he even managed to place one of his people in the secretariat of AKEL's general secretary, Ezekias Papaioannou. Not only did he keep files on every leftist, but he also commissioned dossiers on every Cypriot who played any role on the island; his collecting frenzy knew no bounds, not

1 Interview of the author with Vassos Lyssaridis am 12. November 2007.

2 Clerides, *op. cit.*, II, p. 315; Makarios Drousiotis, *Apo to ethniko metopo stin EOKA B'* (Lefkosia,1994), p. 72.

3 Heinz A. Richter, *Geschichte der Insel Zypern*, II, p. 165.

even shying away from the most private areas. His mistrust even went so far as to have his own staff monitored. All this was fatally reminiscent of a surveillance state, as we knew it from George Orwell's novel 1984 or from the Eastern Bloc of the time and from Greece in the 1950s.[1]

In 1963, when tensions between the Greek Cypriots and the Turkish Cypriots were rising and a clash with the Turkish underground TMT was looming, he was instrumental in building the paramilitary Organosis. Under the nom de guerre Akritas, he was one of its leaders. As such, he also drafted the notorious Akritas Plan.[2] In 1968, he had to resign as minister because he was involved in the failed assassination attempt by Panagoulis on Dictator Papadopoulos. But after this excursion about Interior Minister Georkatzis, let us return to the founding of the party.

After receiving the green light from Makarios to form the party, Kliridis held talks with Georkatzis and Labour Minister Tassos Papadopoulos, as well as some MPs, businessmen, right-wing trade unionists (SEK) and leaders of the right-wing Peasants' Organisation (PEK - Panagrotiki Enosis Kyprou). According to Kliridis, the political orientation of this party was to be right of centre. On 5 February 1969 it was founded under the name Eniaio Komma (Union Party). In Makarios' eyes, the new party was a political offshoot of the National Front (Ethnikofronon Parataxis). Most of its members came from bourgeois, petty-bourgeois and peasant circles. It provided a home for liberal-conservative forces as well as fanatical nationalists and Enosis supporters, and also for most of the former EOKA supporters who were integrated through Georkatzis. Georkatzis became the party's organising secretary and his networks across the country soon enabled the new party to be present throughout the island.[3]

Kliridis hints in his memoirs that Makarios encouraged other political greats to form parties as well. This sounds quite plausible, because it prevented the conservative camp from being completely united, and it also brought other forces into the game, so that he could continue to play the old game of divide et impera. Indeed, Makarios was at the height of his power at that time, as Kranidiotis writes.[4] It is of course also possible that the future party founders heard something of Kliridis' plans and became active for their part. In response, Lyssaridis founded the socialist EDEK (Eniaia Dimokratiki Enosi Kyprou - United Democratic Union of Cyprus), which took up front against the Eniaio Komma and AKEL.[5] In addition, two right-wing splinter parties emerged. One was the Progressive Front (Proodeftiki Parataxi), behind which was the head of the Cooperative Movement, Andreas Azinas. As he was unable to chair the party himself as a government functionary, the former mayor of Nicosia Odysseas Ioannidis was brought forward. This party was supported by certain bishops and parts of the PEK.[6] The second mini-party was the Progress Party (Proodeftiko Komma) of journalist Nikos Sampson, which consisted of radical nationalist fol-

1 Heinz A. Richter, *Geschichte der Insel Zypern*, III, pp. 261-266.
2 *Ibidem*, pp. 282-287.
3 Clerides, *op. cit.*, II, , p. 315. In the Greek edition of his memoirs he speaks of *Enotiko Komma*. Glafkos Kliridis, *I katathesis mou* (Lefkosia: Alitheia, 1989). II, p. 330; Servas, *op. cit.*, III, p. 168; Zavou, *op. cit.*, p. 246
4 Nikos Kranidiotis, *Anoxyroti politeia. Kypros 1960 - 1974,* I (Athina: Estia, 1985), p. 556.
5 Interview by the author with Vassos Lyssaridis on 12 November 2007. Zavou, *op. cit.*, p. 243.
6 Zavou, *op. cit.*, p. 271.

lowers of Sampson. Sampson had acquired a dubious reputation as a Turk-killer in the 1963-64 riots.[1] Both parties differed little in orientation from the Eniaio Komma except that their leaders harboured a distaste for Georkatzis and advocated enosis, but in a less militant way. The DEK, revitalised by the new foundations, wanted to push forward the struggle for union with Greece.[2]

The National Front

Those forces that thought democratically and agreed with Makarios' course of independence, or at least had come to terms with it for the time being, organised themselves in the parties. However, since the emergence of the Republic, there had been a radical right-wing fringe of Cypriot society whose supporters continued to fanatically strive for enosis and radically rejected independence. These extremists did not form a homogeneous group: there were the followers of Grivas, but they only took orders from him. In addition, a number of independent extremist cliques and groupings existed, such as Ieros Lochos (Holy Company)[3] or the Ethnikos Syndesmos Agoniston EOKA (National Association of EOKA Fighters).[4] Many of these extremists were old EOKA fighters or members of militant Christian anti-communist groups such as the OXEN at the time of the liberation struggle.[5] They were also found on the right fringe of the new parties, with the exception of the EDEK. When political parties emerged, the leaders of these groups saw this as a betrayal of the national cause, because Makarios' independence course stabilised the status quo, and they decided to take violent action against it. As in the past, a secret armed organisation was to be formed for this purpose.[6] According to Woodhouse, part of the episcopate, led by Makarios' old rival Bishop Anthimos of Kition, also supported the EM.[7]

The mass of ordinary members of all these groupings were young people whose idealism and naivety and faith in enosis were abused by their leaders. At the same time, their sense of romance and adventure was appealed to: Following the oath sworn by the members of the EOKA, its members also take an oath. For example, the members of the National Front swore to fight for national freedom and unification with the motherland with all their strength. They promised iron discipline, obedience to their leadership and silence even under torture.[8] There were groups who dreamed of an uprising under the leadership of Grivas. Others hoped to bring about a state of anarchy, thereby forcing the Greek government to

---

1 Clerides, *op. cit.*, II, p. 316; Servas, *op. cit.*, III, p. 169f; Zavou, *op. cit.*, p. 274; Richter, *Zypern*, Bd. 3, p. 299.

2 Drousiotis, *op. cit.*, p. 73; Patrick, *op. cit.*, p. 151.

3 Allusion to the 300 Thebans who defeated the Spartans, who were more than twice as strong, during the Peloponnesian War in 375 and 371 BC under the leadership of Pelopidas and Epameinanondas respectively. Since then, elite units of the Greek armed forces have repeatedly called themselves by this name.

4 Among them were Chountikoi, Georkatzikoi, Makariakoi, Sampsonikoi. Only the Grivikoi would have been missing, because they were already preparing to organise the EOKA B. Papageorgiou, *Fakelos Kyprou*, p. 224.

5 Kranidiotis, Anochyroti politeia, I, p. 558. According to the Ministry of Home Affairs, there were four other organisations apart from EM. *Cyprus Mail* (23 May 1969).

6 Clerides, *op. cit.*, II, p. 321.

7 C. M. Woodhouse, *The Rise and the Fall of the Greek Colonels* (New York: Franklin Watts, 1985), p. 75. The ecumenical journal *Publik* 3:11 (13 March 1970), p. 4 reported that Anthimos, in a weekly newspaper in late February 1970, "*accused Makarios of betraying the idea of enosis and therefore called on the priests and people to launch a 'national crusade to achieve annexation to Greece'.*"

8 Kranidiotis, *Anochyroti politeia*, I, p. 558.

intervene. Some even wanted to assassinate Makarios. All wanted a government that vigorously pursued the goal of enosis.[1]

The most eminent grouping was the Ethniko Metopo (EM - National Front), whose centre of gravity was in Limassol and Nicosia. Activities began as early as autumn 1968, when four extremists (including Andreas Gastriotis and Andreas Evthymiou) approached the former EOKA area commander, Christakis Tryfonidis, and asked if he would be willing to take command of a secret organisation whose aim would be to persuade Makarios to remove from the government and his entourage all those who did not support Enosis and to return himself to the policy of union with Greece. Tryfonidis, who was a staunch supporter of Makarios, is said to have informed him of the plans without naming names and warned him that the extremists were serious, but Makarios took the matter lightly.The most eminent grouping was the Ethniko Metopo (EM - National Front), whose centre of gravity was in Limassol and Nicosia. Activities began as early as autumn 1968, when four extremists (including Andreas Gastriotis and Andreas Evthymiou) approached the former EOKA area commander, Christakis Tryfonidis, and asked if he would be willing to take command of a secret organisation whose aim would be to persuade Makarios to remove from the government and his entourage all those who did not support Enosis and to return himself to the policy of union with Greece. Tryfonidis, who was a staunch supporter of Makarios, is said to have informed him of the plans without naming names and warned him that the extremists were serious, but Makarios took the matter lightly. According to his own statements, he had nothing against the establishment of a "national" organisation as long as his leadership role was respected. Apparently he did not realise that the EM had wider aims.[2] According to his own statements, he had nothing against the establishment of a "national" organisation as long as his leadership role was respected. Apparently he did not realise that the EM had wider aims.[3]

Since Makarios' control over the National Guard was slipping away and he was not entirely sure about the police either, he apparently did not mind if another paramilitary organisation emerged, such as those of Lyssaridis or Sampson, which would also contribute to the intra-Cypriot balance of power. The head of Makarios' bodyguard, the police officer Athanasios Poulitsas, must have seen things similarly, because he sent the EM some weapons from his arsenal in the basement of the archbishop's palace.[4]

Apparently, the conspirators learned that Tryfonidis had informed Makarios and stopped him cold. Afterwards they are said to have tried to win Georkatzis over to their plans, but he is said to have demanded the leadership, which was not accepted. Georkatzis then allegedly infiltrated his own people into the EM, who kept him informed about the EM's internal de-

---

1 Patrick, *op. cit.*, p. 147.

2 Clerides, *op. cit.*, II, p. 321.

3 Drousiotis, *op. cit.*, p. 77. To infer from this that Makarios was the leader of the EM, as is done by Athanasiou, is absurd. Andreas N. Athanasiou, *O agnostos polemos Athinon - Lefkosias* (Athen: Tzionis, 1989), p. 128.The fact is, however, that the EM never attacked Makarios, but the explanation is relatively simple. An attack on Makarios himself, given his popularity, would have been absolutely counterproductive and would have harmed the EM.

4 *Ibidem*, p. 80. A. Poulitsas was from Greece and had been a gendarmerie officer there. When Makarios returned to Cyprus from exile in the Seychelles via Greece, Poulitsas was assigned by the Karamanlis government to Cyprus as a permanent escort for the Archbishop, where he remained after independence and became head of the security group. At the same time, he is said to have worked for the Greek secret service (KYP).

velopments.[1] The Cypriot journalist Makarios Drousiotis tried to reconstruct the details of these intrigues, but ended up with wild conspiracy concepts.[2] The fact is that the leadership of the EM came under the influence of the Greek officers serving in the 2nd Bureau of the General Staff of the National Guard (GEEF - Geniko Epiteleio Ethnikis Frouras), the offshoot of the KYP at the Greek Embassy in Nicosia and the ELDYK. It almost goes without saying that all these officers were militantly anti-communist and many were very close to the junta, if they had not participated in the 21 April coup themselves, such as the commander of the Cypriot commando unit, Colonel Dimitrios Papapostolou. These officers took charge of the National Front groups, supplied them with weapons and made it possible for them to go into hiding in the ELDYK camp if the Cypriot police were on their heels.[3]

On 21 March 1969, the National Front (EM) spoke out publicly for the first time in a leaflet: the EM had been founded to defend Cyprus against external enemies. It would make Cyprus a Greek island. The government had to be purged of traitors and rehabilitated. It must be cleansed of the corruption of the political environment and the regime. Other leaflets said that the government's policies were the biggest obstacle on the road to enosis.[4] Many leaflets were written by the Greek officers, as is clear from the choice of words and syntax.[5]

The first terrorist attacks were directed against the Left, because this allowed the extremists to show the national-minded that communism was the main enemy to be fought. Apparently, the extremists hoped to gain sympathy among the middle classes. The first bomb exploded on 1 April, the anniversary of the start of the EOKA struggle. It targeted PEO offices in Famagousta,[6] and in the village of Tersefanou near Larnaka, the walls of the PEO office there were smeared with anti-communist slogans and other slogans exalted the junta. On 20 July, a bomb exploded in the stadium of Famagousta, where a festival of the communist youth organisation EDON was to take place.

The next target was left-wing journalists. Behind this attack was the head of the 2nd Bureau, Colonel Pantelis Lalounis, who directed the anti-communist propaganda in the press and repeatedly invited Cypriot journalists to Athens on "fact-finding trips". The EM published a leaflet calling on the editors of the newspapers Fileleftheros, Agon and Machi to dismiss certain journalists because they were AKEL members and allegedly made propaganda for international communism. The Cyprus Radio (RIK - Radiofonikos Idryma Kyprou) was asked to dismiss the head of the news department and a director because they were communists.[7] The culmination of this campaign was a revolver attack on the government spokesman and head of the Public Information Office (Grafeio Dimosion Pliroforion), Mil-

1 *Ibidem*, p. 82f.
2 *Ibidem.*, pp. 77-83
3 Miltiadis Christodoulos, *Oi scheseis Athinon Lefkosias. Poreia exarsis kai katapontismou, anadysis kai anaplasis* (Lefkosia: Proodos, 1999), p. 99; Spyros Papageorgiou, *Makarios poreia dia pyros kai sidirou* (Athen: Ladias, 1976), p. 57.
4 Christodoulos, *Scheseis*, p. 98; Drousiotis, *op. cit.*, p. 75. Further leaflets of the EM partly as facsimile in: Panagiotis Papadimitri, & Andreas Nofytou, *Polykarpos Giorgatzis. Oi teleftaies tou stigmes* (Nicosia, 1994), pp. 217-227 and Theofanis Dimitriou, *Politika enklimata. Agnostes istorikies ptyches 1960-1978* (Lefkosia: Epifaniou, 2007) *passim*. Unfortunately, the author often gives only vague evidence for other quotations.
5 Dimitriou, *op. cit.*, p. 402.
6 *Cyprus Mail* (2 April 1969).
7 Servas, *op. cit.*, p. 173; Drousiotis, *op. cit.*, pp. 79, 85.

tiadis Christodoulos, on 21 August because he was a leading member of AKEL; he survived seriously injured.[1]

Another target of the EM was the police. Already on 3 March 1969, an attack had been made on the Chief of Police of Cyprus, Charalambos Chasapis.[2] In leaflets, the higher ranks were accused of having no national spirit. The lower ranks should renounce allegiance to the wretched state.[3] Another leaflet announced that the police were considered part of the Greek army, whose orders had to be obeyed.[4] The EM tried to bring the police under its control through a double strategy: They appealed to the patriotism of ordinary policemen and tried to intimidate the leadership. On 1 April, Chasapis, who had resumed his duties, was again threatened and on 1 May 1969, he was again assaulted by unknown persons as he was picking fruit in his orange grove. An anonymous telephone caller to the newspapers stated that the attack was made because the police chief was a collaborator, probably meaning one of the government of Cyprus.[5] Chasapis was one of those incorruptible, absolutely correct police officers of the British school who would have insisted on the efficient prosecution of the terrorists while on duty, but so he went on an extended holiday. His deputy Savvas Antoniou was cut from a different, softer cloth.[6] On 18 April, an explosion followed outside the house of Justice Minister Stella Souliotou; her father, the well-known lawyer Panagiotis Kakogiannis, received threatening letters and calls.[7] On 21 April, the newspaper Alithea claimed that even police officers belonged to the EM.[8]

On 22 May, the Minister of Interior presented a report on the EM to the Interior Committee of the Cypriot Parliament, stating that it was the objective of the EM, *"to promote the national issue by every means and to hand out merciless punishments on opponents of the national issue as well as those government officials who, in view of the organisation, abused their position."*[9] The MPs criticised the poor security situation: the police had no documents or information about the EM. This was hardly surprising, as the EM had infiltrated the police. The officer in charge of police operations, Michalis Pantelidis, and the head of the Cypriot KYP, Georgios Georgiadis, were extremists from Sampson's entourage and worked for the EM. Other police officers and leadership cadres sympathised with the EM's aims on their own initiative and supported it or became members. No wonder the EM leadership was aware of every strike planned against them.[10] On 14 May, Makarios, together with the new Minister of the Interior, demanded that the police take decisive action against the EM. This was the first reaction from the government side against the EM and it probably happened because shortly afterwards the parliamentary committee on interior affairs met and before it a police officer claimed that there was no danger from the EM. Despite Makarios' request to the police to do something against the EM, nothing happened.

1 Drousiotis, *op. cit.*, p. 88.
2 *Cyprus Mail* (3 March 196).
3 Servas, *op. cit.*, p. 173.
4 Drousiotis, *op. cit.*, p. 83.
5 *Ibidem*, p. 75.
6 *Ibidem*, p. 84.
7 *Cyprus Mail* (18 April 1969).
8 *Cyprus Mail* (22 April 1969).
9 *Cyprus Mail* (23 May 1969).
10 Drousiotis, *op. cit.*, p. 85. In the coup of 15 July 1974, Sampson appointed Pantelidis as police chief and Georgiadis, who had been fired in the meantime, as head of the KYP again.

The EM had apparently already penetrated the security apparatus to such an extent that it was able to drag things out.[1]

At the end of May, Grivas supporters joined the EM who liked the Enosis course. They were told that Makarios was behind the EM. In the meantime, Makarios realised that the security apparatus as a whole no longer obeyed him, and he instructed a police officer named Filippos Evripidou to set up a special unit to crack down on the extremists. The EM reacted immediately: on 27 July, two EM hitmen shot Evripidou on his doorstep in Ag. Dometios; the assassins were police officers. A leaflet demanded the end of the intercommunal negotiations and the resignation of Kliridis. On 11 August a leaflet circulated with wild allegations against the head of the cooperative movement Andreas Azinas. On 15 August, the EM detonated a bomb in the vestibule of parliament. This was followed on 21 August, as already mentioned, by the attack on government spokesperson Christodoulou, prompting Makarios to issue his first public condemnation of the EM. The EM responded by condemning Christodoulou as an organ of international communism in a leaflet on 26 August.[2]

After the attacks on the journalists, the editors of the newspapers concerned had complained to Makarios, calling on the government to act. On 23 August, the Turkish Cypriot newspaper *Halkın Sesi* called on Makarios to take legal action against EM, after all, Turkish Cypriots also felt threatened by right-wing terror.[3] Makarios had not taken the EM's activities seriously and believed he could make it dissolve itself through appeals. But now he realised that action had to be taken. On 28 August, the Council of Ministers held a special meeting, which was also attended by Parliamentary Speaker Kliridis, and decided to declare the EM an illegal organisation.[4] The EM countered on 5 September with a leaflet claiming that among Makarios' ministers and staff there were collaborators, agents of foreign powers, impostors, traitors, etc. At the same time, however, it tried to give the impression that Makarios was actually tolerating them. Makarios rejected this in sharp words the next day. The EM responded with a new leaflet regretting Makarios' statement but avoiding an open break with Makarios. Instead, it tried to give the impression that Makarios, despite his verbal attacks on the EM, was secretly behind it.[5]

This strategy became public knowledge when, in 1970, some of the extremists were put on trial and told that they had only joined the EM when they were assured that Makarios was the secret padrone of the front. Makarios, they said, was publicly advocating independence, but this was only a ruse to prevent a Turkish invasion and to buy time, while secret Greek Cypriot forces were preparing for the day when enosis would be declared.[6] So, on the one hand, the EM leadership wanted to instrumentalise Makarios and his prestige for their own purposes, but on the other hand, they wanted to isolate him from his partisans by sowing discord. They tried to divide Makarios and his close associates and, for example, to turn Georkatzis against him and to alienate Kliridis and T. Papadopoulos from him. The aim was to weaken Eniaio Komma.[7] That these conclusions were not speculation was shown by an

1 *Ibidem*, p. 87.
2 *Ibidem*, p. 88f.
3 Servas, *op. cit.*, p. 174
4 Drousiotis, *op. cit.*, p. 90.
5 *Ibidem*, p. 92.
6 Patrick, *op. cit.*, p. 149.
7 Drousiotis, *op. cit.*, p. 94.

internal EM strategy paper which fell into Georkatzis' hands at the beginning of September and was passed on by him to Kliridis. On 16 October this paper was published as an EM leaflet.[1]

The paper was directed against the "anti-national triumvirate" consisting of Kliridis, Georkatzis and T. Papadopoulos. The text attributed EM activities to the triumvirate. It said that the bombings so far - a detailed list followed - were only the first phase of the coup plan. In the second phase, the bombings would continue, but at the same time assassinations would be carried out against friends and relatives of Makarios, creating a climate of fear. This would lead to the declaration of a state of emergency and the assumption of the post of Minister of the Interior by a member of the conspiratorial triumvirate, who would be presented as the only strong man capable of fighting the terrorists. The next step would be to remove or overthrow Makarios as president and replace him with the person designated by the constitution. After that, the Cyprus problem should be solved once and for all in cooperation with Turkey. To this end, a central government should be set up with the highest-ranking member of the Triumvirate at its head. At the same time, a Turkish and a Greek administrative structure should be established. The strong man of the conspiracy leadership was to head the Greek one.[2] The authors thus insinuated that Kliridis had ambitions for the presidency and Georkatzis wanted to return to the office of interior minister. The former would certainly have been incorrect during Makarios' lifetime, as Kliridis was one of his most loyal followers. The statement about Georkatzis is probably true, but the inclusion of Papadopoulos in this circle was certainly wrong, for there was no triumvirate. The Eniaio Comma was led by Kliridis and Georkatzis, so at best it was a duumvirate. Be that as it may, Makarios described the EM's activities before the press as treason.[3]

But the argumentation of the paper is also revealing in another way - certainly not intended by the authors - because it allows conclusions to be drawn about plans of the EM itself: Makarios was to be eliminated, power taken, the island divided and double enosis accomplished. The ideas were fatally similar to Acheson's enosis-per-coup plan (see Vol. 3 p. 514) and clearly came from the Athenian junta environment and may have been introduced into the discussion by Colonel Papapostolou. The question arises as to who in the Athens junta pursued these radical aims.

There is no way that Papadopoulos was ready to act against Makarios himself even at this stage. On the contrary, he was pro-Makarios and against the activities of the EM, as we shall see.[4] The evil spirit of this plan was the ESA chief Ioannidis, who hated Makarios. Theodoros Kouloumbis described the ESA chief as follows: *"Ioannides, a shadowy and paranoid head of the Greek military police [...]. He reserved for himself the exercise of real power, but he operated from the sidelines. [He ...]remained for years in virtual anonymity. He had formed a reputation of being fanatically anti-Communist and uncontrollably anti-Makarios. He was a deep believer in enosis. His reputation was that of an asexual, ascetic person with no appetite for material pleasures and desires. His hatred toward Makarios*

1 *Ibidem*, p. 95.

2 The full text in Dimitriou, *op. cit.*, pp. 202-205. If Georkatzis had been a member of the EM, he would hardly have forwarded this paper to Makarios.

3 *Ibidem*, p. 95.

4 According to Ambassador Alexandrakis, relations between Makarios and G. Papadopoulos were said to have been very good until November 1970. Papadimitris, *op. cit.*, p. 205.

verged on the pathological and dated back to the time Ioannides had served in Cyprus in the early 1960s. Unlike Papadopoulos, who was prepared to see Makarios fall through the use of political pressure, manipulation, and assassination techniques, Ioannides had no inhibition against using large-scale military force in order to remove his bitter rival from the political scene."[1] The latter may have been at best a vague possibility in Ioannidis' mind at the time, but the fact is that he was remotely controlling the EM from Athens.

The focus of the EM was - as already mentioned - in Limassol, where there had already been opposition circles from the corner of former EOKA fighters and frustrated Grivas supporters against Makarios and the central government in 1960, which had been crushed by Georkatzis.[2] In September 1969, the Grivas people took over the leadership there and soon controlled Paphos and Larnaca from Limassol. Michalakis Rossidis and Christakis Tryfonidis were at the top. Subordinate to them were Andreas Gastriotis, Andreas Efthymiou, below whom stood Stavros Papouis, Kostas Papadouris, Rogyros Theocharous and Panagiotis Rossidis. With the entry of the Grivas supporters, the character of the EM changed; it became a paramilitary organisation. According to Makarios Drousiotis, the General Staff of the National Guard is said to have devised some 40 operations for the EM, which would have led straight to civil war, the overthrow of Makarios and the attack on the Turkish Cypriots, which in turn would have provoked a Turkish invasion. The end result would have been double enosis.[3] As fantastic as this may sound at first, it seems plausible when seen against the background of the enosis-per-coup plan and compared with the events of the summer of 1974. Here, apparently, the first planning steps were taken in this direction.

As is well known, Georkatzis had maintained his contacts with the security forces even after his resignation as Minister of the Interior and had even expanded his private networks. It fits into this pattern that Georkatzis also infiltrated people loyal to him into the EM in order to be informed about what was going on in the EM. His aim was to return to the power structure. It was quite enough for him to be in the second row again; he wanted to pull the strings in the shadows and not be in the limelight and let others exercise the real power. For this reason, he had also become one of the deputy party leaders of the Eniaio Komma. As a member of the three-member party leadership (triumvirate), he thus definitely had a perspective for a political future when elections would be held in a year or so. The party's certain victory in the elections would put Kliridis back in the office of Speaker of Parliament and certainly bring him back into the government.

The repeatedly expressed assumption that Georkatzis had got involved with the junta and conspired against Makarios misses the reality, because the junta was divided on Cyprus policy: Junta chief Papadopoulos was friendly to Makarios, and only the head of the Greek Military Police (ESA), Dimitrios Ioannidis, conspired against him. Why should Georkatzis take part in a conspiracy against Makarios when he could safely achieve his goal through the political route. A coup d'état would hardly have promoted him to the top, at best for a short time, which was not a prospect for him. Ioannidis and his clique wanted the annex-

1 Theodore Couloumbis, *The United States, Greece and Turkey: The Troubled Triangle* (New York: Praeger, 1983), p. 79.
2 Richter, Zypern, Band 2, p. 268.
3 Drousiotis, *op. cit.*, p. 97.

ation of Cyprus to Greece. Had the annexation to Greece taken place, Georkatzis' role as a string-puller in the background would probably have ended forever. Enosis would have been counterproductive to Georkatzis' ambitions.

Moreover, there is no evidence of a real quarrel with Makarios that would have led Georkatzis to such hatred that he would have been willing to take part in a real conspiracy including assassination against Makarios. However, such ethical or emotional criteria would have had only limited effect, because Georkatzis was a Machiavellian in relation to himself: He wanted to get back to the levers of power and to that end he did whatever seemed useful. This meant that Georkatzis would also have turned against Makarios if it had benefited his ambitions. But in those months in the autumn and winter of 1969/70, nothing was visible that pointed in that direction.

The ban on the EM on 28 August caused it to temporarily suspend bombings and assassination attempts, but it struck again as early as October 1969 when it detonated an explosive device in front of the house of AKEL Secretary General Papaioannou on 14 October. The latter promptly accused the CIA of authorship, which earned him sharp criticism from the government.[1] On 27 October, unknown persons threw two explosive devices from a moving car over the entrance gate of the presidential palace, only one of which exploded. It is about 200 metres from the gate to the presidential palace; Makarios was in the Archbishop's Palace in the old city of Nicosia at the time of the attack.[2] The police quickly arrested two suspects who denied everything, but it was clear that the EM was behind the attack. Makarios then told the press that the moral instigators were still at large.[3] This interpretation is also supported by Makarios' relatively calm reaction. Makarios is said to have even asked Georkatzis to come to him and ask him for help against the EM.[4]

Increased police activity led to the discovery of a weapons cache in the building of a Christian association (ThOI - Thriskeftiko Orthodoxo Idryma - Religious Orthodox Association) in Omorfita on 19 November.[5] The police questioned more than 70 witnesses and arrested five people in the following days, two of whom were quickly released for lack of evidence. Among the weapons found were explosive devices identical in construction to those found in the presidential palace compound, suggesting that there was a connection between the two actions.[6]

---

1 *Cyprus Mail* (16 & 17 October 1969).

2 *Cyprus Mail* (28October 1969).

3 *Cyprus Mail* (6 November 1969). They were the transport entrepreneur Andreas Fekkas and the taxi driver Mikis Paras'chos from the village of Kato Zodeia, south of Morfou. Drousiotis claims that the two were close associates of Georkatzis and that he was the "instigator". However, he does not provide any valid evidence for this. Moreover, in this case the question of the benefit to Georkatzis would arise. Even if the two had relations with Georkatzis, in this case they were acting as EM supporters and not on behalf of Georkatzis. The two arrested were released a few days later for lack of evidence.*Cyprus Mail* (10 November 1969). Also Dimitriou, *op. cit.*, p. 209 insinuates that Georkatzis was the instigator without providing any evidence.

4 Drousiotis, *op. cit.*, p. 98.

5 This organisation was financed by the church and was always a rallying point for arch-conservative or extreme right-wing forces. Many EOKA fighters emerged from its ranks during the liberation struggle. The EOKA B was also able to draw on this organisation for the recruitment of members.

6 *Cyprus Mail* (11, 12, 18, 20 November 1969). The three arrested were PIO employee Georgios Chatzisavvas, secret police officer Antonios Michail and teacher Michael Spyrou. According to Drousiotis, the first two were close associates of Georkatzis. Drousiotis, *op. cit.*, p. 98. The same logic should apply to them as already noted. They were acting on behalf of the EM and not Georkatzis.

On 24 November, a policeman was shot in Limassol for arresting a youth who had distributed EM leaflets a few days earlier. In one leaflet, EM claimed to have nothing to do with the bombs.[1] On 25 November, the cabinet discussed the situation. One day later, the parliament dealt with the situation. It was suggested that a commission of enquiry be set up. At the same time, the government appealed to the newspapers not to give the EM additional publicity by quoting passages from leaflets. On 27 November, the government passed a bill authorising the use of the National Guard against terrorism and lawlessness. A 500-strong special unit was to be set up for this purpose. At the same time, it became known that the government was planning to reorganise the police. These decisions bordered on the declaration of a state of emergency.[2] On 4 December, the parliament passed this bill unanimously. On 12 December, it was announced that Makarios would visit Eastern Africa in early January. On 16 December, the Cypriot public learned that a retired senior police officer named V. Sakellariou would be coming to Cyprus to advise the government on the fight against terrorism.[3]

In mid-December, the British government took a stand against the military junta in Greece in the Council of Europe, promptly followed by a number of attacks on the British base in Akrotiri.[4] On 19 December, there were attacks on British targets in Nicosia.[5] On 31 December 1969, members of the EM stole 2,300 sticks of dynamite from a warehouse at the Kalavasos copper mine, located about 10km southwest of Skarinou. In order not to disturb Makarios' travel plans, Interior Minister Komodromos concealed this raid, but informed Foreign Minister Kyprianou. On the same day, masked members of the Front raided an arms depot near Limassol at gunpoint and stole weapons and a large quantity of ammunition.[6] On 3 January 1970, Makarios began his trip to Africa by first flying to Athens. There he learned of the raid, which caused quite a commotion.[7] On 8 January, dictator Papadopoulos strongly condemned the activities of the EM. *"I wish to declare in the most catagoric manner [...] the the Greek Government has neither offered nor is offering encouragement or support in any form to any such organization in Cyprus, regardless of aim or name. The only 'organization' with which the Greek Government is collaborating and shows solidarity, exclusively with regard to the handling of the Cyprus question and without interference in any other subject of the island's domestic affairs, is the Government led my Archbishop Makarios."*[8]|

While Makarios visited Tanzania, Zambia and Kenya between 2 and 16 January, Acting President Glafkos Kliridis ordered the police to collect all registered weapons. At the same time, he announced further drastic security measures. On 10 January, it became known that the Attorney General had prepared a bill that would allow terror suspects to be interned for three months without trial. Such a measure had been used by the British against the EOKA in the past, but it had been indefinite. The police set up checkpoints to control people. On 12

1 Drousiotis, *op. cit.*, p. 100. *Cyprus Mail* (25 November 1969).
2 *Cyprus Mail* (28 November 1969); Dousiotis, *op. cit.*, p. 117.
3 *Cyprus Mail* (12, 16 December 1969).
4 *Cyprus Mail* (17 December 1969); Drousiotis, *op. cit.*, pp. 101-108.
5 *Cyprus Mail* (20 December 1969).
6 *Cyprus Mail* (8 January 1970).
7 *Cyprus Mail* (3, 4 January 1970); Dimitriou, *op. cit.*, p. 215.
8 *Keeseing's Contemporary Archives*, p. 23.897;*CM* (9 January 1970). *" The activities [...] meet with our complete disapproval."*

January, the anniversary of the 1950 plebiscite, controls were tightened to prevent riots.[1] On 13 January, Kliridis told journalists: *"I know who the leaders of this organisation are. I personally feel that they lack brains and reasoning powers. [...] If they had any brains or reasoning power they would realise that what they are doing supposedly for Enosis is not leading to Enosis but to partition."* The internment law would be discussed by the Council of Ministers the next day.[2]

In fact, the bill was discussed on 14 January and approved by the cabinet the following day. On 16 January, the government called on the population to hand over all unregistered weapons to the authorities within 10 days, otherwise they would face severe penalties. At the same time, it announced that 800 registered weapons had already been confiscated.[3] Makarios, who returned to Athens on 17 January, approved of these measures.

Assassination and coup plans[4]

On the same day, Makarios held talks with dictator Papadopoulos and Foreign Minister Pipinelis, in the presence of Kyprianou and Ambassador Kranidiotis, on the state of inter--communal negotiations. At the same time, Makarios took the opportunity to inform his interlocutors about acts of terrorism committed by the EM. According to a report in the *Eleftheros Kosmos* newspaper of 13 August 1970, which was very close to the junta, Papadopoulos is said to have warned Makarios of attempts on his life. Makarios is said to have confirmed this, saying he had been warned by a member of a foreign embassy. When Papadopoulos wanted to know what he had done about it, Makarios replied: "Absolutely nothing."[5] The communiqué then said that the Greek government had heard this with great interest and strongly condemned the terrorist activities aimed at overthrowing the Cypriot government.[6] In an interview granted to Cyprus Radio, Papadopoulos then took an even stronger stand against the National Front.[7] On 18 January, Makarios met with King Constantine in Rome to mediate between him and the junta. He returned to Cyprus on 19 January.

In the meantime, the security measures there had been tightened because the warning of a possible assassination attempt on Makarios was taken seriously. The warning by a foreign diplomat in Nairobi mentioned by Makarios had the following meaning: In an interview with the Italian journalist Oriana Fallaci in 1974, he reported on it.[8] Laurence Stern published a longer version: *"We were about to have lunch. I was late in arriving and someone in the American Embassy insisted that he had an urgent message. We were in a hurry and I was not very pleased at the interruption, but I agreed to hear him. The message was this: 'According to reliable sources, when you go back to Cyprus there are plans for your assas-*

1 *Cyprus Mail* (10, 11, 13 January 1970).

2 *Cyprus Mail* (14 January 1970).

3 *Cyprus Mail* (17 January 1970); Drousiotis, *op. cit.*, p. 119.

4 The literature also published on this subject is to be used with restraint. The book on Georkatzi's last days by Papadimitri and Neofytou, published in 1994, is essentially a compilation of newspaper articles, with reports sometimes translated into dialogue to heighten the drama, but this does not necessarily increase the informative reliability.

5 Papageorgiou, *Poreia*, p. 32.

6 Makarios, *Apanta*, XI, p. 315.

7 Pavlos Tzermias, *Geschichte der Republik Zypern* (Tübingen: Francke Verlag, 1991), p. 421; Woodhouse, *op. cit.*, p. 75.

8 Oriana Fallaci, *Interview with History* (New York: Liveright, 1976), p. 317.

sination at the airport in Nicosia.' This was the first time I had heard of an attempt being made on my life. I smiled and said, 'Thank you very much, but I don't think it is probable.' Actually, I didn't think the airport would be a suitable place for an assassination. But the American said, 'Be careful.'"[1] As is well known, nothing happened on his return, but the warnings had a background that was to be taken quite seriously.

Among the Cypriot students studying in Athens there were also radical supporters of Grivas and the EM who fanatically sought immediate enosis. One of them, a certain Adamos Charitonos was even ready to kill Makarios. He told this to the president of the Cyprus Students' Federation EFEK (Ethniki Foititiki Enosi Kyprion - National Cyprus Students' Federation), Stelios Christidis, during his Christmas holiday in Cyprus. When the latter wanted to know if Grivas had been informed about this, he ordered him to keep quiet. When they met again in Athens a few weeks later, Charitonos announced that he would kill Makarios in Athens. Grivas supporter Christidis is said to have refused to join his students in providing the cheering background for the assassination, whether at the airport or in front of the Grand Bretagne hotel in Syntagma Square. [2] This made the assassination impracticable.

More significant than the confused assassination plan of this fanatical student, however, is the fact that he was supported by the commander of the LOK, Dimitrios Papapostolou. Papapostolou was in Athens at the beginning of January 1970 and, according to the potential assassin himself, gave him his own service weapon for the attack. At the same time, he had advised him to claim that he had acted on behalf of Georkatzis in the event of his arrest. When Charitonos objected that Georkatzis would certainly defend himself against this accusation, Papapostolou is said to have replied that a dead man cannot deny anything.[3] If this remark is correct, it means that Georkatzis could hardly have been part of the conspiracy orchestrated by Papapostolou. But before we turn to this conspiracy, let us first register further developments in Cyprus itself.

On 20 January 1970, EM members raided the Limassol port police station and captured a large quantity of weapons.[4] But on 20 January, the newspaper *Ta Nea*, edited by Lyssaridis, claimed that the authorities had accurate information about an imminent assassination attempt on Makarios.[5] On 22 January, another EM attack took place, this time on the police officers guarding the Limassol district administration building. Consideration was given in government circles to dismissing police officers suspected of EM membership and setting up the aforementioned 500-strong special police unit. However, as Makarios was suffering from a cold, no decisions were taken for a few days.[6]

Meanwhile, gun deliveries continued and on 24 January, the authorities stated that 90 per cent of the registered guns had been delivered. Even Sampson delivered 15 home-made machine guns. In the last days of January it became known that Makarios was in favour of the internment law, but Lyssaridis and Sampson and the PEO opposed it on grounds of prin-

1 Laurence Stern, "Bitter Lessons: How We Failed in Cyprus" *Foreign Policy* 19 (Summer 1975), p. 44.
2 Papageorgiou, *Poreia*, p. 30.
3 Drousiotis, *op. cit.*, p. 123; Adamos Charitonos, *Exomologisi* (Lefkosia,1985), p. 27.
4 *Cyprus Mail* (20 January 1970).
5 Dimitriou, *op. cit.*, p. 224
6 *Cyprus Mail* (21-23 January 1970).

ciple. Nevertheless, it was passed by parliament on 30 January, with 17 MPs voting for and 7 against, and a day later Makarios signed the law into law. At the same time it was announced that the law would not be applied if things remained quiet. The EM then announced a ceasefire. In mid-February, hopes were raised that the EM would dissolve.[1]

In the following weeks, the police continued to hand over and confiscate weapons. In total, 300 rifles, 60 machine guns, 400 light machine guns and submachine guns, 800 pistols and revolvers, 1,200 hand grenades and 340,000 rounds of ammunition were collected between January and April. On 24 March, police uncovered an arsenal of 200 firearms in the basement of a Greek house in Nicosia. It may be assumed that this was only a small percentage of the weapons actually present in Cyprus.[2]

In an interview with the Athens newspaper Acropolis on 24 February 1970, Makarios condemned the activities of the EM. The membership itself was absolutely not homogeneous. There were many nationally-minded people among them who had been seduced. Makarios admitted that some police officers had also joined the EM because they believed that the EM was pursuing patriotic objectives. This, of course, was no excuse to be taken seriously and the officers would have to expect punishment.[3] In another interview with representatives of the Association of Athens Daily Newspapers, Makarios repeated these arguments and expressed his hope that the EM would dissolve.[4] Makarios obviously believed that the threat of a tougher stance would deter the EM from further action. He therefore did not take seriously another warning, this time from US Ambassador David Popper: The warnings conveyed in Nairobi had been confirmed. An attack would be attempted in the next two weeks.[5]

But it was not only the Americans who observed the developments in Cyprus with concern, but also the Soviet Union. On 19 February 1970, the Soviet Union's representative to the UN presented the Secretary General with a statement distributed by the TASS news agency, which stated that in Cyprus there was a terrorist organisation called the National Front, which, together with other reactionary forces, was linked to the Greek military regime. They were also trying to establish a dictatorship in Cyprus on the Greek model. A small clique of reactionary Greek officers, who still held important posts in the Cypriot National Guard, was responsible for this. These plans are an integral part of a NATO plan to solve the Cyprus problem by military means. The forces were trying to create a pretext for

1 *Cyprus Mail* (1, 3 February 1970).
2 Patrick, *op. cit.*, p. 148f.
3 Makarios, *Apanta*, XI, p. 608.
4 *Ibidem*, p. 614.
5 In his book *The Wrong Horse*, p. 87 Stern embellished this second warning: He reported a telephone conversation between Georkatzis and his successor in office, in which Georkatzis informed him about the planned assassination. The minister advised his interlocutor to stay out of it. *"You will bring the country a lot of misery [...] you should not carry a personal grudge this far. Georhadjis replied, the other man later recalled: 'Don't worry, the future is with us. The Americans are behind us.'."* Stern cites no source for this story; moreover, the name of the minister he mentions is completely wrong (T. K. Anastosiou). The correct name was Komodromos. See also Fallaci, *Interview*, p. 317. There it says: *"A few days later, in Cyprus, they conformed the information to me, adding that the attempt would take place within two weeks."* Laurence Stern, *The Wrong Horse. The Politics of Intervention and the Failure of American Diplomacy* (New York: Times Book, 1977).

NATO to intervene. The Soviet Union leadership was following the development with concern.[1]

The action was welcome to Makarios as support for his tough course against the EM on the one hand, but on the other hand it was of course embarrassing, because he did not want a row with the junta. Therefore, a government spokesperson denied the Soviet accusations that the junta supported the reactionary forces in Cyprus. They were working closely with Athens and held the same views on the solution of the Cyprus problem.[2] Three days later, Pravda said that preserving the independence of Cyprus was also in the interest of the Soviet Union and Izvestia claimed that the EM was plotting to assassinate Makarios and NATO circles wanted to turn Cyprus into a NATO base.[3] Obviously, Moscow was also well informed through the comrades of AKEL and its own services that something was brewing in Cyprus.

Popper's warning and the references in the newspapers had a real background, for there were indeed plans for a coup, on which the staff of the National Guard and the Commando Unit (LOK) under Colonel Papapostolou had been working for some time. The basic concept was apparently similar to that of September 1969: assassination of Makarios, seizure of power by the military and then bringing about the double enosis. The prerequisite for the success of the plan was, of course, the removal of Makarios. The military apparently left the execution of the assassination to the EM. They themselves planned a staff coup for the end of May. On 27 January 1970, the final version, Operations Order 3, the coup plan was available. The four-page order envisaged the seizure of power in Nicosia by the Commando Unit (LOK) at 11.30 p.m. on 28 May 1970, in close cooperation with units of the National Guard and armed groups of the EM. The form and language of the order leave no doubt that the text came from a trained Greek staff officer.[4] If this plan was to be carried out successfully, precise timing and cooperation between the various forces was necessary. But this is exactly what did not work and therefore coordination breakdowns occurred. The planners had neither managed to bring the additional National Guard units needed in the coup under their control, nor to have larger units of the EM ready at the time. Although it was still possible, when the time of the assassination became clear, to order a holiday ban at short notice for the LOK from 7 to 9 March, the units planned for the coup did not take up initial positions, but were only to go into action after the successful assassination. The execution of the assassination itself was rather amateurish. When the assassination attempt on Makarios took place on 8 March 1970, the military were obviously not yet organisationally ready to strike.

The feared assassination attempt on Makarios was carried out in Nicosia in the early hours of 8 March 1970. In the days before, it had become known that Makarios would go to the monastery of Machairas on that day to dissolve a mass there in memory of the EOKA hero Grigorios Afxentiou. There had been rumours that there would be an attempt on Makarios' life there. Deputy Police Chief Antoniou informed Makarios and he had those responsible for his security, Athanasios Poulitsas and Colonel Dimitrios Papapostolou, come to him.

---

1 United Nations, *UN Yearbook 1970* (New York: UN, 1971), p. 290f; Servas, *op. cit.*, III, p. 175f.
2 Tzermias, *op. cit.*, p. 422.
3 Drousiotis, *op. cit.*, p. 159.
4 Text of the plan in Papageorgiou, *Poreia*, pp. 50-53.

He informed them of the rumours and asked them to take the necessary security measures. It was decided to concentrate a larger number of security forces in Machairas, including Makarios' personal security, under the command of Poulitsas, leaving Makarios virtually without protection in Nicosia. The officers of the security forces, including Poulitsas and Papapostolou, were to leave at 5 a.m. on 8 March from the police headquarters for Machairas to lead the security measures there.[1]

The usual flights started at the Presidential Palace, where the helicopter was also stationed. When Makarios made a trip on Sundays, it always started at the Archbishop's Palace in the Old City. Whenever he took a flight from the latter, it was announced beforehand; in this particular case, it had been known for a week. At 7.02 a.m., the pilot, Greek Major Zacharias Papadogiannis, landed the President's helicopter on the forecourt of the palace. As Makarios had not yet appeared, the pilot got out and opened the passenger door of the helicopter through which Makarios would enter, thus making it difficult for the assassins waiting on the flat roof of the Severis Library of the Pankyprian Gymnasium opposite to see Makarios. These were the already known assassin of Athens, the student Adonis Charitonos, the broker Georgios Taliadoros, the policemen Antonakis Genagritis and Polykarpos Polykarpou. A second group around the policeman Antonakis Solomontos and the newspaper editor Kostas Ioannidis had taken up position on the flat roof of an apartment block to the west.

Precisely at 7.06 a.m., Makarios left the archbishop's palace alone, came down the stairs. Surprisingly, despite the rumours, he was alone; normally the head of his bodyguard, Poulitsas, or another of his bodyguards accompanied him on such flights. The fact that Makarios was flying unaccompanied was odd, given the situation.[2] Be that as it may, Makarios sat down in the seat to the left of the pilot. The assassins did nothing; their aim was to set the helicopter on fire and bring it down. The pilot closed the door and secured it, walked around the helicopter and sat in his seat, put on his seatbelt, put on his headset and began the ascent. When he reached about the height of the roof of the Archbishop's Palace, he turned the helicopter about 150 degrees towards Troodos and began the rapid climb. When he had gained about 10 metres in height, the pilot heard a shot and registered that the shot had been fired from the left rear and had hit the helicopter. A moment later, a machine gun shell hit the helicopter and a bullet hit him in the abdomen causing violent internal bleeding. More shots were fired and hit the helicopter. The pilot lost all feeling in his lower body and realised that he was about to lose control of the helicopter and had to land as soon as possible. Therefore, he steered the helicopter to a vacant lot north of the house of Dragoman Chatzigeorgakis Kornesios, corner of Isokratous and Partriarchos Gregorios Streets, avoided an electric and telephone line and landed.

The pilot, fearing an explosion, shouted to Makarios to leave the helicopter immediately, which he did. When the Archbishop was about five metres away, he too struggled out of the helicopter in great pain and bleeding. When he had dragged himself about 20 metres, he collapsed. Makarios called for help. Local residents rushed over and took the pilot and Makarios in a Volkswagen to the general hospital emergency room, where the pilot received first aid. The assassins left their weapons, threw a hand grenade on the road between the school

1 Dimitriou, *op. cit.*, p. 240f.
2 *Ibidem*, p. 258.

and the palace to cover their escape and fled through the back exit of the school. They left the scene in a waiting rental car. The car was later found abandoned at Ag. Antonio's market.[1]

While Makarios was still at the hospital, Colonel Papapostolou suddenly appeared in his private car, who should have been at Machairas to supervise the security measures. Makarios had apparently become suspicious and therefore refused to go alone with the colonel to the presidential palace and enlisted a prison officer who happened to be there to stay by his side. Then Makarios decided to return to the Archbishop's Palace in Papapostolou's car. The latter urged Makarios to go to the presidential palace outside the city after all, in order to address the public from there in a radio statement. Makarios refused and made Papapostolou drive the car himself, while he and his "bodyguard" sat in the back. The reason for Makarios' refusal was probably the realisation that there in the presidential palace he would have exposed himself to unhindered access by the LOK, whose one camp was only a few kilometres away.

In the meantime, Makarios' personal physician Vassos Lyssaridis, Interior Minister Epaminondas Komodromos, the chairman of the cooperative movement Andreas Azinas, the deputy police chief Savvas Antoniou and others had arrived at the archbishop's palace. Makarios sent for his official car, driven by his brother, and without hesitation Papapostolou, who in the meantime was posing as Makarios' bodyguard, climbed into the back of the car. Shortly before leaving, Makarios is said to have told Interior Minister Komodromos that Georkatzis should be arrested.[2] This would mean that Makarios also suspected Georkatzis of being involved in the attack, but since Georkatzis was only questioned and his house searched, it is unlikely that Makarios ordered his arrest, but only his questioning. This is also supported by Makarios' later instruction to the head of the Presidential Security Group, Andreas Potamaris, to search Georkatzis' home.[3] The suspicion that Georkatzis might be involved in the attack was also expressed by Grivas in Athens on the same day.[4]

Former government spokesman Miltiadis Christodoulou added an interesting hypothesis to the discussion about those behind the attack: the Athens junta had wanted to get rid of both Makarios and Georkatzis. Papapostolou had been the executive organ. He had made Georkatzis believe that Makarios wanted to use the EM to kill him. Through Makarios' chief bodyguard Poulitsas, he had told Makarios that Georkatzis was planning an attempt on his life. In this way, he succeeded in getting Georkatzis to use his men against Makarios.[5] The author overlooked the fact that it was not the junta that wanted to eliminate Makarios, but the ESA leader D. Ioannidis and his clique. Moreover, it may be assumed that both Makarios and Georkatzis would have been clever enough not to fall for such an intrigue and allow themselves to be played off against each other in such a transparent manner. The former partisans of Georkatzis who took part in the crime carried out the assassination on their own decision under the influence of the EM and Papapostolou.

---

1 Testimony of the pilot. Papageorgiou, *Poreia*, pp. 41-43; Clerides, *op. cit.*, II, p. 362f; Drousiotis, *op. cit.*, p. 171. An exact listing of the weapons left behind in Dimitriou, *op. cit.*, p. 250.

2 Drousiotis, *op. cit.*, p. 177.

3 *Ibidem*, p. 179. Dimitriou suspects that an arrest was not made because Georkatzis knew too much and could have spoken out. Dimitriou, *op. cit.*, p. 280.

4 Papageorgiou, *Poreia*, p. 47.

5 Christodoulou, *Poreia*, p. 530f.

The search of Georkatzis' flat was carried out by Potamaris at around 10 pm that evening. He paid little attention to the lockable filing cabinet where Georkatzis kept his "dossiers" and tapes that he had taken with him when he left the ministry, but confiscated two pistols that Georkatzis had received as a gift from Makarios. As Potamaris left, police chief Chassapis and his deputy Michalakis Pantelidis showed up to ask Georkatzis questions. Before the conversation began, Kliridis called to ask what was going on. Georkatzis informed him of their presence and said that he would come and see him after the interview was over. After hanging up the phone, Pantelidis said that he had better stay at home for security reasons because many people suspected him of being involved in the attempt on Makarios' life. Georkatzis agreed and admitted that people distrusted him. Pantelidis wanted to know who was behind the attack on Makarios, for example the EM. Georkatzis denied it. The EM had split, perhaps the assassins belonged to the hard core of the EM, Pantelidis replied. Georkatzis thought this was possible, but he did not know anything for sure. Georkatzis mentioned that there had been a conspiracy by Grivas in the past. When Pantelidis wanted to know if this was still the case now, Georkatzis did not answer. Pantelidis prodded: had he informed Makarios of this? Georkatzis replied that the Archbishop had not received him. The two policemen realised that Georkatzis would say nothing more and left him, after advising him again not to leave his flat.[1]

On the afternoon of 8 March 1970, Parliament met and condemned the attack in strong terms.[2] A crowd gathered outside the building, from among whom it was shouted that Georkatzis and his men had carried out the attack.[3] Thus began the hunt for Georkatzis. In the evening, dozens of leading personalities sought out the Archbishop's Palace to assure Makarios, who had meanwhile returned from Machairas, of their sympathy and to congratulate him on his rescue. All the ministers and MPs, the police leadership and others close to Makarios appeared. Among the well-wishers was the head of Makarios' bodyguards, Poulitsas, who had been in Machairas at the time of the attempted assassination. Lyssaridis heard him say that Georkatzis had to be killed. Greek officers of the National Guard also made similar remarks. The remarks were picked up by those present and passed on. For Sampson, it was clear that Georkatzis was behind the attack.[4] The rumour mill began to run at full speed and was deliberately fed with disinformation, which in turn was picked up and spread by all those who disliked Georkatzis. It was obvious that the real perpetrators were looking for a scapegoat to hide behind. Georkatzis was suddenly all alone.

Kliridis remembered: *"Yiorkadjis began to show signs of being extremely worried. According to what he said to various people who saw him during those days, there were two sources of concern which worried him. He expressed the fear that his enemies would incriminate him in the attempt on he life of Makarios and that fanatical supporters of Makarios would kill him."*[5]

On the evening of 9 March, the police arrested G. Taliadoros, one of the assassins, whose testimony led to the arrest of Adamos Charitonos. On 9 March, Nicosia was full of

---

1 Drousiotis, *op. cit.*, p. 181 auf der Basis der Gerichtsakten.
2 Papageorgiou, *Poreia*, p. 64.
3 Dimitriou, *op. cit.*, p. 245.
4 Drousiotis, *op. cit.*, p. 182; Dimitriou, *op. cit.*, p. 246.
5 Clerides, *op. cit.*, II, p. 369.

people who had come to the capital from all parts of Cyprus to express their support for Makarios. Throughout the week, Georkatzis tried again and again to contact Papapostolou or Makarios. But the former did not answer the phone and the latter refused any contact. On 11 March, Solomontos, Geragritis and Polykarpou were arrested. On the same day, Makarios gave an interview to the correspondent of the German ecumenical magazine Publik, in which he made it clear: *"I know my opponents on the island. But unfortunately they receive active support from abroad. I have not yet given up hope that the foreign backers will see reason. But here on the island I will ensure peace and order through tough laws. I will not allow a small group of fanatics to terrorise the loyal majority."*[1]

On the evening of 12 March, the trial of Georkatzis for illegal possession of weapons took place. As rumours were circulating that he was to be murdered either on the way to court or in the courtroom, his party supporters had taken tight security measures. Nevertheless, he went to the courthouse alone. The courtroom was filled to capacity. Georkatzis sat down on the defendant's bench. He pointed out to the court that the two revolvers had been a gift from Makarios, but that he had forgotten to declare them. The judge sentenced him to a fine of £150 for illegal possession of weapons.[2] If there had been concrete evidence of Georkatzis' involvement in the conspiracy, the judge would certainly not have let him off so cheaply.

Georkatzis realised that the situation was becoming difficult for him and decided to present his knowledge of the actual activities of the Greek officers in Cyprus to Makarios. He tried to get a meeting with Makarios through the intermediary of the editor of the newspaper *Fileleftheros* Michalakis Chatziefthymiou, but in vain. In view of this situation, Georkatzis decided to leave the country and informed his former bodyguard and friend Kyriakos Patatakos. The latter and other friends thought this was a sensible solution. It was decided that Georkatzis should leave the island on 13 March by plane to Beirut. One of the friends procured an anonymous plane ticket.[3] Before he went to the airport the next morning, accompanied by two friends, he declared his resignation from Eniaio Komma. He had registered that rumours were now circulating that Kliridis was involved in the attempt on Makarios' life because he wanted to become president. Georkatzis hoped to limit the damage.[4]

Georkatzis passed through police passport control without any problems and boarded the plane, which taxied for take-off but suddenly turned back. The explanation was relatively simple, the military security department (OAS - Omades Asfaleias Stratou) was monitoring the airport and when their people spotted Georkatzis at the airport they made sure that his departure was prevented because it would have been more than embarrassing if Georkatzis had spilled the beans abroad about the activities of the Greek officers. The OAS headquarters informed Poulitsas and he intervened with Makarios, who agreed to prevent Georkatzis' departure. The police, "on the orders of Makarios", ordered by radio the return of the plane to the parking position. The pilot obeyed the tower's instructions and when he returned to

1 Rolf W. Schloss, "Makarios: Ich kenne meine Feinde" *Publik* 3:11 (13. März 1970), p. 4. Since the magazine was published on 13 March 1970, the interview must have taken place at least two days earlier. Makarios, *Apanta*, p. 623 mentions 14 March 1970, which is hardly possible given the publication date of the magazine.

2 Drousiotis, *op. cit.*, p. 187f.

3 *Ibidem*, p. 193.

4 Makarios, *Apanta*, XI, p. 629.

his starting position, the rear door of the plane was opened and a mobile staircase was brought in. Some police officers went into the aircraft and asked Georkatzis to follow them. Georkatzis did so and returned with them to the airport. There he got into Patatakos' car and he drove back to the city and took him to his flat. Georkatzis had only been prevented from taking off, but not arrested.[1]

After arriving at Patatakos' flat, Georkatzis tried to contact Papapostolou by telephone through the National Guard Staff (GEEF), but he allowed himself to be denied. Only when he called in under a different name did he manage to speak to the colonel. A meeting was arranged on the road from Nicosia to Famagousta near the electricity company's substation at 7.30 pm. The reason for this meeting was probably the following: Georkatzis feared being killed by Papapostolou or his people because of his knowledge of the attempt on Makarios' life. In order to prevent this, he had only one option, he had to threaten the colonel with revelations that would be highly dangerous for him, and by the logic of the matter these could only be revelations about the coup plan. It may be assumed that Georkatzis already had certain information about it at this point, but it was not yet concrete enough to make Papapostolou hold back when he confronted him with it. At the same time, he probably tried to sound out Papapostolou.[2] This interpretation is supported by the course of the meeting.

Georkatzis went to the meeting point accompanied by Patatakos and another policeman named Solomou. The two confidants drove ahead in Patatakos' car and Georkatzis followed at some distance in Solomou's car. The meeting took place at the appointed time and place. Georkatzis and Papapostolou spoke privately in Solomou's car. Since there were no witnesses, what was spoken between the two was never known. On the way back from the meeting point in Patatakos' car, Georkatzis allegedly said in response to questions from his confidant that a coup d'état and further attacks were planned against Kliridis, Attorney General Tornaritis or government spokesman Christodoulou.[3] Georkatzis' mention of the coup may be taken as an indication that he had indeed brought up the coup plan in conversation with Papapostolou, but had obviously failed to obtain his objective, some kind of guarantee of his safety, because his "evidence" had not been weighty enough. So Georkatzis had to provide evidence that was beyond doubt and present it to Papapostolou at a new meeting.

A first meeting between the two, arranged by telephone for the evening of 14 March, was postponed to the evening of the next day following a telephone call from Georkatzis. Late in the evening of 14 March, at around 11 pm, police officer Ioannis Metaxas appeared at the flat where Georkatzis was staying and delivered a file containing documents from the National Guard Staff (GEEF), which had previously been stolen by Cypriot Lieutenant Kikis Channidis. Georkatzis took one look at the file and ordered Metaxas to take it to Patatakos so that he could copy it with the machine in Georkatzis' office. Afterwards, the original was to be returned to Channidis so that he could put it back in its place. The copies themselves were to be taken by Patatakos and kept in a safe place in Aglantzia. On Sunday 15 March, Patatakos came to the flat where Georkatzis was staying. The latter instructed

---

1 Drousiotis, *op. cit*, pp. 194-196.

2 Clerides, *op. cit.*, II, p. 371. *"Yeorkadjis [...] told Patatakos that he met Papapostolou in order to obtain information about the coup certain military officers were planning."*

3 Drousiotis, *op. cit.*, p. 197f.

him that if anything should happen to him at the forthcoming meeting with Papapostolou, he should hand over the copies to Kliridis so that he could pass them on to Makarios.[1]

Georkatzis spent Sunday at a friend's house. At around 7.30 pm he had Vasos Tofas drive him in his car to an agreed meeting point with Patatakos. Mrs Tofas sat in the passenger seat and he in the back seat. They met near the Aglantzia bypass and from there Patatakos drove ahead, the others following. About two kilometres before the village of Mia Milia, Georkatzis made his driver flash his lights to signal the Tofas ahead to stop. Georkatzis got out and came to Patatako's car and said he would drive. Georkatzis got behind the wheel and Patatakos got into the passenger seat. Tofas was told to wait at this point until the end of the meeting. Georkatzis and Patatakos continued towards the village of Neo Chorio Kythreas. The meeting was to take place on a dirt road between Mia Milia and the Lakkovounaro forest area. As they approached the dirt road, they saw a car with parking lights parked there at some distance. Georkatzis reduced his speed and prepared to turn left into the dirt road. He told Patatakos to leave the car and wait for him at that spot. Patatakos warned him that this was dangerous. Georkatzis replied that he would not stop if he did not see Papapostolou, but would continue towards the forest. Patatakos got out.

Patatakos testified in court about the subsequent development as follows: *"I followed his instructions. From the point where I got off to the position of the stationary car there was a distance of about 200 meters. I proceeded on foot through the fields and I saw his car getting near the stationary vehicle. I noticed him stop*[2] *and in a few seconds I heard four to five shots and I realized that something was going on. I fired two shots with my service pistol towards them to frighten them. After my shots I heard automatic fire from a different gun than the first. I realized that there was something serious. I moved about 30 meters from the side-road and I hid behind a bank of earth. I noticed the car of the unknown persons with its side lights on go towards the main road with speed. I did not manage to see the number of the car or how many persons were in it. It was a small saloon car. I noticed that the said car took the direction towards Kythrea village."*[3] Georkatzis had been executed. He was only 40 years old at the time of his death.[4]

Patatakos ran to the scene hoping that Georkatzis was still alive. He found the dead Georkatzis, still in the driver's seat, with his foot on the accelerator. His head was just a bloody mass and his body was also hit several times. The car's engine was still running, Patatakos pulled Geokatzis' foot off the accelerator and turned off the engine. Then Patatakos ran to Mia Milia. At the first house he knocked on the door, hoping to get a car there to get to Nicosia. The resident advised him to try the kafeneion in the village. On the way there, he met Tofas and his wife. Together they drove to Nicosia. There they came across a police Landrover and stopped it. Patatakos let the police officers drive him to Kliridis' flat and Tofas drove to the Director General of the Ministry of the Interior, Georgios Anastasiou, and informed him of Georkatzis' death.[5]

---

1 Makarios, *Apanta*, XI, p. 632.

2 Since Georkatzis stopped, it can be assumed that he saw Papapostolou, otherwise he would have continued his journey. Dimitriou, *op. cit.*, p. 291.

3 Clerides, *op. cit.*, p. 373. According to Drousiotis, op. cit., p. 207, there was supposedly an LOK camp there at the time.

4 *Keesing's Contemporary Archives*, p. 23.897.

5 Drousiotis, *op. cit.*, pp. 205-208; Makarios, *Apanta*, XI, p. 632.

There are still wild speculations about this murder in Cyprus today. Depending on political sympathies, the most diverse views are held. There are those who attribute the murder to police officers loyal to Makarios who were convinced that Georkatzis was behind the attack on Makarios: allegedly they would have killed Georkatzis at another location and then put him in the car and taken him to the murder site. Others are convinced that the EM perpetrated the attack, which sounds equally unlikely, since the EM had hardly any operational killers left, because the teams of the attack on Makarios had been arrested. If one concludes from the "efficiency" - as opposed to the one on Makarios - of the attack on the perpetrators, then the two perpetrators, the automatic and the pistol shooter could only have been professionals. The escape route taken towards the LOK camp suggests that the killers were members of the LOK. Whether they were Greek officers or fanatical Cypriot LOK fighters is not known.[1] The fact is, however, that the murder was absolutely counterproductive for the coup plans of Papapostolou or D. Ioannidis, because now Makarios was informed about the plans. The coup planners had to start all over again.

Kliridis writes about the minds of these officers: *"It was exponents of this school of thought, serving in Cyprus as Greek officers, who brought about the fusion of anti-Makarios elements with pro-Makarios elements, who had been badly disappointed and disillusioned by Makarios abandonment of Yiorkadjis, which led to the Interior Minister's fall from office. In this way a common interest was created for the removal of Makarios from office. Since this was not possible by political means, it had to be done by assassination. Only in such way could a regime be created in Cyprus, which would remove the communist threat, inspire confidence in the West and re-open the road to Enosis. [...] It was, however, these very few officers who master-minded the attack on the life of Makarios. Papadopoulos on a subsequent visit by Makarios to Athens, referring to the attempted assassination on his life, told him: 'I should have put certain colonels before a firing squad, but unfortunately I could not'."*[2]

Around 9.30 pm Patatakos arrived at Kliridis' house and rang the doorbell. Kliridis opened the door: *"There stood Patatakos whom I knew. He looked agitated, dishevelled and was covered in dust and blood stains. He said 'They killed Yiorkadjis, you must leave at once, they will kill you and then a military coup will follow.' I said 'Come in, calm down and tell me what exactly are you talking about'. After he told me what had actually occurred I took him to the Archbishopric to see Makarios."* When they arrived at the Archbishop's Palace, Makarios had just been informed about the events by telephone by the Director General of the Ministry of the Interior, Anastasiou, to whom Tofas had reported in the meantime. Any doubts about the contact between Georkatzis and Papapostolou were removed when a piece of paper with Papapostolou's telephone number was found in the breast pocket of Georkatzis' jacket. Kliridis suggested to Makarios that the Greek ambassador Alexandrakis and the Greek commanders be called in. He himself went with Patatakos to Aglantzia to fetch the photocopies with the coup plan that he had hidden there.[3] Makarios called the

1 Dimitriou, *op. cit.*, p. 304. Dimitriou, who took part in the investigation at the time, reported in his memoirs that he suspected at the time that the chief of the 2nd Bureau of the National Guard Staff, Colonel Pantelis Lalaounis, and the chief of Makarios' bodyguard Athanasios Poulitsas were the shooters. However, his "evidence" seems somewhat weak.

2 Clerides, *op. cit.*, II, p. 368.

3 *Ibidem*, p. 374f.

Greek ambassador, Menelaos Alexandrakis, and asked him to come to the archbishop's palace, as he had something serious to discuss with him.[1]

When Kliridis returned to the archbishop's palace with Patatakos, he met Alexandrakis in the staircase. Kliridis informed Alexandrakis of the situation: Greek officers had shot Georkatzis and a coup by the Greek army was imminent. They had written evidence from the staff of the National Guard GEEF). Alexandrakis went to the Archbishop's office. Makarios was calm and said that any had killed Georkatzis. Alexandrakis would certainly hear a lot about Greek officers and about a planned coup. He, Makarios, did not believe this talk. The document in question was either a forgery or of no significance. When Alexandrakis said goodbye, he told Makarios that he should call in the commanders of the military units and give them orders. Makarios repeated that he did not believe in the rumours and saw no need to summon the commanders.[2]

Alexandrakis returned to the Greek embassy and sent for the commanders and told them about what had happened. Then he asked them to accompany him to Makarios despite the late hour. There he heard that Makarios had already gone to bed, yet he insisted that he be woken up. A little later Makarios appeared in a blue monk's robe and sandals. Alexandrakis said the commanders were awaiting his orders. Makarios replied that there was no cause for alarm. The information about a coup was false, he said. Alexandrakis returned to the embassy and confronted Papapostolou: his name had come up in connection with the attempt on Makarios' life and the murder of Georkatzis. Papapostolou protested his innocence. In his memoirs, however, Alexandrakis noted that during the trial of the assassins of Makarios, Papapostolou's name was mentioned as an accomplice, making it clear that he considered Papapostolou to be a liar.[3]

It would be a mistake to attribute gullibility to Makarios, as has been done.[4] The opposite is true, for he realised that he faced a dilemma. If he publicly acknowledged the coup plot as genuine, he would have to expel Papapostolou and his clique from the country and possibly more officers. This would inevitably lead to a confrontation with Athens, ruin his good relations with G. Papadopoulos, lead to an inevitable closing of ranks of the junta around Ioannidis and strengthen the forces around him in Greece and Cyprus. Therefore, in a press statement on 17 March, he announced that he considered the document to be a forgery. He did not believe the rumours that Greek officers were involved in the murder of Georkatzis. These only served to undermine the psychological unity between the people and the army, which was one of the main pillars of Greekness in Cyprus.[5] These were fine words used for damage control and to divert attention from the truth.

But Makarios' attempt to defuse the situation through this linguistic arrangement only succeeded to a limited extent, for the *Spiegel* of 16 March 1970 spoke of the existence of a three-stage Hermes plan through which enosis was to be achieved: "overthrow of Makarios; separation of the Greek and Turkish populations; annexation of Cyprus to Greece." This is

---

1 Alexandrakis, *op. cit.*, p. 60.

2 Kranidiotis, *Anochyroti politeia*, II, p. 17 speaks of faneriotic politics and probably means a politics that was committed to the reason of state.

3 *Ibidem*, p. 61.

4 Woodhouse, *op. cit.*, p. 75.

5 Makarios, *Apanta*, XI, p. 638f.

strongly reminiscent of the ideas of the already mentioned EM leaflet of October 1969. The generally very well-informed Athens *Spiegel* correspondent Kostas Tsatsaronis was only mistaken in one detail when he assumed that this plan came from Papadopoulos and that he had commissioned Ioannidis with its implementation. The implementing body, according to *Der Spiegel*, was the National Front.[1] Apparently, information about that EM leaflet of October 1969 had reached the always well-informed Spiegel correspondent, who had somehow linked it to the name Ermis (Hermes). But the Hermes Plan, as it was called by *Der Spiegel*, had nothing to do with the content of the coup plan. It is true, as the author knows from his own experience, that Tsatsaronis occasionally heard the grass grow in the Athens of the junta, but his ears certainly did not reach the planning department of the staff of the National Guard in Cyprus. Nevertheless, the Spiegel article proved helpful for internal Cypriot enlightenment. The AKEL paper Charavgi, which had journalists who knew German because they had studied in the GDR, wrote on 17 March about a conspiracy plan aimed at separating the Cypriot ethnic groups and double enosis. The word *Ermis* was deleted by the censors.[2] Be that as it may, Makarios stuck to his language regime in the weeks that followed, even in his Spiegel interview, which appeared in the 6 April 1970 issue. There he stated that the assassination attempt on him had been carried out by Greek Cypriots and denied that a "foreign finger" had fired. He did not mention the assassination of Georkatzis.[3] However, the coup plan has since been called the Ermis Plan in the literature.

Georkatzis' funeral took place on 17 March. Only Tassos Papadopoulos from the government attended. Glafkos Kliridis represented the Einaio Komma. Since Georkatzis could no longer defend himself, he became everyone's scapegoat from then on, and everyone made an effort to cover up the true facts. The great cover-up of the truth began, in which all sides concerned participated. The first to ensure a "cover-up" were the Greek military. As early as 16 March 1970, Chief of General Staff Odyssefs Angelis instructed Brigadier General Grigoris Bonanos to go to Cyprus and investigate, by means of interrogations under oath, the allegation that Greek officers stationed in Cyprus were involved in the recent assassinations. Bonanos flew to Cyprus the same day and spent four days interrogating those involved. It is clear from his memoirs that he was convinced of Georkatzis' involvement in the assassination attempt on Makarios, for he cited Makarios' alleged order of 8 March to arrest the former interior minister. It is little wonder, therefore, that his investigation had no result. When he returned to Athens on 20 March, he reported to dictator Papadopoulos himself. The latter was very disturbed by the idea that something had happened to Makarios and wanted to know whether Bonanos would be prepared to take over the command of the Greek troops in Cyprus, which the latter, however, refused. This can probably be interpreted as an indication that Papadopoulos did not trust the commanders stationed in Cyprus. Bonanos, however, recommended the dismissal of Colonel Papapostolou and Lieutenant Georgios Aslanidis for reasons of psychology.[4]

1 *Der Spiegel* 12 (16 März 1970), p. 129.
2 Drousiotis, *op. cit.*, p. 220. Since Der Spiegel was printed before the coup plan fell into Georkatzi's hands, Drousiotis assumed that Der Spiegel must have special channels to the junta. He did not realise that the so-called Hermes Plan had a completely different content.
3 *Der Spiegel* 15 (6. April 1970), p. 128.
4 Bonanos, *op. cit.*, pp. 92-96.

On 17 March, the police leadership and the investigating magistrates in charge of the case met at the Presidential Palace, chaired by Interior Minister Komodromos. The minister lectured on the case, relying mainly on the testimony of Patatakos, and finally asked whether there was evidence to justify questioning Papapostolou and searching his car. Prosecutor General Tornaritis stated that this depended solely on the investigating judges, he saw no legal obstacle. One of the police officers doubted Patatakos' statement: it was not even certain whether Georkatzis had met Papapostolou at the first meeting. Another policeman, Fanis Dimitriou, was of the opinion that that piece of paper with Papapostolou's phone number was probably enough proof of contact. No one objected, but no decision was taken to arrest Papapostolou. In the end, the minister ordered that no action would be taken against the colonel until he ordered it.[1] At a second meeting, this time chaired by Makarios, it became clear that Makarios had understood who was behind the attempt on his life, but had to cover up the case for reasons of reasons of state. Further investigation of the Georkatzis murder case was taken away from Dimitriou because he had come dangerously close to the truth. The further investigation was delayed and the facts that did come to light were covered up.

The trial of the assassins of the Makarios attack began on 21 April 1970 and ended on 13 May. The accused were Kostas Ioannidis, Antonakis Solomontos, Adamos Charitonos, Georgios Taliadoros, Antonakis Genagritis and Polykarpos Polykarpou. Already at the beginning of the trial, Prosecutor General Tornaritis dropped the charges against Polykarou because the evidence was insufficient. The court found the evidence against Ioannidis insufficient and let him go. The four remaining defendants claimed that they had been incited to commit their crime by Georkatzis, and Prosecutor General Tornaritis stressed that relations between Makarios and Georkatzis had been bad. The four defendants were found guilty of attempting to overthrow the government through the use of violence, together with Georkatzis and other unknown persons, and were sentenced to 14 years in prison, of which they only served two, as Makarios' Christian clemency allowed them to serve the rest of the sentence.[2]

Last actions and the end of the Ethniko Metopo

The "successful elimination" of Georkatzis encouraged Papapostolou to continue, even though the attempt on Makarios had failed. He made contacts with Bishops Anthimos of Kition, Kyprianou of Kyrenia and Gennadios of Paphos to bring them into line with the EM. A member of the Greek embassy learned of this and informed Makarios. Papapostolou arranged for the EM to set up a youth organisation along the lines of the EOKA. The EM, or rather the radical organisation Ieros Lochos (IL), which was linked to it, prepared for a new strike against the government with the aim of taking power in order to achieve enosis.[3]

In early April, IL leaders allegedly met with a Greek officer who told them to draw up plans to attack the Limassol police headquarters and then occupy the city's strategic points. A two-man EM group led by Michalakis Rossidis would attack state targets in Nicosia. In order to bring the resulting chaos under control, the National Guard will be deployed. They

1 Drousiotis, *op. cit.*, p. 232f; Dimitriou, *op. cit.*, pp. 308-315.
2 Drousiotis, *op. cit.*, p. 242; Dimitriou, *op. cit.*, pp.365-380; Kranidiotis, *Anochyroti Politeia*, II, p. 16.
3 Drousiotis, *op. cit.*, p. 245f.

will take over and within 24 hours Enosis will be realised.[1] Whether the Greek officer was Papapostolou himself is not known, but the plan he drew up is very similar to the original EM plan of September 1969 and the plan of March 1970.

Of course, the IL could not implement such a plan off the cuff either, so intensive military training and precise planning work on the details of Operation Astrapi (lightening) began over the next few weeks. Since the IL leadership did not trust the general EM leadership of Limassol, Tryfonidis, Efthymiou and Gastriotis were to be kidnapped before the operation began, which it did. On 22 May 1970, an armed group of the IL, said to have numbered about 70 men, attacked the Limassol police headquarters. They disarmed the police officers present there, captured some Land Rovers and a large number of weapons: 205 rifles, 21 automatics, 42 pistols, 5 heavy machine guns, 100 hand grenades and 20,000 rounds of ammunition.[2]

But this time the state power struck back. Makarios himself went to Limassol. Police officers from Nicosia took control. Members of the IL revealed the weapons caches and gave names. The planned uprising in Nicosia did not take place. Within a few days, dozens of IL members became members. In the short term, consideration was given to starting a guerrilla war, but it was discarded due to impracticality. The investigating authorities worked more and more efficiently, arresting more and more until eventually about 100 IL members were in custody. It became clear that about 70 per cent of the police officers in Limassol were secret supporters of the EM. Even police officers were members of EM in Limassol. But in Nicosia they found that the infiltration was extreme there too, even the head of the KYP, G. Georgiadis, and the deputy police chief, Michalakis Pantelidis, had links to the EM.[3]

At a meeting in early June attended by the Interior Minister, the police commanders, the Attorney General and Makarios, the latter wanted to know from those gathered whether it made sense to charge all 100 arrested. Interior Minister Komodromos advised moderation. There was agreement and dissent. Finally, it was decided to try only the leaders, 22 people in total. The trial ended in December 1970. The 22 were sentenced to four or five years in prison. Some tried to talk their way out of it by claiming that they had only become members of the EM when they were assured that Makarios was behind the EM. His public advocacy of independence, they said, was just a ruse to keep Turkey from invading. In the meantime, the EM was building up military forces to repel them on that day when Enosis was declared.[4] In January 1971, Makarios pardoned them, which turned out to be a big mistake, as many of them later joined the EOKA B. The EM itself disbanded.

The attack on the police headquarters ultimately led to the cleansing of the police, on whom Makarios, unlike the "uncleaned" National Guard, could from now on rely again. Members of the presidential security group made it known to Athanasios Poulitsas that they were aware of his activities. Poulitsas left for Athens at the end of June 1970, from where he never returned to Cyprus. A few days after him, Papapostolou also left Cyprus for good. He left the army and became an official of the Greek Sports Federation. In September 1974

1 *Ibidem*, p. 247.
2 *Ibidem*, pp. 247-252; Dimitriou, *op. cit.*, pp. 391-401.
3 *Ibidem*, pp. 253-261.
4 Patrick, *op. cit.*, p. 149; Dimitriou, *op. cit.*, pp. 426-434.

he was arrested for conspiring against the new Karamanlis government. After his release, he withdrew from public life.[1]

1 Drousiotis, *op. cit.*, p. 268.

HENRY KISSINGER AND CYPRUS

Many Greeks and Greek Cypriots are convinced that Henry Kissinger was the sinister architect of the Cyprus problem. The following opinion was expressed in an internet forum in May 2006: : *"It starts to become obvious that Henry Kissinger had one hell of a lot to do with the existing status in Cyprus. If you're looking for a scapegoat, somebody to blame for the atrocities, look to Kissinger. He played Greece, Turkey, England all as if they were dummies. His clinical disregard for the consequences of his actions defies belief. This man was a complete and utter bastard. Right up there with Hitler, Stalin et al. with his almost sociopathic contempt for the lives of millions of people. [...] Kissinger is the foundation on which the misery that has befallen Cyprus was based."*[1] There are many such statements on the internet. If one takes a closer look at the arguments put forward in this forum, it is easy to see that they have a lot to do with preconceived opinions and projections of prejudices and emotions, but little to do with historical truth.

One might regard these opinions as unqualified nonsense and not take them seriously, but these ideas are partly based on widely circulated publications that claim to be serious. These publications all have one thing in common: they are based on conspiracy theories. The first in the series of "conspiracy theorists" was the Washington Post journalist Lawrence Stern, who assumed in his 1977 book that the coup of 21 April 1967 in Greece as well as the one against Makarios on 15 July 1974 were equally due to the sinister machinations of the CIA, and that Kissinger pursued a similar policy towards Cyprus as Metternich and Castlereagh did towards the Greek War of Independence after 1821: *"Like Metternich [... Kissinger] insisted that humanitarian considerations were subordinate to maintaining 'the consecrated structures of Europe,"* which in this case was the cohesion of NATO. *"In the case of Greece and Turkey the military relationships conceived in the name of NATO became the driving imperatives of foreign policy [...] rather than a component of a policy in which social and humanitarian considerations were given serious weight."*[2]

The second author in this series is the British journalist Christopher Hitchens, who expressed the same opinion in his 1984 book dedicated to Laurence Stern. His account of the events in Cyprus in 1974 is dazzlingly written and his conspiratorial theses are presented convincingly and with verve, but his presentation of the facts is far from accurate and is often based on rumours that have been circulated. He describes Kissinger as the patron of extremists in Greece and Turkey. For him, Kissinger's foreign policy on the Cyprus issue is the counterpart of Nixon's Watergate scandal in American domestic politics.[3] Hitchens' theses fitted into the political environment of the time and so his book went through a second edition a few years later under a different title.[4] In the following years, Hitchens delved so deeply into Kissinger's involvement in crimes in Indochina, South America, East Timor and, of course, Cyprus, that his new book became a veritable indictment in which he accused Kissinger of war crimes and crimes against humanity.[5]

---

1 "Kissinger: sinister architect of the Cyprus Problem?" http://www.cyprus-forum.com/cyprus5873.html.

2 Laurence Stern, *The Wrong Horse. The Politics of Intervention and the Failure of American Diplomacy* (New York: Times Book, 1977), pp. 95, 160f.

3 Christopher Hitchens, *Cyprus* (London: Quartet Books, 1984).

4 Christopher Hitchins, *Hostage to History. Cyprus from the Ottomans to Kissinger* (New York: The Noonday Press, 1989).

5 Christopher Hitchens, *The Trial of Henry Kissinger* (London: Verso, 2001). Parts of it were printed in Harper's Magazine in March 2001.

The books by John L. Scherer[1] and Willam Mallison[2] ultimately also belong to this category because they draw on elements of conspiracy theories at crucial points in the account. The most extreme example of conspiratorial historiography is the book by the two British journalists Brendan O'Malley and Ian Craig. The title alone, "The Cyprus Conspiracy", is programmatic.[3] For these two authors, the Cypriot catastrophe is the result of an international conspiracy that began in colonial times, took on concrete contours during President Johnson's term in office and whose goals were finally realised in 1974.

However, such a view of the history of Cyprus is not limited to English-language historiography. One of the earliest such publications in German describing the development of Cyprus towards the catastrophe of 1974 is by Niels Kadritzke.[4] All authors describe conspiracy scenarios running through decades that correspond to the fears and ideas of the readership, which tends to belong politically to the left spectrum, and are therefore eagerly received. These books all have one thing in common: they are based on extremely thin sources and on speculation. The argumentation of all these authors is so similar that one could speak of a conspiracy school. The Anglo-Saxon conspiratorial view of the history of Cyprus naturally had its impact on Cypriot historiography, where Makarios Drousiotis' publications are typical examples of such a view of history.[5] Since there are now a great many quite different sources from some of the states involved in the events, it is time to present an objective account based on the sources. Of course, there will be voices in the reading community that regard such an approach as naïve, but this risk will probably be bearable.

The Cyprus Policy of the Johnson Administration

Leaving aside the American contribution to the resolution of the colonial conflict in its final phase in 1958 by Secretary of State John Foster Dulles, which took place mainly behind the scenes with the aim of eliminating an internal NATO conflict and ultimately led to the Zurich and London Agreements,[6] there has really only been an American Cyprus policy since the inter-communal riots in Cyprus in 1963-1964. When these broke out at Christmas 1963, a direct Greek-Turkish clash threatened very quickly. To prevent this, the Americans under President Johnson sought a solution within NATO: Secretary of State George Ball flew to the region in February 1964 to push through the adoption of a NATO Peacekeeping Force.

1 John L. Scherer, *Blocking the Sun. The Cyprus Conflict* (Minneapolis: Minnesota UP, 1997).

2 William Mallison, *Cyprus. A Modern History* (London: Tauris, 2005), p. 75: "*The two-state Turkish invasion of Cyprus in the Summer of 1974 was the culmination of ten years of planning by various U.S. government sectors, initiated with the 'Ball/Acheson' plan for double enosis in 1964, in secret connivance with the Turkish armed forces, with the British government looking on.*"

3 Brendan O'Malley & Ian Craig, *The Cyprus Conspiracy. America, Espionage and the Turkish Invasion* (London: Tauris, 1999), p. X: "*This book argues that the Cyprus crisis was no failure of American diplomacy, but a deliberate Cold War plot to divide the island and save the top secret spying and defence facilities from the twin threats of a communist takeover or British withdrawal.*"

4 Niels Kadritzke & Wolf Wagner, *Im Fadenkreuz der NATO. Ermittlungen am Beispiel Cypern* (Berlin: Rotbuch Verlag, 1976).

5 Particularly clear Makarios Drousiotis, *Cyprus 1974: Greek Coup and Turkish Invasion* (Möhnesee: Bibliopolis, 2006).

6 Heinz A. Richter, *Geschichte der Insel Zypern, II, 1950-1959* (Mannheim; Bibliopolis, 2006), pp. 504-526, 581-592.

London, Athens and Ankara agreed to the plan, but Makarios rejected it. Since the Soviet Union supported Makarios, a UN blue helmet force, the UNFICYP, was sent.[1]

But before the UNFICYP troops arrived in larger numbers, the crisis in Cyprus escalated again. At the end of May 1964, President Inönü ordered a military invasion of Cyprus for the beginning of June. Only through massive pressure in the form of a threatening letter was Johnson able to avert the invasion at the last moment. The harsh tone of this letter angered Inönü to such an extent that it set Turkish foreign policy on a course of greater independence from Washington. The extent of the alienation process is shown by the fact that Ankara began a kind of flirtation with Moscow that had unbelievable consequences: Ankara interpreted the 1936 Montreux Straits Agreement in such an extremely liberal way that it was possible for the Soviets to bring a fleet into the Mediterranean, where it caused NATO strategists headaches for years as the so-called Eskadra.

The renewed trouble with Makarios prompted the Americans to intervene again. In close cooperation with the British, the former Secretary of State Dean Acheson developed various plans for the solution of the Cyprus problem, all of which had one thing in common: The state existence of Cyprus was to be eliminated and Cyprus was to be annexed to Greece. In this case, the Turks could receive territorial compensation from Greece. This concept went down in history as the double enosis. Ankara agreed in principle, only the then Greek Prime Minister Georgios Papandreou had qualms about imposing such a solution on Cyprus, which displeased Washington and ultimately had far-reaching consequences for Greek domestic politics.

Ankara had abstained from the invasion, but the Turkish air force intervened in the renewed fighting at Kokkina in the Tillyria region and napalmed Greek Cypriot villages. When the Soviet Union interfered, Athens reacted rather nervously: in talks with the Americans and the British, a concept was developed that went down in history as "enosis by coup": Greece was to organise a coup d'état in Cyprus and remove Makarios. Afterwards, the annexation of Cyprus to Greece was to be proclaimed immediately. The Americans and British would dissuade Ankara from reacting hastily. As soon as the situation calmed down, Athens would agree with Ankara on territorial compensations. Although this plan was not carried out in 1964 for various reasons, it had developed the blueprint that the Greek military tried to implement in 1974 under completely different foreign policy circumstances. By the end of 1964, however, it had become clear to the Americans that neither enosis nor double enosis was a solution to the Cyprus problem - both were alternately unacceptable to the Cypriot communities - but only independence. Consequently, Washington withdrew from active Cyprus policy for the time being and left the field again to the guarantor powers or Makarios.[2]

The Johnson administration's next interference in Cyprus occurred in the wake of the Kofinou crisis of November 1967.[3] On the night of 15 November, the commander-in-chief of all Greek and Greek Cypriot forces in Cyprus, Grivas, had launched an attack on the Tur-

---

1 Heinz A. Richter, *Geschichte der Insel Zypern, III, 1960-1965* (Ruhpolding; Rutzen Verlag, 2007), pp. 325-347.

2 *Ibidem*, pp. 439-527. Claude Nicolet, *United States Policy Towards Cyprus, 1954-1974: Removing the Greek-Turkish Bone of Contention* (Mannheim: Bibliopolis, 2001), pp. 263-289.

3 On the Kofinou crisis Heinz A. Richter, *Geschichte der Insel Zypern, IV, 1965-1977* (Ruhpolding; Rutzen Verlag, 2009), pp. 98-110.

kish Cypriot village of Kofinou, unauthorised by Athens, prompting strong reactions from Ankara. On the morning of 15 November, Foreign Minister Çağlayangil warned the Greek ambassador that if there was fighting in Cyprus, it might not be confined to the island.[1] To US Ambassador Hart, Çağlayangil said that the Turks would never forgive it if the Americans intervened again as they did in 1964 and prevented them from coming to the aid of the Turkish Cypriots.[2] The Secretary General of the Turkish Foreign Ministry threatened air strikes if the attack did not end, and as the Americans learned from another source, the Turkish forces were indeed preparing for an operation.[3] Çağlayangil demanded a return to the status quo ante.[4] The Americans realised that the situation was becoming critical and intervened in Athens. From there, the order went out to Grivas to stop the attack and withdraw his troops.[5]

Grivas obeyed, but continued his provocations, albeit at a lower level; obviously he did not realise that he was playing with fire. In Ankara, meanwhile, the national waves were running high and the government was authorised by parliament to use military means, even against Greece, if necessary. Around midnight on 16 November, Foreign Minister Çağlayangil handed over a kind of ultimatum to the Greek ambassador, demanding not only the recall of Grivas but also the withdrawal of the Greek troops who had been stationed illegally in Cyprus since 1963. Washington observed this development with concern and intervened by presenting a five-point programme. According to this, Turkey should once again recognise the inviolability and independence of Cyprus. All troops stationed in Cyprus, with the exception of the two legal contingents, were to be withdrawn. The role of UNFICYP was to be strengthened and the Turkish Cypriots in Kofinou were to be compensated. As Athens took its time in responding to the plan, the tension escalated: the Turkish side mobilised part of its forces, and the landing preparations were carried out in all openness. On 22 November, the Americans determined on the spot that Turkey was on the verge of breaking loose. To prevent this, Johnson instructed former Secretary of Defence Cyrus Vance to act as his personal representative to prevent a Greek-Turkish war and a Turkish landing on Cyprus.[6]

The history of the Cyrus Vance mission is complicated and has been described by me in detail elsewhere,[7] so we can content ourselves here with presenting the results. Outwardly, there were no victors and no vanquished. Vance had avoided the international press, the Greek press was under censorship, and the chauvinist statements of the Turkish press were virtually unnoticed outside Turkey because of the language barrier. As Vance himself admitted, the fact that there was a dictatorship in Greece was useful to him. Under democratic conditions, the concessions Greece had to make would probably not have been so easily en-

1 Sonyel, *Aftermath*, p. 226. Zeki Kuneralp, *Just a Diplomat* (Istanbul: Isis Press, 1992), p. 110: *"Turkey and Greece were on the brink of war."*

2 Parker Hart, *Two Nations at the Threshold of War. Cyprus, a Firsthand Account of Crisis Management, 1965-1968* (Durham & London: Duke University Press, 1990), p. 52. Çağlayangil spielte auf Johnsons Brief vom 5. Juni 1964 an. Richter, *op. cit.*, III, pp. 447ff.

3 *Ibidem.*

4 Sonyel, *Aftermath*, p. 226.

5 Hart, *op. cit.*, p. 52.

6 Richter, *op. cit.*, IV, pp. 110-118.

7 *Ibidem*, pp. 118-131.

forceable.[1] Vance's success in this mission was also largely due to his discretion, his integrity, his restraint and, above all, the support of the State Department and the White House, which gave him full freedom of decision. At the same time, he benefited from the fact that neither Turkey nor Greece actually wanted war. Makarios wanted to risk it because he naively trusted that the Americans would not allow it. Since he was always playing for high stakes, Vance finally had to outsmart him for the sake of peace. Seen in this light, the Vance mission was a complete success.[2] Vance saved the peace, prevented the collapse of the right wing of NATO, and improved US relations with Turkey again, which had suffered greatly as a result of the Johnson letter.

The clear loser was Greece. The dream of annexing Cyprus to Greece was over for the time being, because it would mean war. But some of the colonels had not completely given up the idea of annexing Cyprus to Greece: In their eyes, the main obstacle was Makarios; if they got rid of him, they might be able to reach a bilateral agreement with Turkey. When Makarios later granted asylum to the anti-junta forces, these considerations became an obsession for some in the Greek junta, as we shall see.

The moderate part of Turkey's leadership, on the other hand, could be satisfied, because it had won its demands: Grivas was out of the way and the Greek division was withdrawn. The hawks would of course have liked to see the opportunity seized, the matter closed once and for all and part of Cyprus annexed.[3] The withdrawal of the Greek division under pressure from the motherland strengthened the self-confidence of the Turkish Cypriots, whose leadership now became more intransigent. They realised that Makarios was not in a position to impose his will on them by force, and as early as December 1967 they took the first step towards their own statehood by forming a "Temporary Separate Turkish Administration".

Analysing the outcome from Makarios' point of view, there are positive and negative outcomes. The most important positive outcome was that Grivas, who had triggered the crisis through his irresponsible behaviour, had to disappear from the scene. Talbot had already characterised Grivas' behaviour on 20 November as "monumental stupidity" without equal.[4] UNFICYP Chief of Staff Harbottle regarded Grivas' attack on Ag. Theodoros as his personal Waterloo.[5] On the one hand, the withdrawal of the Greek division weakened the Cypriot defence force, but on the other hand it also reduced the danger of a coup against Makarios, because a large number of Greek officers who sympathised with the ideas of the junta in Athens had to leave the island. It remained a cause for concern, however, that the majority of the officers of the National Guard still belonged to the Greek army, and thus the junta could still exert influence on Cypriot domestic politics, which is why Makarios also demanded complete demilitarisation.[6] Since he was unable to push this through, Makarios thus had to continue to expand the police in order to build up a counterweight. Overall, Makarios'

---

1 *FRUS 1964-1968*, XVI, p. 699.
2 Hart, *op. cit.*, p. 101f.
3 Tozun Bahcheli, *Greek-Turkish Relations Since 1955* (Boulder: Westview Press, 1990), p. 74.
4 Nicolet, *op. cit.*, p. 365.
5 Michael Harbottle, *The Impartial Soldier* (London: Oxford UP, 1970), p. 174.
6 The claim that Vance had demanded the disbandment of the National Guard and that this had been rejected by Makarios appears again and again in the literature. Tzermias, *Republik*, p. 389 and also Glafkos Clerides, *Cyprus: My Deposition* (Nicosia: Alithia, 1989), II, p. 211. But this clearly contradicts Makarios' desire for total demilitarisation.

course of independence was strengthened. The desire for enosis remained among Greek Cypriots, but it lost considerable appeal among the majority of Greek Cypriots in the face of dictatorship in Greece, and in foreign policy terms enosis was out of the question, as it could not be achieved without war with Turkey. It was a dream that was slowly fading.

The question now was whether Makarios would use the newly won leeway to reconcile with the Turkish Cypriots. If he did not succeed in building new trust among the Turkish Cypriots so that they would be willing to disarm, hard domestic political battles were ahead, for the Turkish Cypriots would defend their rights by all means and once again call for help from the motherland. The all-important question now was whether Makarios would succeed in changing course. Nancy Crawshaw is right when she describes the Kofinou crisis as the turning point in Cyprus' post-colonial history.[1] For the next few years, Cyprus remained quiet.

New American Considerations

On 17 January 1968, the State Department presented the President with a strategy paper for a solution to the Cyprus conflict. It stated that the study group under Ambassador Yost had recommended doing everything possible to bring about a long-term solution. Although this could lead to disagreements with Athens and Ankara, only the USA was in a position to bring the parties to the conflict together. They should work closely with the British and especially with the Canadians, who have their own plan, and with the UN Secretary-General.[2] At the US National Security Council meeting on 24 January, Cyrus Vance, who had been invited to the meeting, gave his impressions: *"'The situation is still held together with paste and glue, and more paste than glue.' If it flares up again, war cannot be avoided. The majority of Turks had wanted to go to war in November. The Greek people felt humiliated and many of them are anxious for a chance to have a go at the Turks. The Cypriots are fatalistic. He believed that the US should take an active role in trying to achieve a settlement. The pace of the problem is quicker than the pace of the UN Secretary General. He hopes the problem can be solved within the framework of the UN, but he is 'not sanguine'."* Deputy Secretary of State Joseph Sisco agreed, saying that U Thant would soon have reached the end of his Latin. Rusk said it was necessary to talk to the Turks and the Cypriots. In summary, it was stated that one should work with U Thant but in the meantime appoint a mediator and prepare him for his task so that he would be ready for his task when the time came.[3]

Indeed, the British and the Canadians submitted their plans to the Americans a day later. The British thought of a three-phase model. In the first phase, lasting until somewhat March 1968, living conditions on the island were to be improved. In the second phase, bi-communal talks on a new constitution were to take place, which could last until 1969, and in the third, the three guarantor powers were to sanction the results. The Americans did not think

1 Nancy Crawshaw, *The Cyprus Revolt. An Account of the Struggle for Union with Greece* (London: Allen & Unwin, 1978), p. 378.

2 *FRUS 1964-1968*, XVI, p. 738.

3 *Ibidem*, p. 740f.

the plan was bad, but the question was whether they would be willing to participate in phases two and three, or whether they wanted to leave that to the UN.[1]

The Canadian plan was similar to the British, except that it was more concrete. The Canadians had understood that the crux of the Cyprus problem lay in certain provisions of the constitution. The idea was to get the two communities to talk about it, and they were quite optimistic about the results: *"It is just conceivable that the Turks might eventually be willing to abandon certain of their veto rights and their built-in over-representation in Government organs if they could be solidly assured of a significant degree of local control with respect to security arrangements in particular. It is also just conceivable that Makarios might see sufficient advantage in the return of Turkish Cypriots to participation in a more centralized regime than the 1960 version so that he would be willing to admit some kind of limited and relatively inconspicuous local autonomy."* One could imagine that Glafkos Kliridis and Rauf Denktaş could negotiate such a compromise, and indeed this is exactly what happened a few months later.[2]

There was disagreement between the three governments on the timing and nature of the intervention. The Americans were in favour of immediate direct intervention. The British wanted to wait until the inter-communal talks and the Canadians wanted to stay out of it, the ethnic groups should solve the problems without outside interference. A compromise was agreed upon: U Thant should continue with his good offices and be supported by the three states as long as he made progress. Should his initiative flag, they could become active again themselves. So the Americans accepted that the Cypriots should decide their own fate under the aegis of the UN, but not entirely, as we shall see.[3] So Washington, London and Ottawa decided to wait and see.

Security Advisor Kissinger and Cyprus

In the USA, presidential elections were held in the autumn of 1968 and the Republicans emerged victorious. In January 1969, Richard Nixon became president and Spiro T. Agnew, of Greek origin, became vice-president. Behind Agnew was the Greek-American business tycoon Tom Pappas, who controlled a $200 million investment empire in Greece (Esso--Pappas). Pappas had contributed massively to the cost of Nixon's election campaign and ensured that his friend Agnew became vice-president. Pappas' economic interests in Greece necessitated a good relationship with the ruling colonels and his positive attitude was passed on to Agnew, who made junta-friendly statements during the election campaign and denounced Andreas Papandreou as a communist friend.[4] The arms embargo against Athens imposed by the Johnson government was officially renewed, but in fact lifted, as arms deliveries resumed in February 1969. [5] William Rogers became the new Secretary of State and Harvard professor Henry Kissinger was appointed Security Advisor. Ambassador Talbot, who was critical of the junta, was replaced and Henry J. Tasca was nominated as the new ambassador in September.

---

1 Nicolet, *op. cit.*, p. 383.

2 *Ibidem*, p. 383f.

3 *Ibidem*, p. 384.

4 Maurice Goldblum, "United States Policy in Post-War Greece", in: Richard Clogg and George Yannopoulos (eds.), *Greece under Military Rule* (London: Secker & Warburg, 1972), p. 245.

5 C. M. Woodhouse, *The Rise and the Fall of the Greek Colonels* (New York: Franklin Watts, 1985), p. 63.

In September of the same year, Colonel Muhamar el-Gaddafi launched a coup in Libya, and shortly afterwards he demanded that the Americans and the British vacate their bases in his country. In December 1969, students in Izmir attacked members of the US Navy so massively that US warships had to leave the port. It became clear that both the US Air Force and the US Navy would have to look for new bases. Since such anti-American riots were unthinkable in junta Greece, the Greek dictatorship suddenly gained a new attractiveness in the eyes of the Americans. On 8 January 1970, the US Air Force began to vacate its base in Libya, and on 10 January the vacant ambassadorial post in Athens was filled by Henry Tasca.[1]

Tasca had no scruples about establishing a good relationship with the leading junta members. In his eyes, the military dictatorship in Greece was a completely normal phenomenon in the country's development. For Tasca, the security interests of the USA had priority, and this included the full lifting of the arms embargo, for which he lobbied massively from then on. In September 1970, arms deliveries were indeed resumed in full; the culmination of this policy was then the decision in 1972 to make Piraeus, or the Bay of Faliron, the home port of the US 6th Fleet.[2] Washington was pursuing realpolitik in this area of the world. Nixon's new security advisor, Henry Kissinger, saw things somewhat differently. *"Our larger interests require that we have good relations with both Greece and Turkey; in consequence, we are impartial as to the formula for a Cyprus solution."*[3]

When Makarios also paid a visit to Nixon in October 1970 in connection with his trip to New York for the UN, the memorandum prepared by Henry Kissinger to prepare Nixon for this conversation showed that the latter did not have much idea about Cyprus and its problems: *"The principal U.S. concerns in Cyprus have been: (1) that tension between Greek and Turkish Cypriot communities not erupt and draw Greece and Turkey into war; (2) that the well organized Communist party not achieve predominance."* But as long as Makarios was in power, there was no reason to worry. The important thing was that Makarios continued to tolerate U-2 flights over VAR territory from British bases.[4] During the conversation between Nixon and Makarios himself on 25 October, Makarios stressed that there was no communist danger in Cyprus. He was in full control of the Cypriot communists.[5]

When renewed tensions over Cyprus emerged in June 1971 despite the intercommunal talks, President Nixon commissioned a review of American policy on Cyprus.[6] This was presented on 6 August[7] and discussed on 11 August. The Assistant Secretary of State for Near Eastern Affairs, Joseph Sisco, explained the situation to the panel of representatives from the State and Defence Departments, the Joint Chiefs of Staff, the CIA and the National Security Council: if a crisis arose, Makarios would immediately turn to the UN for mediation. The USA would not be able to stop this, although the Turks would urge them to do so. A dialogue developed between Sisco and Security Advisor Kissinger:

---

1 *Ibidem*, p. 74.
2 *Ibidem*, pp. 70-73; Stern, *op. cit.*, pp. 66-73.
3 Nicolet, *op. cit.*, p. 394.
4 *FRUS 1969-1976* , XXIX, p. 881. Die VAR (Vereinigte Arabische Republik) war ein zeitweiser Zusammenschluss Ägyptens und Syriens zu einem Staat.
5 *Ibidem*, p. 883f.
6 Ibidem, p. 904f.
7 *Ibidem*, p. 910.

Mr. Kissinger: *My impression of Makarios is that he is a very cool customer. We can't antagonize him.*

Mr. Sisco: *He is an evil man of the cloth. Even though the Greeks are more amenable now to cooperation with the Turks on Cyprus, when the chips are down they will inevitably back the Greek Cypriots.*

Mr. Kissinger: *So we would have to choose between Turkey and Cyprus.*

Mr. Sisco: *We have generally supported Turkey all along.*

Mr. Kissinger: *If we came out against UN mediation, what would be the cost?*

Mr. Sisco: *It's a question of the impact on Greece and Turkey. I believe we would have to give some support to Turkey. If we supported Makarios' efforts - which would mean, in effect, supporting the status quo - we would increase Turkish nervousness and possibly encourage Turkish thinking that they might have to take military action. We would inevitably be in the middle of two of our principal allies.*

Sisco considered the continuation of inter-communal talks to be the best solution. However, an American mediating role had to be avoided. The Acheson formula that has been valid until now is that one accepts the solution that the parties agree on. Makarios would not provoke anything because he feared a Turkish invasion.[1]

On 1 September 1971, the new strategy paper formulated by the responsible State Department official, Thomas Boyatt, was available. After an overview of the possible options for mediation, Boyatt stated that the most important thing was to keep the Cyprus problem at the level of negotiations and to become diplomatically active again in this sense. *"Our goal should be to insure that in the case of a real stalemate in the inter-communal talks and increasing violence on the Island a mediation effort can be quickly and efficiently mounted. The ideal kind of mediation would be [...] a UN-sponsored effort stimulated by the parties and involving a mediator and guidelines previously agreed upon. [...] The US role should be that of an amicus curiae providing behind the scenes ideas and support."* To this end, Sisco should talk to the ambassadors of the three states and ask them to state their positions and at the same time signal to them that the USA was committed to negotiations. They could also suggest the possibility of the UN Secretary General participating in the negotiations. During the forthcoming visits of the three foreign ministers to the UN in New York, Secretary Rogers could, if necessary, take action in the same sense.[2]

The second part of the paper analysed strategies to be applied in case of outbreaks of violence in Cyprus. The most interesting proposal concerned the case of an imminent military invasion to divide the island. In such a case, the Turks would have to be convinced that they were harming themselves. The first thing to do was to encourage UNFICYP to oppose the Turks, which would not have much effect in the case of a Turkish invasion. Secondly, in coordination with Britain and other interested states, Ankara should be made to understand that this would lead to a conflict with Athens. The international community would regard this as aggression and the Soviet Union would certainly react with hostility. Thirdly, the UN must be activated by requesting an emergency meeting of the Security Council. Fourthly, as in 1967, NATO must be involved. Finally, as in 1964 and 1967, a special presidential envoy

1 *Ibidem*, pp. 911-915.
2 *Ibidem*, pp. 919-923.

could be sent to stop the fighting. Once the crisis had been defused, a solution could be sought.[1]

The application of this plan could have avoided a catastrophe for Cyprus such as a Turkish invasion. It can be assumed that Kissinger, the president's security adviser, was aware of the plan, since he chaired the discussion on 11 August and decided to wait until the paper was available before making any decisions. In view of this detailed description of crisis management in the event of a threatened Turkish invasion, Kissinger's behaviour in 1974 is astonishing.

The next time Henry Kissinger dealt with Cyprus was in February 1972, when it was reported by the US Embassy in Nicosia that, according to Kliridis, a coup against Makarios was imminent in Cyprus. Kliridis' report prompted another meeting of the Special Actions Group in Washington, chaired by Kissinger. Although doubts were raised as to whether a coup was actually being planned, it was agreed that something had to be done. Kissinger wanted to inform the president accordingly.[2] This was done, and *"American Ambassador Henry J. Tasca was therefore instructed to warn the Greek junta against any 'violent change'. The junta replied that Greece would not tolerate any foreign intervention, a statement that was explicitly 'also addressed to our friends - to them above all'. So, although the junta rejected outside interference on principle, it followed our basic recommendation and declared its renunciation of the use of force on 4 March 1972."*[3] Kliridis was informed of this intervention.[4] The crisis was over and Makarios remained the victor of this first round in the confrontation with Athens. An American diplomatic démarche had thus been enough to stop Greek coup plans.

Secretary of State Kissinger and Cyprus

In September 1973, Henry Kissinger had become US Secretary of State. Barely in office, the following events occupied his attention between October 1973 and June 1974: the Yom Kippur War, his trip to Moscow, the first trip to the Middle East, another trip to China, the Geneva Conference, the shuttle diplomacy in the Middle East and finally the energy crisis triggered by OPEC and, above all, the Watergates scandal, which was gaining ever greater importance.[5] In fact, the Watergate crisis was at its peak in the first six months of 1974. The US had virtually no fully operational government. A senior US diplomat recalls Kissinger's role: *"And in that vacuum stepped Henry Kissinger. [He] became, in effect, president for foreign policy. Both during the final stages of Nixon, because Nixon was without power, and during the Ford administration because Ford really didn't have any capabilities in that area, Kissinger truly 'ran' foreign affairs."*[6] In view of this situation and Kissinger's commitment to world politics, it was hardly surprising that Greece was not an issue for him until the Ioannidis coup. In early December 1973, Ambassador Tasca told his Dutch colleague

1 *Ibidem*, pp. 923-925.
2 *Ibidem*, pp. 986-993.
3 Henry Kissinger, *Jahre der Erneuerung. Erinnerungen* (Gütersloh: Bertelsmann, 1999), p. 164. The friends probably meant the Turks.
4 Clerides, *op. cit.*, III, p. 133f.
5 Henry Kissinger, *Memoiren 1973-1974* (München: Bertelsmann, 1982), *passim.*
6 Ambassador Boyatt's Presentation at Foreign Service Institute September 30, 1992, p. 4. In: Foreign Affairs Oral History Collection of the Association for Diplomatic Studies and Training. (ADST).

Barkman that in view of the global security problems Kissinger wanted to avoid a dispute with Athens at all costs.[1]

On 25 November 1973, the head of the military police, Dimitrios Ioannidis, overthrew the previous dictator Papadopoulos in a coup that had been planned since the beginning of October. Neither the uprising of the students of the Athens Polytechneion nor the so-called Seminario tis Romis played any role in this. The Americans also had nothing to do with the change of power, even if this was repeatedly claimed.[2] The change from Papadopoulos to Ioannidis was a disaster for Cyprus. Papadopoulos had been a realist politician with regard to Cyprus, who had been angry with Makarios' policies in February 1972 and had asked him to resign, but had then calmed down and returned to the previous sensible course. Its parameters were as follows: Independence and resolution of the problem through extended inter-communal negotiations. He knew that any attempt to impose enosis meant war with Turkey, and this would end in defeat for Greece and the partition of Cyprus, if not the annexation of the island by Turkey. Ioannidis had no idea of this problem, nor was he capable of learning, as his behaviour had shown several times in the past. This meant that the slightest occasion could lead him to set fire to Cyprus and this would lead to disaster.

After Ioannidis' coup in November 1973, Ambassador Tasca had asked the State Department to think about what course to steer towards the new regime. A paper was then prepared in the State Department between January and March 1974. But it was not until Ambassador Tasca was summoned to appear before the Foreign Affairs Committee of the House of Representatives at the end of March 1974 and reported that there could be another coup in Greece that Kissinger was prepared to deal with the Greek problem on 20 March.[3]

The paper said: The new Greek regime is reactionary and far less capable than the people around Papadopoulos to deal with the political and economic problems at hand. *"The new regime is not a group of 'Atlanticists' who see their relationship with the US and NATO based on shared values. Virtually inexperienced in the world outside Greece, their point of view is narrowly nationalistic. Their fanatic anti-Communism is based on deep fear of a threat from the North that impels them to value their ties to the United States and NATO. They tend to believe, however, that we need Greece at least as much as Greece needs us, so that their approach to us is likely to be one of hard bargaining over such issues as base rights and homeporting - adversarial in style rather than cooperative. Their nationalistic orientation is also likely to make them highly sensitive to foreign meddling in Greek affairs - e.g., efforts to press them to restore democratic institutions."*[4]

The paper then discussed the options for American policy. There were basically two positions: "hands-off" or "intervention". The paper ruled out the first option: *"Given the Greek belief that the United States strongly influences Greek politics, non-interventionism is illusory. A hands-off approach is seen as support for the incumbent government and is thus a form of intervention on its behalf. Our close military association with Greece underlines this consideration. Because of this belief we in fact have considerable leverage on the*

1 Carl Barkman, *Ambassador in Athens* (London: Merlin Press, 1989), p. 144.

2 John Sakkas, "The Greek Dictatorship, the USA and the Arabs, 1967-74" *Journal of Southern Europe and the Balkans*, 6:3 (Dec. 2004), p. 255.

3 *FRUS 1969-1976*, XXX, pp. 46, 51 Footnote 4.

4 *FRUS 1969-1976*, XXX, p. 32.

Greek political scene if we choose to use it." The analysts had thus clearly recognised the foreign policy maxim of all Greek politicians, which was "ti thelei o xenos paragontas?" (what does the foreign factor want?). Henry Kissinger was expected to decide on the course to take.

During the subsequent discussion with the ambassador, it became clear from the questions asked by Kissinger that he had little idea about Greece, as had been established on previous occasions. Tasca did try to explain the problems at hand, but he did not really succeed. When Kissinger followed up, Tasca got to the crux of the matter: *"Greece has had a foreign factor since 1821 and since the revolution. We're right in the internal Greek foreign institutions, whether you like it or not; we're part of their value system, part of their political process. And we ought to get out of it. But it's going to take time to get out. In the meantime, we're going to be responsible."*Tasca made it clear that the US, as a "foreign factor", was so deeply involved in Greek politics that even non-interference would be interpreted as interference, as reinforcing the status quo, i.e. in this case supporting Ioannidis. Kissinger sighed: *"Well in that case we cannot change our policy because whenever we change to a neutral stance, we're going to be accused of interference or non-interference."* One of the panellists suggested a continuation of the previous policy of gently trying to influence those in charge in Athens towards democratisation, but for the last few months, since Rogers was no longer in office, no one had commented on this. Tasca wanted instructions so that he could answer the senators' questions. Kissinger could not or would not make a decision and told Tasca to refer the senators to him.

Tasca, however, was not satisfied with that and made a push: *"May I put one other note on the security side - because I want to be sure that's put on the table too. There's one thing about these people that is worrisome, and that is: They're very primitive in their foreign-policy approach. And there's evidence now that they could easily get into an argumentation with Turkey on the question of the Aegean Sea and Cyprus. I think the oil-exploration problem in the Aegean Sea does tend to indicate that these people might get into a real confrontation with the Turks on that. And I think that would raise all the problems that Cyprus did."*Kissinger said that this was probably a foreign policy problem that could be judged. Undeterred, he wanted to know what the purpose of the meeting was. *"When do I have to make a decision? I mean, I don't even know what the decision is that I'm being asked to make."* The answer was clear: *"That's the whole point. It's not that you're asked to make decisions. There is a feeling that perhaps incrementally you might slide into a posture - but maybe the right posture, that someone should know you're doing it."* Kissinger admitted that Greece might be a special case, but there was no danger that he would adopt a particular posture. After further discussion, it was agreed that decisions should be postponed and that the present policy should be continued.[1] It was obvious that Kissinger's staff was worried about problematic spontaneous solo actions by their boss. But they could rest assured that Kissinger did not care about this issue because he was making world policy and did not realise that something was brewing in Cyprus. A warning like the one in March 1972 would

---

1 *Ibidem*, pp. 47-60. At Stern it reads like this: *"Kissinger insisted that Tasca make no waves. Kissinger's don't-rock-the-boat attitude towards the Athens junta contrasted sharply with the well documented covert US intervention [...] against the elected government of the late Salvador Allende in Chile."* Laurence Stern, "Bitter Lessons: How We Failed in Cyprus" *Foreign Policy* 19 (Summer 1975), p. 48.

have been overdue.[1] Presumably, such a warning would even have prevented the catastrophe of the summer of 1974, but Kissinger failed to issue such a warning and was thus guilty of negligent omission more or less out of ignorance of the facts.

The question arises as to why Kissinger behaved in this way. In volume 2 of his memoirs, published in 1982, he claims: *"I had always expected that the next domestic crisis in Cyprus would trigger a Turkish intervention."*[2] If this is not a realisation ex post for his memoirs, which he included in them to disguise his failure on such an important issue, so if this statement is correct, then he either acted grossly negligent or absolutely irresponsible, or else he agreed with the direction in which things were going. In the third volume of his memoirs, published in 1999, Kissinger described Makarios as the *"proximate cause of many tensions in Cyprus"*.[3] This remark is revealing because it implies that if the causes of the tensions were eliminated, the problem would be largely solved. Kissinger thus seems to have regarded Makarios as the root of all evil. No wonder, then, that he did not object to Ioannidis planning the elimination of the archbishop and that Kissinger did not take the corresponding indications and warnings of his people on the spot seriously, neither interfering nor calling Athens back. Apparently, however, he did not realise the consequences of an attack on Makarios, because Ioannidis' aim was not the removal of Makarios but Enosis. Athenian interference in Cyprus with this aim not only implied danger, rather it was bound to lead to Turkish intervention and, as a consequence, to a partition of the island. Yes, with the Aegean conflict simmering since October 1973,[4] the danger of the outbreak of a Greek-Turkish war was palpable. Kissinger tries to talk his way out of it in his memoirs by claiming that nothing had indicated an imminent crisis: *"After the coup in Cyprus, self-styled investigative journalists claimed to have discovered intelligence warnings that the administration - blinded by dislike for Makarios and caught up in geopolitical thinking - had ignored. What the outsider hardly understands is the fact that in a large government apparatus one can always find one or another document predicting a certain event. This is how the bureaucracy safeguards itself for all the vicissitudes of life. What really matters, however, is the context and the people to whom the warning is brought to their attention."*[5] This raises the question of whether there were in fact clear warnings that came to Kissinger's attention, or whether he might not have wanted to take note of them.

The coup of 15 July 1974

In February 1974, the State Department desk officer in charge of Cyprus, Thomas Boyatt, realised that something was brewing in Cyprus. Boyatt, who was fluent in Greek, had served as the first embassy secretary at the US Embassy in Nicosia from 1967 to 1970. He then became special assistant to the Assistant Secretary of State for the Middle East, Joseph Sisco. From 1971 to 1974 he was Director of the Cyprus Division of the State Department and as such had to follow developments in Cyprus closely. In a lecture to the Foreign Service Institute in September 1990, he reported that from late 1973 and increasingly from early

1 Kissinger, *Erneuerung*, p. 164.
2 Henry Kissinger, *Memoiren*, II, p.1.388.
3 Kissinger, *Erneuerung*, p. 161.
4 Zum Ägäis-Konflikt Heinz A. Richter, *Friede in der Ägäis? Zypern -Ägäis - Minderheiten* (Köln: Romiosini, 1989), *passim*.
5 Kissinger, *Erneuerung*, p. 165.

1974, he realised that the junta, the Greek secret service KYP and the Greek military were supporting those forces in Cyprus that wanted to overthrow Makarios and annex Cyprus to Greece. From his experience on the ground, he knew that this was bound to lead to a Turkish invasion. *"I knew that if Turkey invaded Cyprus we'd have two armies fighting each other, illegally, with American weapons and [...] that it would damage our position in the eastern Mediterranean for a generation and provided [...] opportunities for the Soviets."*[1]

In view of this situation, he formulated a message with instructions to Tasca, instructing him to seek out Ioannidis and *"tell him in words of one syllable that even he will understand, that the United States [....] strongly opposes any efforts by any element of the Greek government, overt or clandestine, to mess around in the Cyprus situation. And that we particularly oppose any efforts to overthrow Makarios and install a pro-Athens government. Because if that happens the Turks are going to invade."* Copies should be sent to the embassies in Nicosia and Ankara.[2]

But Boyatt's superior, the Deputy Assistant Secretary of the Middle East Department, Roger Davies, stopped him: *"'We can't do that.' And I said, 'We have to do that.' He said, 'Nobody in this town wants to alienate the Greek government.' And I said, 'You would prefer a war?' Anyway, we argued back and forth, he refused to clear the cable. So I went back and I redrafted it, and I toned it down but with essentially the same message, and I came back with another try. This time he said, 'Okay'."* Both went to the next higher instance, where the dialogue just described was repeated.[3] Boyatt reformulated again. As we have already seen, Kissinger avoided any specification at that conference on 20 March and only instructed Tasca not to make waves in Athens.[4] Two days later Kissinger had to deal with the issue again, because the Soviets informed the State Department that they had warned the Greeks and Turks not to intervene in Cyprus and take any irresponsible action.[5] Surely the Americans should take part in this démarche. Kissinger wanted to know on the basis of what information the Soviets had acted. It was not ruled out that the Cypriots were behind it, and therefore Kissinger did nothing.[6]

On 9 April 1974, the three department directors for Greece, Turkey and Cyprus put Cyprus and Greek-Turkish relations on the agenda of the weekly meeting of the Bureau for Near Eastern Affairs. Boyatt warned again.: *"[He] was less concerned that the Turks were up to something than by the prospect of the Greeks putting the Turks in a position where they would have to react."* The Director for Greece agreed that it was quite possible that Ioannides could do something in Cyprus. Assistant Secretary of State Kenneth Rush, who was present, did not respond. This was the first time that Cyprus was officially discussed in the State Department in 1974. Boyatt insisted and a few days later managed to raise the matter again with Second Assistant Secretary of State Joseph Sisco: *"I said, 'God damn it, Joe, we have to do something,' And he said, 'Look, this is very difficult. Nobody in Wash-*

1 Boyatt, *Presentation*, p. 4.
2 *Ibidem*, p. 5.
3 *Ibidem*.
4 *Ibidem*.
5 The Soviet Union spoke out in favour of independence, sovereignty and territorial integrity and against any outside interference. *DocBritPol V*, p. 29.
6 Ivar-André Slengesol, "A Bad Show? The United States and the1974 Cyprus Crisis" *Mediterranean Quarterly* 22:2 (2000), p. 102; Nicolet, *op. cit.*, p. 415f.

ington wants to do this, particularly they don't want to hear anything anti-Greek in the White House. Don't ask me why. I don't know why, but I know that's how they feel over there.' So we had the same argument again."[1] It was obvious that Kissinger's finger--off-the-junta policy was working and engendering anticipatory obedience in the upper echelons of the State Department.

In mid-April 1974, the CIA presented a situation report for Greece: The regime in Athens had failed to win support outside the military. It was more inclined to adventure with regard to Cyprus and Turkey than Papadopoulos'. The economic problems are enormous, especially the galloping inflation, and there was no adequate financial and economic policy. The military was divided into factions. It was expected that the regime would soon be overthrown. The silent majority of officers were in favour of a return to civilian government under Karamanlis, but he would probably demand a free hand, and these officers were also hesitant to give it to him. In terms of foreign policy, the regime was continuing its previous policy, but the officers who controlled the government were more provincial and nationalistic than their predecessors, but feared a military confrontation with Turkey. Ioannidis himself was particularly interested in Cyprus. He deeply distrusted Makarios and had exaggerated ideas about the communist danger on the island. At the moment, Ioannidis posed no threat to Cyprus because he was preoccupied with domestic problems, especially the consolidation of his position within the armed forces. If he succeeded, he might attempt to overthrow Makarios, which would of course strain relations with Turkey, which were already strained by the dispute over the extension of territorial waters and over oil under the Aegean.[2]

Kissinger came to Cyprus on 7 May. Makarios played the role of host at a meeting on neutral ground between Soviet Foreign Minister Andrei Gromyko and Henry Kissinger as part of the latter's mediation mission between Israel and Syria. Makarios was quite relaxed: nothing indicated an imminent crisis. Then follows a sentence in Kissinger's memoirs that once again shows how little Kissinger had recognised cause and effect in this matter, for he claims that Makarios had set out to question Greece's status on the island; in reality, it was Ioannidis.[3]

Next, in his memoirs, Kissinger tries to talk his way out of the reaction to the May 1974 prognosis paper written by Thomas Boyatt. It had been forwarded to him during the period of his shuttle diplomacy between Syria and Israel. He acknowledged that Boyatt had correctly predicted the development and noted that the Acting Foreign Minister had agreed to Boyatt's recommendation to approach Ioannidis and warn him against the use of force and any other steps.[4] He himself saw no need to take personal action. At about the same time, the Chairman of the Senate Foreign Relations Committee, Senator J. William Fulbright, received specific warnings that the junta was sending Greek officers to Cyprus to prepare for the overthrow of Makarios. Fulbright called Kissinger and urged him to do something about it. Kissinger refused on the grounds that he could not interfere in Greece's internal affairs.[5]

---

1 Boyatt, *Presentation*, p. 5.
2 *FRUS 1969-1976*, XXX, pp. 62-68.
3 Kissinger, *Erneuerung*, p. 164.
4 *Ibidem*, p. 166.
5 Slengesol, *op. cit.*, p. 10f; Christopher Hitchens, "The Case Against Henry Kissinger, Part II Crimes Against Humanitiy," *Harper's Magazine* 302:1810 (March 2001), pp. 49-74.

On 7 June came the next serious warning: *"On 7 June 1974, the National Intelligence Daily, essential breakfast reading for all senior State Department, Pentagon and national security officials, quoted, an American field report dated 3 June which stated that: 'Ioannides claimed that Greece is capable of removing Makarios and his key supporters from power in twenty-four hours with little if any blood being shed and without EOKA assistance. The Turks would quietly acquiesce to the removal of Makarios, a key enemy. [...] Ioannides stated that if Makarios decided on some type of extreme provocation against Greece to obtain a tactical advantage, he is not sure whether he should merely pull the Greek troops out of Cyprus and let Makarios fend for himself, or remove Makarios once and for all and have Greece deal directly with Turkey over Cyprus's future.'"*[1]

On 14 June 1974, Ioannidis informed Ambassador Tasca of his ideas: He did not want a war with Turkey, because the winner would only be the Soviet Union. Greece would not attack first, but would preserve its rights in the Aegean and Cyprus. The USA could prevent a Greek-Turkish war by selling the Greeks enough arms to deter a Turkish attack. The usual American practice of always selling the Turks twice the amount of weapons afterwards was not helpful. The Americans could use the Souda Bay in Crete as before. As far as Cyprus was concerned, he saw two alternatives: *"Either Cyprus will slowly drift left and become a Cuba of the Mediterranean [...] or the 80 percent Greek majority will achieve union with Greece. The only thing that cannot happen is union with Turkey."* The oil in the Aegean is Greek property: no rights will be granted to Turkey. Should there be a Greek-Turkish war, even the expatriate Greeks would return to help the homeland.[2] On 20 June, Ioannidis told his CIA contact that if Makarios continued his provocations, the Greeks would have only two options: *"To write-off Cyprus, with its sizeable Greek majority, or eliminate the Archbishop as a factor."*[3]

On 21 June 1974, the American intelligence services presented a jointly prepared memorandum on the "likelihood of a conflict between Greece and Turkey". This analysis was primarily concerned with the consequences of the oil discoveries near the island of Thasos. Although the tension between Greece and Turkey had increased, there was no immediate danger of war in the Aegean at the moment. Both sides are counting on negotiations. Should a military clash occur, it would remain localised, as both sides were not materially capable of waging a long war. Cyprus would probably not be drawn into such a conflict, but intercommunal tensions would increase again as a result. Ankara would in any case be able to cut off the lines of communication between Cyprus and Greece and carry out a landing.

---

1 Christopher Hitchens, *Cyprus* (London: Quartet Books, 1984), p. 79. *"This statement and its contents have since been authenticated before Congress by CIA Athens staff serving at the relevant time."* Der Sachbearbeiter für die Türkei meinte: *"The CIA official added that he was convinced that the Greeks were prepared to overthrow Makarios. I agreed with the analysis."* Slengesol, *op. cit.*, p. 105. Im *Pike Report*, p. 80 hieß es: *"The National Intelligence Daily warned that Ioannides was actively considering the ouster of Makarios if the Archbishop made an extremely provocative move."*

2 *FRUS 1969-1976*, XXX, p. 69f.

3 US Congress House Select Committee on Intelligence, *Report (P. 69)*, reprint in: *The Village Voice* 21:7 (16 February 1976), p. 80. Since the Republican majority in Congress prevented the publication of this report, it was leaked to Daniel Schorr, a reporter for the Village Voice magazine, which printed it almost in its entirety in a special edition under the bar headline on the outside cover "The Report on the CIA President Ford doesn't Want You to Read". This report became known as the "Pike Report" soon after the committee's chairman Otis Pike. It will be cited as such from now on.

"Ankara would take such action only in the unlikely event of a Greek attempt to take over the island or in order to protect a threatened Turkish minority on the island."[1]

Finally, on 29 June, a rather watered-down version of Boyatt's original February call to stop Ioannidis went out. It said that the situation between Athens and Nicosia was tense. It said that there were reports that Ioannidis seriously intended to overthrow Makarios. *"In our view, an attempt to remove Makarios through force entails unacceptable risks of creating chaos, a possible cause of a Greco-Turkish confrontation, the involvement of the Soviets in the Cyprus situation, and complications in the course of US-USSR détente. We know that Ioannides has long been obsessed with issue of Communism, both in Greece and in Cyprus, and that his dislike for Makarios has bordered on the pathological."* Tasca should go to Ioannidis and make it clear to him that the USA is against any adventure in Cyprus: *"You should send a signal to Ioannides. Through whatever channel and means you deem most appropriate, our view that any effort to remove the Archbishop from power by violent means could have disastrous consequences not only for the two communities on the island, but also for Greece and Turkey and that, therefore, we would be strongly opposed to any move of this nature."*[2]

Robert Dillon, the director of the Turkish section of the State Department, had suggested sending this message to Ioannidis through CIA channels so that he would really understand what was going on. But the State Department refused: the US government does not communicate with foreign government officials through such channels.[3] But now Tasca was stonewalling: *The ambassador in Athens instantly came back with a cable, which is his right, saying, 'Those are terrible instructions that you've given me. I can't possibly do that. If I do that it's going to alienate the Greek government, and we won't have any influence with the Greek government. I reject these instructions. You've got to change them.' So I had to fight the fight all over again, but with one more enemy. And by this time the CIA and the Defense Department had discovered what I was up to and they were both opposed [...] because of home porting [...] because they had a relationship with Ioannidis."*[4] Stern's claim that Tasca refused to pass on the message to Ioannidis for reasons of prestige because he was just a cop does not sound convincing, even if it is repeated by Kissinger.[5] Tasca's behaviour was indeed unprofessional. He had got on so well with Papadopoulos that Kissinger regarded him as a mouthpiece of the junta and left him on the sidelines.[6] Tasca's appointment, as is well known, had been at the insistence of Tom Pappas (Esso-Pappas), who insisted that he remain in office even when it became clear in March 1974, in connection with the hearing, that he was not cutting a good figure. He had also shown little cooperation in the

---

1 *Ibidem*, pp. 70-76.

2 *Pike Report*, p. 81; *FRUS 1969-1976*, XXX, p. 273.

3 Robert S. Dillon interview by Charles S. Kennedy in: Foreign Affairs Oral History Collection of the Association for Diplomatic Studies and Training. (ADST).

4 Boyatt, *Presentation*, p. 5.

5 Stern, *Wrong Horse*, p.100; Kissinger, *Erneuerung*, p. 166: "Later, Tasca was accused of not having carried out his mission with the necessary vigour. There was no evidence of this; moreover, the same diplomat had carried out a similar mission two years earlier extremely effectively." In that case, Tasca had intervened with Papadopoulos, who was in charge.

6 Statements by Assistant Secretary European Affairs Wells Stabler in: Foreign Affairs Oral History Collection (ADST): *"Tasca was in fact not a great deal more than the spokesman for the junta - to the extent that there really was no communication between [Kissinger] and the Ambassador in Athens."*

past.[1] Be that as it may, Boyatt reworded his telegram for the eighth time and sent it to Athens again on 5 July 1974.[2]

Tasca had gone on leave there in the meantime, and the deputy chief of mission gave the paper to the embassy's political counsellor, Elisabeth Brown. To make sure Brown really understood the importance of the assignment, Sisco called her. From the telephone conversation which Dillon overheard, it was clear that she had understood nothing: *"She did not indicate that she had understood that the issue was a very serious one that required special attention and care."*[3] Later it turned out that Brown had not gone directly to Ioannidis either, but conveyed the message to the powerless Prime Minister Androutsopoulos and Archbishop Serafeim, who had close relations with Ioannidis. One can imagine how little such a demarche impressed the ESA chief, especially since it had been delivered by a woman. Boyatt's rescue attempt *"had been carried out in a halfhearted manner at best by the embassy in Athens."*[4] This was probably more of an understatement, as the Athenians directly torpedoed the very purpose of the message's message by the manner of its delivery. The Pike Report is absolutely right in its judgement of the embassy's failure: *"It is clear, however, that the Embassy took no steps to underscore for Ioannides the depth of US concern over a possible Cyprus coup attempt. [...] Ioannides had much ground to believe that in the light of the direct contact he enjoyed with the CIA station, he would have received a stronger, more categoric warning if the US were genuinely exercised about protecting Makarios. All this leads to one basic conclusion: I believe that strong US representation to Ioannides would have prevented the crisis."*[5]

On 10 July, the Athens CIA chief and Ioannidis met. Two days later he reported to Washington, as Boyatt recalls: *"'We have been in touch with General Ioannidis, and we have been assured by General Ioannidis that the Greek government is not, and will not be involved in any clandestine activity designed to overthrow Archbishop Makarios, and to damage the situation in the eastern Mediterranean.'* [6] *That was a weekend, so all right, we'd had it from the horse's mouth. I went home. And about 3:00 a.m. on Monday morning [15 July], I*

---

1 Stanley I. Kutler, *Abuse of Power: The New Nixon Tapes* (New York: Free Press, 1997), p. 218: *"Haldeman: Pappas is extremely anxious that Tasca stay in Greece [...] Our plan was, you know, to remove him and put somebody else in Greece, [...] Nixon: Good. I understand. No problem. Pappas has raised the money for this other activity or whatever it is."*

2 Before the Greek Parliament's Committee of Inquiry, the then Secretary General of the Greek Foreign Ministry, Angelos Vlachos, claimed that Tasca had shown him two telegrams from Kissinger at the end of June, in which the latter had asked him to go and see Ioannidis and to make it clear to him that he should not do anything against Makarios. Averof, on the other hand, told the committee that Tasca had shown him three (sic!) telegrams at the same time.Vouli ton Ellinon (ed.), *Porisma tin exetastikis epitropis gia to 'Fakelo tin Kyprou'* (Athen: Eleftheri Skepsi, 1989), p. 80. Both cannot be true, because Kissinger did not send any telegrams to Tasca during this period. This is also supported by the fact that a few months after his testimony before the Committee in the summer of 1987, Averof corrected it and stated that Tasca showed him these telegrams after the coup on 15 July 1974.

3 Dillon, *Interview*.

4 Boyatt, *Presentation*, p. 5.

5 *Pike-Report*, pp. 80, 81.

6 The Pike Report read like this: *"On July 3, 1974, a CIA report stated that an individual, later described as 'an untested source', had passed the word that [...] Ioannides had changed his mind: there would be no coup after all. For reasons still unclear, this CIA report was embraced and headed until July 15, the day of the coup. The Intelligence Community post-mortem, appears to have concluded that the 'tip' was probably a ruse."* Pike *Report*, p. 80.

got a call from the Ops Center at the State Department and the person said, 'You better get in here. There's fighting in Nicosia, and something is going on and it doesn't look good.'"[1] Boyatt went to the State Department Operations Centre. The officer on watch presented him with two messages: Ioannidi's assurance to do nothing and the first report from the US Embassy in Nicosia on the coup against Makarios. Boyatt described his reactions: *"There we were, sitting there with the entire intelligence establishment of the United States in all of its majesty, having been conned by a piss-ant Greek Brigadier General, on the one hand; and on the other hand the disaster which I had been trying to avert, and avoid, coming true like your worst nightmare. Well, it was in the fan, clearly."*[2] The National Intelligence Community Bulletin of 15 July 1974 was headed: *"Ioannides is taking a moderate line while he plays for time in his dialogue with Archbishop Makarios."*[3]

Before we proceed with the account of Kissinger's behaviour on 15 July 1974, the day of the coup against Makarios, a brief evaluative review of Kissinger's previous policy and behaviour is in order. He himself was not aware of any blame: *"What caused the situation to spiral out of control was not so much Washington's wrong action as the behaviour of Makarios, who was once again testing his art on the high wire, but this time with disastrous results. On 2 July, he let the Greek president know that since he was reducing the strength of the National Guard, he was demanding the withdrawal of the Greek officers who controlled it. With these two steps, Athens' influence in Cyprus would have been greatly reduced, if not eliminated. Makarios would have relied even more on the Communist Party internally and on the Non-Aligned externally."*[4] The claim that this letter was the trigger for the coup against Makarios is false. The coup had been a done deal since early June. Makarios' letter therefore had no influence whatsoever on the decision-making process. Moreover, it was addressed to the wrong person, because President Gizikis had no say in the matter. The decisions were made by dictator Ioannidis. Implicitly, Kissinger's argument justified the junta's coup. So it was the victim's fault, Kissinger said in the pose of Pontius Pilatus, and cooperation with the communists was an unforgivable crime in his eyes. When Kissinger was cornered by the journalists at the press conference on 22 July, he tried to talk his way out of it with the argument that *"the information was not exactly lying on the street."*[5]

At the beginning of August, in front of his staff, he began to gloss over the image of Makarios in retrospect and his own role: *"We never saw in him, even for a moment, the 'Castro of Cyprus'. If we had had our way, there would have been no coup and we would have continued to get along well with him. It wasn't even a question of coexistence, because we didn't think he was particularly anti-American. His biggest disadvantage, if there is one, is that his talent for this island is too great and he may therefore be tempted to play along*

1 Boyatt, *Presentation*, p. 5.

2 *Ibidem*, p.6.Statement ofDeputy Chief of Mission Linsay Grant in Nikosia in: Foreign Affairs Oral History Collection of the Association for Diplomatic Studies and Training. (ADST): *"My wife had already left, because I knew this was coming. I remember drafting a telegram saying, 'We think they're going to try to kill Makarios' We said this in the summary of that telegram. The Ambassador [Rodger Davies], newly arrived, said, 'We can't say that people are going to kill a foreign head of a state just like that, in the summary.' So we took it out of the summary, but left it in the body of the message."*

3 *Pike-Report*, p. 80.

4 Kissinger, *Erneuerung*, p. 166.

5 *Department of State Bulletin* (12 August 1974), p. 261.

at a level that is worrying - not for us, but for the other parties involved in the Cyprus question." Makarios appeared "troublesome" to him, but not "threatening".[1] But, he further claimed, he had not been personally informed and therefore had not intervened.[2] Neither was true, as we have shown; they were protective claims to deflect attention from his own accountability. When, in a conversation with the Chinese Vice Foreign Minister on 2 October 1974, the latter said to him: *"You surely knew something of the situation before the event,"* and asked *"Why didn't you take steps to prevent it?"*, Kissinger answered: *"When the coup occurred I was in Moscow. My people did not take these intelligence reports seriously as such reports had been very numerous in the past. Every three months there was a rumor of a possible coup. An intelligence officer even told Makarios about these rumors, but he didn't believe them. He was away on a weekend holiday. If I had known about the report, I would have stopped it [the coup]."*[3]

It may be assumed that Kissinger would indeed have intervened if he had recognised the far-reaching consequences, but since he had not dealt with the problem of the potential consequences, he let things take their course; after all, it was only the stumbling block, Makarios, that was to be removed. This fatal tendency was reinforced by several factors, some of which directly affected Kissinger and others the State Department. Kissinger was constantly travelling during the crucial days: *"From 10 to 18 June, I accompanied Nixon on his trip to Egypt, Saudi Arabia, Syria, Israel and Jordan. From 27 June to 3 July, I was by his side at his last summit in Moscow. This was followed by several days of consultations in Brussels, Paris, Rome, Munich, London and Madrid. Finally, on 9 July, I watched the World Cup final - a clear indication that I did not sense a looming crisis."*[4] In his memoirs, the former Secretary of State at the State Department, George Ball, was quite biting about this shuttle diplomacy à la Kissinger: *"Trying to run the State Department singlehandedly from an airplane, Secretary Kissinger knew nothing about Cyprus and did not bother to inform himself. As a result, he absentmindedly let the Greek junta mount a coup in Cyprus [...]. Effective diplomacy for a great nation requires a constant high quality institutional vigilance. That is not possible when all decisions are preempted by an individual virtuoso with a lust for travel."*[5] In addition, the Watergate crisis was nearing its end in those days; on 23 June, the definitive evidence had been found that led to Nixon's resignation on 9 August.

In view of this burden, Kissinger would have been well advised to delegate partial competencies. Instead, he relied on the State Department apparatus to warn him of dangers in good time. He overlooked the fact that his attitude in the past had prevented him from doing exactly that with regard to the Cyprus question. The upper echelons of the State Department practised - as mentioned - anticipatory obedience, i.e. its members behaved as they thought Kissinger expected them to. This tendency was reinforced by a restructuring in the State Department ordered by Kissinger. Presumably because the directors of the departments responsible for Greece, Turkey and Cyprus were annoying him with their constant warnings, he placed them under the European Department on 1 July and appointed a new Assistant

---

1 Kissinger, *Erneuerung*, p. 160.
2 Nicolet, *op. cit.*, p. 419.
3 Slengesol, *op. cit.*, p. 105.
4 Kissinger, *Erneuerung*, p. 165.
5 George W. Ball, *The Past Has Another Pattern* (New York/London: Norton, 1982), p. 359.

Secretary and his deputy for the ad hoc Southern European Department. Until then, these three departments had belonged to the Middle East Department, and this had caused friction several times in the past because the heads of this department understood something of the Cyprus problem and had supported the three departments. Since the European Department and the new Southern European Department had no clue about the Cyprus problem, Kissinger was able to decide sovereignly on Cyprus policy.[1]

Another point should also not be left out of consideration: Henry Kissinger's arrogant hubris. He thought he could see through any problem with his high intellect, but in this case he failed because of his inability to comprehend the stupidity and bigotry of a Greek military policeman's brain. He did not think it possible that someone could commit such an insane act as Ioannidis did. Yet, unfortunately, this was precisely the reality. Let us summarise the main points that prevented the US government from intervening effectively in time: From what has been presented so far, it seems clear that there was no American conspiracy with the Athens military junta to overthrow Makarios. Kissinger is quite right when he wrote in his memoirs: "*The very last thing he [Nixon] or I could think of at that time was fomenting a crisis between two NATO allies in the eastern Mediterranean.*"[2] A coup could have exploded the tension between Greece and Turkey, dangerously heightened by the Aegean conflict, and affected the whole eastern Mediterranean. Makarios was no longer seen in Washington as the Castro of the Mediterranean; this view belonged to the Johnson era. The US intelligence services did nothing to foment the crisis, which does not exclude the possibility that some simple CIA agent was talking nonsense, but Ioannidis was experienced enough in this profession to realise the weight of such statements. Nicolet's differentiated judgement can only be agreed with: *"Bureaucratic problems and Kissinger's style of centralizing decisions led to the loss of valuable time and further misjudgment. Rather than bad faith, it had been inadequate handling, bureaucratic breakdowns, misjudgment and, finally, some bad luck, therefore, that had been responsible for the U. S. failure."*[3] With regard to CIA involvement, the Pike Report got to the heart of the matter: "*In terms of both its immediate and long-range consequences, the sum total of US intelligence failure during the Cyprus crisis may have been the most damaging intelligence performance in recent years.*"[4] But after this excursion on Kissinger's responsibility for the developments leading up to the coup of 15 July 1974, let us return to the coup itself.

Henry Kissinger was woken up in the early hours of 15 July 1974 with the news of the coup in Cyprus. The memorandum submitted to him by the National Security Council Staff in his capacity as Advisor to the President on National Security Matters, formulated by

1 Monteagle Stearns, *Entangled Allies. US Policy Toward Greece, Turkey, and Cyprus* (New York: Council on Foreign Relations Press, 1992), p. 9; Nicolet, *op. cit.*, p. 422, based on an ADST interview. The Pike Report states: *"Cypriot experts within State and CIA were in the process of being shuffled around in a bureaucratic reorganization of area responsibilities. In addition State Department Washington experts on all three countries concerned, as well as the Ambassador to Greece, were removed from their posts at one time or another during the crisis." Pike-Report*, p. 81; similar to the statement of Assistant Secretary European Affairs in: Foreign Affairs Oral History Collection of the Association for Diplomatic Studies and Training. (ADST).

2 Kissinger, *Erneuerung*, p. 165.

3 Nicolet, *op. cit.*, p. 423; ähnlich John C. Campbell, "The United States and the Cyprus Question, 1974-1975" in: Van Coufoudakis (ed.), *Essays on the Cyprus Conflict* (New York: Pella, 1976), p. 18.

4 *Pike-Report*, p. 80.

Rosemary Niehuss at 6 a.m. Washington time, contained information about the coup and Sampson's government statement based on the telexes from the US Embassy in Nicosia. Regarding the possible Turkish reaction, the memorandum saw two possibilities: *"If any fighting associated with the coup begins to spill over into the Turk Cypriot Community and seriously threatens it, Turkey may move to fulfill its promise of immediate military assistance and all the implications that such a move would have for a broader Turkish-Greek confrontation."* If the Turkish Cypriots were left alone, Turkey might stay out of it. Sampson's government declaration contained the right elements. The Soviet Union was watching developments closely and was against Cyprus being "natoised".[1] Obviously, R. Niehuss completely misjudged the reaction of the Turkish government.

At 10:15 a.m., the Special Actions Group met in the White House situation room, chaired by Henry Kissinger. The State Department, the Department of Defence, the Joint Chiefs of Staff, the CIA and the National Security Council were represented. Kissinger opened the meeting by asking CIA Director William Colby to give a status report. The military had no information on the situation yet, but thought it wise to keep an aircraft carrier that was near Spain there so that no wrong signals would be sent. Secretary of State Sisco said that the situation was so confused that it was probably best to wait and see. At the same time, one had to keep a clear eye on one's own aims and these were: *"(1) do what we can to avert war between Greece and Turkey; and (2) do what we can to avert Soviet exploitation of the situation. [...] What is important is that the integrity and political independence of Cyprus be maintained."*So far, the dispute has been limited to the Greek ethnic group. *"Whether this is a limited objective coup inspired by Greece or will lead to a prolonged civil war will depend partly on whether Makarios is alive and whether his Communist supporters and others will fight. Our best interests are protected within the framework of the territorial integrity of Cyprus. I suggest that we continue to operate quietly, that not to internationalize the situation would be in our best interests."*

Kissinger agreed: one had to keep the Soviets out and prevent internationalisation. One had to tell the Turks that one wanted to preserve the status quo (ante). They should not allow themselves to be provoked. They would be supported in the question of maintaining their rights in Cyprus. They should also tell the Greeks that they are against any change in the status of the island. He summarised: *"It seems to me that our immediate objective is to keep this thing from becoming internationalized, the Greek-Turk problem, the Soviet angle. There is really nothing we can do at this time internally but we can keep it from becoming an international issue."* He even rejected UN interference in Cyprus. It was obvious that Kissinger did not know what to do and therefore stuck to Sisco's proposals. Finally, it was agreed to continue the debate at the next meeting.[2]

During the day, more precise news of Ioannidis' involvement in the coup arrived in Washington from Athens. Kissinger briefed Ambassador Tasca along the lines of Sisco's arguments: the US wanted a unified, sovereign and independent Cyprus. No change in the status of Cyprus by the Greek government would be accepted. The continuation of the inter-communal negotiations was a priority. They appealed to all parties to show restraint. A similar telegram was sent to the Turkish government. In two telephone conversations with Soviet

1 *FRUS 1969-1976*, XXX, p. 275f.
2 *Ibidem*, pp. 277-281.

Ambassador Anatoly Dobrynin, Kissinger made sure that the Soviets did not want to interfere.[1]

On the afternoon of 15 July, Thomas Boyatt, the head of the department responsible for Cyprus in the State Department, presented a first differentiated danger analysis: In Cyprus, he said, the civil war within the Greek-Cypriot population threatened to turn into a clash between the ethnic groups. The Soviet Union would intervene by appealing to the UN Security Council. Turkey would intervene militarily if it became convinced that the coup was a precursor to enosis. Boyatt analysed the options of American policy: Either nothing could be done, which was impossible in view of the previous involvement in this issue, especially as this would mean losing the possibility of influencing developments. Such a course would give the impression that the USA was de facto supporting the Greek coup, which would provoke massive public protests and criticism in Congress. Or return to the status quo ante. To do this, it would be necessary to make it crystal clear to Ioannidis directly that the USA was against his action and demanded that he reinstate the government of Cyprus and withdraw the Greek officers. This option would certainly be welcomed by Turkey and the Soviet Union, but Ioannidis would ignore this diplomatic demarche. Therefore, according to the third option, the status quo ante would have to be enforced by threatening sanctions such as breaking off diplomatic relations and cutting off US military aid. This option could turn against American interests if Ioannidis closed American military installations in his wake. Boyatt recommended the second option, saying that if it did not work, they could always move on to the third. Undersecretary of State for Europe Arthur Hartman signed Boyatt's memorandum and forwarded it to Kissinger.[2]

A little later came the news that Makarios had survived. Boyatt immediately suggested that he be restored to office. When asked for his opinion, Robert Dillon, the State Department director responsible for Turkey, said, *"that if it were done quickly, they would accede. If time passed, then the Turks might well raise objections."* In an interview with ADST in 1990, Dillon recalled the further development: *"The issue of what we should do next was pushed up to the secretary, Henry Kissinger, who fancied himself an expert on these matters. He immediately developed some grand scheme. He had never liked Makarios and was happy to see him gone. He liked the situation and could only see us as unimaginative bureaucrats at lower levels who could not seize opportunities. He talked about a Clerides solution. (Clerides was the leader of the moderate Greek faction on Cyprus). Boyatt, who knew Cyprus, said that Clerides was a grand man, but he was not the solution. The saga continued and we did nothing to try to get Makarios back."* Kissinger's idea to make Kliridis Makarios' successor actually came from the Cypriot ambassador in Washington, who expressed it to Kissinger that day. The ambassador, as we know, was the brother of the new Cypriot Foreign Minister Dimis Dimitriou.[3]

1 *Ibidem*, pp. 283-286.

2 Nicolet, *op. cit.*, p. 423f; Drousiotis, *Cyprus 1974*, p. In the late afternoon, Ambassador Tasca from Athens also recommended a return to the status quo ante.. *FRUS 1969-1976*, XXX, p. 287 Fußnote 2.

3 Interview of Robert S. Dillon with Charles Stewart Kennedy am 17. Mai 1990 (ADST). Nicolet, *op. cit.*, p. 427. As Kliridis reports in his memoirs, US Ambassador Roger Davies visited him shortly after the coup and told him that Sampson had to resign, otherwise there was a threat of an invasion of Turkey. Clerides, op. cit., IV, p. 25. It is not known whether Kliridis' possible assumption of the presidency was also discussed on this occasion.

Late in the afternoon, a telex arrived in Washington from the US Embassy in Ankara warning of two dangers: Turkey was determined to use force if it was convinced that the declaration of enosis was imminent. This threat was serious and not one of the usual nationalist outbursts. Turkey would invoke the Treaty of Guarantee. If the US government wanted to prevent a war, it would have to prevent Enosis by all means. Nothing should happen to the Turkish Cypriots. It is more important to enforce these two points than to stop the internal Greek civil war in Cyprus.[1]

It should be noted that British Foreign Secretary Callaghan, through the British Embassy in Athens, had urged the Greek government to respect the independence, territorial integrity and security of Cyprus. To Ankara, he showed great understanding for Turkish concerns, but hoped that the Turkish government would not rush into anything. Addressing the embassy in Washington, he told Kissinger that he would be grateful for information about the American plans.[2] It was thus obvious that the guarantor power, Great Britain, was trying to stay out of everything.

All in all, the situation in Cyprus on the evening of 15 July was as follows: The putschists controlled all of Cyprus except for the area of Paphos, but since Makarios had survived, their coup had de facto failed on the first day. There were no significant inter-communal clashes. The Greek government remained ironclad. Since Washington, unlike in 1963, 1964 and 1967, did not take a clear position, Ankara began to prepare the invasion. The next step was to secure it diplomatically and under international law.

Before proceeding with an account of further developments, it seems useful to look at Henry Kissinger's conduct. In the second volume of his memoirs, published in 1982, he claimed that in the last three weeks of Nixon's presidency it had been impossible to make credible threats or credible commitments to influence the course of events. Yet just one page later he reports that by threatening the withdrawal of American nuclear weapons from the region, he forced the Turkish government into a ceasefire on 22 July.[3] So US policy was not quite so powerless after all. In the third volume of his memoirs, published only in 1999, he stated that his only concern was to avoid a war between two NATO allies and to keep the Soviets out of it.[4] At a meeting of his staff on 5 August 1974, it became clear once again how little Kissinger thought of the advice of the experts.[5] They had recommended that he exert pressure, but had not made any concrete proposals. This claim, as the Boyatt/Hartman memorandum proves, was simply not true. Then followed a eulogy on his craftsmanship: *"Our objective in such [a] stage of crisis is that: We are professionals, we are here to serve the national interest. We are not here to conduct our own domestic preferences, we are not here to lead crusades before we know what is going on. Nor are we newspaper commenta-*

---

1 *FRUS 1969-1976*, XXX, p. 287f.
2 *DocBritPol*, p. 67f.
3 Kissinger, *Memoiren*, p. 1300.
4 Kissinger, *Erneurung*, p. 168.
5 Thomas D. Boyatt, "Why Kissinger Was Wrong", in: Eugene Rossides & Van Coufoudakis (eds.), *The United States and Cyprus. Double Standards and the Rule of Law* (Washington: AHIF, 2002), p. 182: *"Kissinger's ignorance of the reality of the situation, combined with his arrogance that he was right about the situation, led to the Cyprus crisis in 1974."* Glen D. Camp, "Greek-Turkish Conflict Over Cyprus" *Political Science Quarterly* 95:1 (Spring 1980), p. 53.

tors. In the early stages of a crisis, it is our responsibility to assess what the balance of forces is; What the likely developments are going to be; How we can shape them, toward the national and public good. [...] Our strategy was to define objectives that would retain United States control, and to adopt tactics in which the United States would have the maximum flexibility as the crisis developed. [...] We want maximum flexibility until the other parties are committed before the United States is committed, so that the United States can sell its commitment in order to achieve its maximum publicity."[1]

These were classic maxims of realpolitik according to Metternich or Bismarck, which fitted into a 19th century Europe. Everyone had a free hand to do nothing as long as their own interests were not disturbed. The prerequisite for the functioning of this policy was, of course, that all participants adhered to these rules of power politics and acted rationally. What Kissinger did not understand was the fact that these rules did not apply in this region of the world. Neither Greece nor Turkey had pursued an independent policy in recent decades, but had always waited to see what direction the "foreign factor" would give. Both were American client states and knew that the Americans would interfere if something did not suit them. If no direction came, it was interpreted as approval.

Kissinger's policy of maximum flexibility was here inverted into a policy of maximum non-commitment, which everybody could interpret to their own liking. This sent the wrong signals to those who were waiting for American signals and now had to assume that the signals supposedly received were due to American wishes. Kissinger's policy of non-interference also meant that he no longer controlled the development, gave it free rein and even accelerated it uncontrollably. The result was that it took exactly the direction that the Americans had tried to prevent for years. Of course, Kissinger's personal inclinations also played a role here. He did not like Makarios. Good relations with Turkey were more important to him than those with Greece.

Since Kissinger held the office of Secretary of State in addition to that of Security Advisor, his behaviour towards his staff had changed considerably: *"As chief of U.S. diplomacy, Henry Kissinger preferred loyal subordinates to independent-minded collaborators. His senior lieutenants, whatever their individual competence, were above all yes-men who carried out policy with a minimum of dissent. Professor Kissinger kept them in line with crude psychological ploys: subjecting them to his sarcasm, playing one off another, belittling them to others. In the first days of the Cyprus crisis, the weaknesses of this management style became evident."*[2] Moreover, Henry Kissinger could not deny his attitude that he had been a professor at Harvard and was therefore superior to everyone in knowledge and otherwise.

Around 10:30 a.m. on 16 July, the Special Actions Group, chaired by Kissinger, met again. When CIA chief Colby reported on the Turkish landing plans, the following dialogue ensued: *Kissinger: "I just can't believe that. I just can't believe they want Makarios back in power." Sisco: "The Turks would intervene to (a) protect the Turk Cypriot community and (b) to prevent enosis from taking place." Kissinger: "It just seems inconceivable to me that they would support him"*Kissinger obviously did not understand what the aim of the

---

1 Nicolet, *op. cit.*, p. 425; Kissinger, *Erneurung*, p. 172.

2 James Edward Miller, *The United States and the Making of Modern Greece. History and Power, 1950-1974* (Chapel Hill: UP North Carolina, 2009), p. 192.

forthcoming Turkish intervention was. After some back and forth in the argumentation, in which Sisco tried to make the actual facts clear to Kissinger, Kissinger came to conclusions that no longer had much in common with reality and showed that he still did not understand anything: *"Our first objective is to prevent the situation from becoming internationalized. We need to put stronger pressure on Athens, and today. We must get our Ambassador in to see the President, or Prime Minister, or whoever it is, and get our views across forcibly. We've got to get somebody in there who will ask the Greeks for a statement of their intentions. I want an unambiguous statement of Greek intentions towards Cyprus from him. We want to defuse the Turk angle. They mainly want to prevent enosis. If civil war develops then we'll have to assess the situation then."* Recognition of the Sampson regime should be avoided for the time being. In the further discussion it became apparent again and again that Kissinger was uncertain and avoided decisions. He instructed his people in Athens and Ankara to find out where things were going.[1]

In Athens, Tasca sent the usual (CIA) contact to Ioannidis, who read him a message from Kissinger about maintaining a sovereign and independent Cyprus. The result was an outburst of anger from Ioannidis: *"After emissary completed message, the General literally blew up, jumped up, backed up, knocked over a table, broke empty glass and uttered a strong obscenity. He continued that one day Kissinger makes public statements regarding non-interference in Greek internal affairs and a few weeks later the USG [US Government] says 'consistent with the above principles ...' and threatens interference. 'No matter what happened in Cyprus I (Ioannides) will be blamed. [...] Some day USG will realize that on 15 July 1974 Cyprus was saved from falling into the hands of the Communists."* When Ioannidis had calmed down again, he claimed that he too was in favour of an independent Cyprus, but the Cypriot nationalists had turned against Makarios without his knowledge. Neither he nor the Cypriots had demanded enosis and the Turkish government had accepted this, understanding that this was a matter within the Greek Cypriot ethnic group. Then Ioannides lashed out at Makarios: *"Makarios had become a rotten priest homosexual; he was perverted, a torturer, a sexual deviate and the owner of half the hotels in the island."* When the emissary doubted that Ioannidis had not had his fingers in the coup, the latter exploded a second time after the same ritual. Makarios was finished, *"'Just who cares; he now has no power and no one, if he believes in principle of non-interference in internal affairs of sovereign nation will assist him - not even the Russians unless Turks ask them to do so and the Turks just don't care.' In reply to question whether Greeks were in direct touch with Turks, General stated we have not bothered the Turks; we have not declared enosis. Turks agree that 'the principal thorn' (i.e., Makarios) is gone and, 'I am not in touch with the Turks.' He expressed view that Greece and Turkey could now proceed at some future time to sit down, talk and solve their differences. [...] Again in reply to direct question, General Ioannides stated that he was not in contact with any Turkish official; however, he added that Turks were officially aware that enosis was not the objective at this point and that Greek Cypriots did not intend any bloody action against Turk Cypriots."* As the emissary took his leave, Ioannidis again stressed that he too believed in an independent Cyprus, just like the Turks and Kissinger; the Cypriots should solve their own problems.[2]

---

1 *FRUS 1969-1976*, XXX, pp. 288-294.

2 *Ibidem*, pp. 296-299; Kissinger, *Erneurung*, p. 174.

This conversation once again proved Ioannidis' total incompetence, even narrow-mindedness. He did not understand that with the coup against Makarios, who was the guarantor of Cypriot independence, he had already taken the decisive step towards Enosis in the eyes of the Turkish government, and that his tactical move of not mentioning it at the moment was such a transparent trick that no Turkish government would fall for it. The least that could have been expected would have been for Ioannidis to contact the Turkish side in order to explain his game and to secure it diplomatically. If he did not do so, this indicates that he was consciously or unconsciously relying on the Americans, who had held back the Turks in the past. But since they did nothing to stop the government in Ankara, disaster took its course.

Kissinger and the Turkish Intervention (Attila I) - 20-22 July 1974

On 17 July, the Special Actions Group met again in Washington. CIA chief Colby reported that Turkey was massing troops on the south coast. It probably intended to establish a bridgehead in the north of Cyprus. The Defence Ministry representative doubted that the Turks would actually make an invasion. *"They may make some noise, but I don't think they'll move."* Colby: *"Oh, I think they'll try to avoid having to move. [...] I think they'll try the diplomatic route first, but may feel in the end that they have to move. [...] To maintain the status quo ante."* Kissinger wanted to know what the Turks' objectives were in Cyprus. Colby said that they wanted to partition the island. This prompted Kissinger to come up with the idea of sending someone to London to talk to Makarios and Ecevit, who were there to negotiate the way forward on the basis of the Treaty of Guarantee. This met with general approval.

In the discussion that now followed, it became clear that Kissinger meanwhile realised that one had to return to the status quo ante, but in his opinion without Makarios. Makarios would lean more heavily on the Eastern bloc after a restoration. Kliridis would be better. It was only a matter of keeping the Turks from intervening, keeping the talks going in London and thus finding a passable constitutional solution. He would talk to Callaghan and inform him that someone would be sent to London. He would talk to Nixon about it. *"We can't let them run loose over there when they don't know our analysis of the situation."*[1]

After the end of the meeting, Kissinger called Callaghan and announced the dispatch of Sisco. Callaghan thought this was a good thing. He was of the opinion that Makarios should be brought back. This was also the position of the other European states. Whether this could be achieved by diplomatic means remained to be seen. But the question, Kissinger said, was how this could be done. Callaghan replied: *"Well, hopefully you would exert your influence on the Greek Government about the national guard officers. [...] We think there is a chance that if there is concerted diplomatic pressure they might calm down by withdrawing some of their officers. [...] The problem is three to one or five to one chance it won't succeed."* Kissinger said this should be discussed with Sisco. Callaghan promised to inform him immediately of the outcome of his conversation with Ecevit.[2]

In order to avoid a development like that of 1964, Ecevit went to London to urge the British government to take joint action on the basis of the Treaty of Guarantee. During an

1 *FRUS 1969-1976*, XXX, pp. 304-308.
2 *Ibidem*, p. 309f; *DocBritPol*, p. 85 Footnote 4.

interruption in the conversation between Callaghan and Ecevit, the former called Kissinger and informed him that the Turks were demanding a joint American-British declaration condemning the Sampson regime and calling for the restoration of the old system. Kissinger and Callaghan agreed that this was too extreme a demand to reject.[1] Around 4:30 p.m. Washington time, Kissinger called Nixon: The Europeans demanded the reinstatement of Makarios and expected the US to exert appropriate pressure on Athens. However, he feared that Makarios was moving closer to the Communists and the Eastern Bloc. He wanted to send Sisco to London to negotiate a compromise that would not necessarily bring Makarios back. The Europeans were aware that Washington was dragging its feet, and they did not know exactly what Washington wanted. *"We cannot openly oppose Makarios, but we can try to slow it down enough so that perhaps we can crystalize enough support for an internal solution. The Europeans are talking a tough game, but we have to defend their position."* Should there be a collapse of the regime in Athens, he feared a takeover by the Left. *"If Makarios is brought back this way, he will have to kick the Greek officers off the island and then the Communists will be the dominant force and to balance the Turks he will have to rely on the Eastern bloc. So the coup will have shifted the balance to the left."*[2]

It became increasingly clear that Kissinger was becoming entangled in contradictions. Since he wanted to keep all options open until the end, he was not allowed to commit himself. A commitment would have required a realistic analysis. But since he did not do this, when he came under pressure he began to look for known elements and to project them onto the situation in Cyprus. He did not realise that they did not apply there. His argument that if Makarios were reinstated the communists would dominate politics was not true, as the past had shown. Moreover, the claim would have applied even more to Kliridis, who would have had less authority than Makarios. The result of this laissez-aller policy was that things took their course and disaster drew ever closer.

In the evening, the British ambassador in Washington, P. Ramsbotham, called Kissinger to explain the background of the draft British Security Council resolution. Kissinger thought everything was too hasty; one would end up in a civil war and strengthen the communists. *"Was there not a risk of doing Makarios's work for him, without tying his hands in any way? It was also surely a mistake to commit ourselves now to Makarios and thus narrow our options when it was far from certain that Makarios could return to power. Kissinger was also concerned at the line we were taking about the withdrawal of Greek officers in the National Guard. Whatever other role they had been playing they had at least acted as a force against communist infiltration in Cyprus. Kissinger was clearly suspicious that Makarios, returned to power in those circumstances, would not hesitate to regard the Russians as his saviours and allow an already strong Communist Party to gain further strength."* Ramsbotham took the liberty of doubting this role of the officers. Moreover, Kissinger should not forget that Makarios was also the ethnarch. But Kissinger wanted Kliridis as president and considered it a mistake to support only Makarios. Sisco would fly to London and explain his thoughts.[3]

---

1 *FRUS 1969-1976*, XXX,, p. 311 Footnote 3.
2 *Ibidem*, p. 311f.
3 *DocBritPol*, p. 91f.

In his telephone conversation with Nixon, Kissinger had been given the green light to send Sisco accompanied by Boyatt, Dillon and others. The briefing is reported by Dillon: *"Just before departure, Tom Boyatt, Joe Sisco, myself and some others went to Kissinger's office. [...]. We were there [...] to discuss what we might do on this special mission. In fact, the meeting consisted of a lecture by Henry Kissinger on history which was totally irrelevant to the issue that we were to address. With a couple of exceptions - Boyatt and I among them -, most of the other participants kept remarking: 'Gee, Mr. Secretary, I never knew the history of the eastern Mediterranean, until I just heard you explain it' and other similar vacuous remarks. That is a slight exaggeration, but that was the tone of the conversation."*[1] About the end of the briefing, Dillon recounted: *"Kissinger asked whether anyone had any questions. I asked a couple, which went essentially unanswered. I tried to use the questions as a way of showing that what we were about to do was not going to work. I thought that our only chance of getting the Turks' attention would have been to threaten to cut off aid. The Turks were never going to take us seriously unless we threatened to suspend aid immediately. I knew that that was the only language the Turks would understand. I was convinced that the Turks would invade without some very strong US threat or action. Tom Boyatt, having watched my performance and having seen how unsuccessful it had been, just said: 'I disagree with you, Mr. Secretary. This isn't going to work!' Kissinger just looked at him and turned away. Nothing further was said and we all got up and left the office, went to the airport and took off."*[2]

Kissinger gave Sisco the following assignment: He was to get Kliridis to become acting president for six months. After that, elections were to be held in which Makarios could also run. In the meantime, inter-communal negotiations were to continue and new agreements were to be negotiated. A President Kliridis would allow Ankara and Athens to save face. In that case, Athens would not have had to deal with Makarios in the intercommunal talks.[3] These instructions proved once again that Kissinger had no idea of the conditions in Cyprus or that he threw warnings to the wind.[4] A change from Sampson to Kliridis would not reassure the Turkish government, because Ankara wanted a return to the status quo ante. Only this could prevent military intervention; and in the case of new elections after six months, the winner would have been Makarios without any doubt anyway.

Sisco knew the region. He had participated in the Ball mission ten years earlier in February 1964.[5] Unlike Sisco, Ball had had massive leverage in 1968. Sisco, on the other hand, was sent on a "mission impossible" without a chance. Boyatt recognised this aspect very clearly: *"I had been around Washington long enough, and had become cynical enough, that I knew that the minute Kissinger sent Sisco, instead of going himself, it meant that he knew that there was no hope, and he didn't want to have a loser identified with himself. So he sacrificed Under Secretary Sisco, and his staff, of which I was one. I mean it's a clear bureaucratic signal that you're not going to win. And we didn't."*[6] The latter sounds a bit dra-

1 Interview Dillon ADST.
2 Interview Dillon ADST.
3 Kissinger, *Erneuerung*, p. 175.
4 Drousiotis, *Cyprus 1974*, p. 194.
5 Richter, *op. cit.*, III, pp. 335-347.
6 Interview Boyatt ADST.

matic, but it shows the frustration of the participants in this hopeless mission. It is actually amazing that Sisco played along and did not resign when he realised the real situation.

Sisco first flew to London, where Ecevit was negotiating with the British about a joint intervention in Cyprus to restore the status quo ante.[1] Sisco held talks with Foreign Minister Callaghan and with Ecevit. During the second conversation between Sisco and Ecevit, it became apparent that the latter was steering a hard course: *"In second session Ecevit took more extreme line presenting some ideas which were tantamount to partition. Ecevit noted that Turkey could not tolerate situation created by coup in Cyprus and believes that creeping enosis is taking place. He calls for two autonomous provisional governments. Also asks for free access to airports and seaports supervised by guarantor powers. Sisco agrees to examine all ideas and discuss situation further with Ecevit in Ankara. Sisco also agreed to visit Ankara evening of July 19. During both Sisco-Ecevit conversations there were indications of a separation in Ecevit's large delegation with pressures from home for a very hard line."*[2] Despite these harsh demands, Sisco believed that Ecevit was nevertheless leaning towards a peaceful solution and asked him not to do anything until he arrived in Ankara on 19 July.

About the time the talks in London were nearing their end, the Special Actions Group was meeting again in Washington. The discussion revolved around the vague possibility of Soviet intervention. Since nothing had been heard from Sisco, nothing was decided except that the vote on a Cyprus resolution in the UN Security Council should be blocked for the time being. Kissinger again made his position clear: *"We have to find out first what is negotiable between the Greeks and the Turks. I agree that an ideal solution would be to get negotiations started, within the Zurich framework, towards a solution on which all sides would agree. I know some of my colleagues believe we are advocating the overthrow of the Ioannidis government, but that is not our policy. We still have the Cyprus problem with Turkish intervention. Our first objective is to avoid a Greek- Turkish war and Soviet intervention. We can worry about Ioannidis later. We do not want to tip our hand on a Cyprus solution yet til we know what will come out of it."*[3] In a conversation with Kissinger's inner circle, the options were discussed again and late in the evening he informed the embassies concerned of his position: *"The thrust of our position at this time, therefore, is to avoid assuming a public posture which commits us to any particular course of action. We view as unlikely the restoration of Makarios and we do not accept a Sampson regime. Consequently, the situation in favor of either one or the other should not be allowed to freeze, thus creating the conditions for the development of a compromise and negotiated settlement which would permit the maintenance of constitutional arrangements in Cyprus, both in their internal and external aspects."*[4] In the meantime, preparations for intervention had long been underway in Ankara, but Henry Kissinger continued to indulge in theoretical considerations on how to keep everything in abeyance in order to reach negotiations.

---

1 On the negotiations in London Richter, *op. cit.*, IV, pp. 401-404.

2 *FRUS 1969-1976*, XXX, p. 320f. According to Barutşu, Ecevit demanded access to the sea for the Turkish Cypriots. Cyprus must be taken under the control of the guarantor powers. After that, the form of the state could be determined. Barutşu, *op. cit.*, p. 21.

3 *FRUS 1969-1976*, XXX, pp. 313-317.

4 *Ibidem*, p. 323.

On 19 July, Sisco flew to Athens and from there to Ankara. For the negotiations in Athens and Ankara, Sisco devised the following tactics, about which he informed Kissinger: He first wanted to get the Turkish side to agree to the following four points: (1) *"The independence and territorial integrity of the Republic of Cyprus and the security and prosperity of all citizens are better served by a return to the previously agreed constitutional arrangements."* (2) Parliamentary Speaker Kliridis should assume the office of President in accordance with Article 44 of the Constitution of Cyprus. (3) Intercommunal negotiations should be resumed without preconditions. (4) Both governments should undertake to eliminate all measures threatening Cyprus. Turning to Kissinger, he added that he had gained the impression in London that Ecevit was favourably disposed towards the Kliridis plan. If the Turkish side accepted these points, he would make a commitment to Ecevit to return to Washington and suggest that the US government lobby the Greek government for the Kliridis solution. The goal, he said, must be the enforcement of the four points. A prerequisite for this plan to work was, of course, that Kissinger receive a promise from the Turkish side that they would not take military action against Cyprus or Greece as long as Sisco's proposals were discussed in Washington.[1] So Sisco understood perfectly well that he was travelling empty-handed. Only if he succeeded in getting the Greek side to make a substantial concession, and only if he got Kissinger to put pressure on the Turkish side to postpone its attack, did his mission make any sense at all.

Boyatt's report on Sisco's stay in Athens is available: *"We flew first to Athens where an ashen-faced ambassador received us and said, "We've made arrangements for you to see the foreign minister." And Sisco said, "I'm not going to see the foreign minister. If I can't see General Ioannidis, I'm leaving.' And we had about a morning's go-around over that, but we eventually got to see General Ioannidis, and Joe Sisco went in there and said, 'If you don't do something we're going to have a war, and you're going to lose the war. Now give me some elements of compromise that I can take to Ankara that we can work with." Whereupon, General Ioannidis launched into an emotional, weird, surreal, description of Byzantine history, and the struggle against the Osmanli Turks, and Constantinople, not Istanbul. We were clearly in real trouble because this guy had disconnected from the world, and he had all the power. And he didn't give us anything."*[2] According to the Chief of General Staff, Bonanos, who was present at the conversation, Ioannidis is said to have expressed that if the Turks wanted war, they could have it.[3]

Sisco obtained two small concessions from Ioannidis, but on the decisive issue Ioannidis remained intransigent: *"I got nowhere on the question which interested the Turks most, namely, a willingness to give the Turkish community access to the sea [via] some port or ports under UN supervision. As I expected, GOG [Government of Greece] saw this proposal as a form of separatism or partition (which it is) and it was therefore politely but firmly rejected. GOG rejected anything smarting of partition, and I did not therefore put forward outright partition proposal which Ecevit gave me in my second meeting yesterday, since it might have cooled them on going to London."* He intends to make the best of the two concessions in Ankara. He feared, however, that he would not get far with them; he needed Washing-

1 Drousiotis, *Cyprus 1974*, p. 200.
2 Interview Boyatt ADST.
3 Grigorios Bonanos, *I Alitheia: 21i Apriliou, 25i Noemvri, Kypriakon* (Athen,1986), p. 232.

ton's support to still stop the Turkish attack. Sceptically, he added: *"I have the distinct impression that no matter what is done in this situation, the Turks see it as an ideal time to achieve by military intervention a longstanding objective, namely, double enosis."*[1]

Kissinger, who was with President Nixon in San Clemente on 19 July, was briefed on Sisco's proposals by Deputy Secretary of State Robert Ingersoll. He sharply rejected them: *"We have to remain as flexible as possible and not proceed with the Clerides suggestion until we make the interested parties recognize by themselves that a compromise solution serves their own interests."* Sisco should not mention the four-point programme in Ankara, he said, and should also refrain from trying to achieve a short-term postponement of Ecevit's intervention by temporarily returning to Washington. He should not put pressure on Ecevit: *"The Secretary of State wishes that you show sympathy and understanding for Turkish anxieties in your approach to Ecevit, and avoid creating any sort of feeling in Turkey that we are letting them down. We must make them feel that we are consulting with them as a friend and an ally."*[2] So, empty-handed and without the possibility of exerting the slightest pressure, Sisco flew to Ankara, where he arrived at around 10 pm. It was indeed a mission impossible.

In the meantime, the order to attack was given in Ankara. It was not until around 1.45 a.m. on 20 July that Ecevit received Sisco. Sisco tried in vain to persuade Ecevit to postpone the attack. Ecevit was not amenable to any argument. The conversation was interrupted and Sisco went to the US Embassy. There he found a message from Kissinger: He strongly disapproved of the Turks' actions. Now the Kliridis solution had to be implemented and he expected the Turks to support it. Sisco replied that both Athens and Ankara rejected this solution.[3] Sisco went to Ecevit again. *"Sisco now produced his last and most persuasive card. He said: 'Mr. Ecevit, give me 48 hours and I will bring you an American plan'. There was utter silence. This sounded attractive - but could one trust the Greeks? Was it worth while suspending all action on the strength of a verbal promise? Could one trust the U.S. ? Would the circumstances ever be so favorable again? Even if the present situation could be straightened out, would not the same thing happen again? Ecevit's response was decisive; 'No! Mr. Sisco, it is now too late. A similar meeting to this was held in this very room ten years ago. On that occasion both Turkey and the U.S. made mistakes. You erred by standing in our way, we erred in listening to you. History may repeat itself, but we are not obliged to repeat the blunders of the past. No! We will not listen to you this time; we will not repeat the mistake we made ten years ago and I hope that neither will you. Because of that error, Turkish-American relations have been embittered for the last decade ...'*[4] *As Ecevit looked at his watch, Sisco burst out; 'Do you mean that I am talking here to no purpose?' Ecevit: 'Yes.' Sisco: 'Has the operation been launched already?' Ecevit: 'It is about to begin. The planes are just about to take off'.*[5]

---

1 *FRUS 1969-1976*, XXX, p. 329f; Kissinger, *Erneuerung*, p. 175.

2 Drousiotis, *Cyprus 1974*, p. 201f.

3 *FRUS 1969-1976*, XXX, p. 333.

4 Interview Dillon ADST: *"Ecevit, savoring every minute, said to Sisco that the Turks don't make the same mistake twice. In 1967 (the Vance Mission), the Americans had urged the Turks not to invade Cyprus and they hadn't. It had been a mistake and the Turks would not repeat it again."* Ähnlich Barutşu, *op. cit.*, p. 23.

5 Mehmet Ali Birand, *30 Hot Days* (London: Rüstem, 1985), p. 18f.

While the Turkish fleet was already on its way to Cyprus, the Special Actions Group was meeting in Washington at 3:30 p.m. on July 19, 1974, which was about 10 p.m. Cypriot time. Kissinger, as mentioned earlier, was in California. The Department of Defense announced that they had moved an amphibious force to the vicinity of Cyprus to evacuate American citizens in case of doubt. The State Department confirmed that preparations had also been made for such an eventuality. Ingersoll reported that Kissinger had called him and reminded him that there was no American plan for Cyprus. Ambassador Robert McCloskey added that the United States was discussing ideas on how to avoid a Greek-Turkish war and establish constitutional conditions (Kliridis solution) in Cyprus. *"It is our thinking that if the Turks insist on the return of Makarios this can have only destabilizing impact on the island and on the area as a whole because we think that Makarios will have to turn to the left inside the country and out in order to remain in power."* Kissinger would see Makarios on Monday (July 22) in an effort to defuse criticism emanating from Congress. At the same time, he said, he would avoid giving the impression that Makarios was recognized as head of state. Ingersoll concluded by saying that it would be necessary to wait for Sisco's report before making any further decisions. At the request of Richard Kennedy of the National Security Council, a working group was set up to react immediately if the Turks did undertake an invasion of Cyprus.[1]

During the first phase of Sisco's conversation with Ecevit, Kissinger spoke by telephone with Secretary of Defense James R. Schlesinger. Kissinger confirmed that the Turkish landing operation had begun. The Turks had assured him that if the Greeks did not fire on them, they would not fire: *"So we're going to pass that message and we're also going to tell the Greeks that we think the best solution now is to have a negotiation as rapidly as possible looking for the return to constitutional government. And that we recommend the Clerides solution under these conditions. That's - that means they have gotten rid of Makarios and they'll have to give up Sampson. And we'll send Sisco back from Ankara. Now we don't think this will really fly but at least it's a slender thread. [...] If the Turks want a piece of the island then in my view we have to work for double enosis and give the Greeks the other part of the island. So my view is there are now two possible outcomes. Either double enosis or Clerides."*[2]

When Sisco's reply arrived that both the Greeks and the Turks rejected the Kliridis solution, Kissinger had reached the end of his Latin. In a telephone conversation with McCloskey he said: *"As to who will be president under those circumstances, Ecevit said government in Turkey does not care. Now, what in the hell does that mean?"*[3] About half an hour later, Kissinger had CIA chief Colby brief him on the military balance of power and the presumed invasion targets. When Colby predicted that the National Guard would fight with their Greek officers and that the situation would therefore become critical, he asked: *Do you have any good idea what we should do?"* Colby replied: *"Well, I think the biggest thing is to get the Greeks not to fight. To say all right, let's negotiate and discuss what ought to be*

---

1 *FRUS 1969-1976*, XXX, pp. 324-328.
2 *Ibidem*, p. 331f.
3 *Ibidem*, p. 333.

done. [...] I think the most important thing is to limit it to Cyprus and not let it go out beyond that." Kissinger agreed.[1]

Kissinger spoke with Nixon another 30 minutes later. After Kissinger had briefly informed him of the situation, the following dialogue ensued: *"Nixon: 'You think this is the kind of thing that requires - that they feel my presence in Washington - that I have to get the hell back there for this thing?' Kissinger: 'Not yet, but if the Greeks attack the Turks, Mr. President, then I think you should go back to Washington. If it leads to a major war.' Nixon: 'Yeah, and then what do we do then?' Kissinger: 'Not much I think ...'"* Kissinger hoped, however, that the matter could be stopped by 22 July if the Greeks accepted the Kliridis solution and they met with the Turks in London. Then Kissinger recommended that they adopt the attitude of Pontius Pilatus. *"We got to posture needless to say that we are not - that we aren't responsible for the damn thing. I don't think - except for a few nuts - that what, that we could have saved this fellow [Makarios] - how could we have saved him.[...] - the question was: could we have brought him back faster. The answer was he didn't even show up in London till Wednesday [17 July] - that night we sent Sisco there ..."*[2]

At about 11 a.m. (4 p.m. UTC) on 21 July, the Special Actions Group chaired by Robert Ingersoll met in Washington, as Kissinger was still in California. Kissinger's position was described thus: Support for a ceasefire, the trilateral talks in London and the restoration of constitutional order in Cyprus. They would support a UN Security Council resolution to that effect. Kissinger had instructed Sisco: *"to be brutal towards the Turks in the sense that he can say that we will withhold all military aid in the event there is an all-out war."* Sisco should induce the Turks to go to London.[3] But only a short time later Kissinger rowed back again and revoked the threat.[4]

While the Americans and the British were trying to get the Turkish government to agree to a ceasefire, the government received information that a Greek convoy was on its way to Cyprus. In fact, it was three Turkish destroyers that had not been correctly detected by Turkish air reconnaissance. At Tasca's request, the Greek government informed him that there were no Greek ships in the region and that they agreed to a ceasefire, which Tasca immediately relayed to his colleague in Ankara. Macomber rushed to Ecevit and told him that Athens accepted the Turkish ceasefire terms and was prepared to send representatives to London for the talks. Ecevit distrusted the Greek promises: The Greeks were fooling both the US and Turkey; the Greek convoy was close to Cyprus and ready to land. Turkish forces had orders to open fire on the convoy's ships as soon as they entered the restricted zone. At about the same time, a message from Sisco reached Ankara that Ioannidis had told him that no Greek convoy was heading for Cyprus. If the Turks found Greek ships in the exclusion zone, they should quietly sink them. In Ecevit's presence, Macomber called Kissinger and informed him of Ecevit's views. He then passed the phone to Ecevit.[5] The following dialogue ensued:

---

1 *Ibidem*, p. 334f.
2 *Ibidem*, pp. 336-339.
3 *Ibidem*, p. 343.
4 *Ibidem*, p. 348f.
5 Drousiotis, *Cyprus 1974*, p. 222, on the basis of American sources..

Ecevit: *We have a problem. We have doubts that Greece can be relied on. Ioannides'word of honour is a joke. We have now found out what joke is behind his words. He says we will shoot at any ship flying the Greek flag. But his ships carry the Turkish flag!*
Kissinger: *So, nobody will blame you if you sink your own ships.*
Ecevit: *No, Dr Kissinger, they are not our ships. They are Greek ships. They are Greek ships flying the Turkish flag.*
Kissinger *Yes, Prime Minister, but you can sink them if they are not your ships and yet they are sailing under the Turkish flag.*
Ecevit: *They use two tricks. We are NATO allies and the Greek pilots know our codes. But they speak Turkish. They speak to our pilots in Turkish and use our slogans. We cannot rely on Greece's word.*
Kissinge *What do you want exactly? Since the days of Harvard I have known you as an intelligent man. But with all due respect - I cannot accept something like this. On this basis, this can go on for another six weeks.*
Ecevit: *They say they want a ceasefire. It is clear that they want to use the ceasefire to concentrate troops on the islands. The Greeks must desist from such methods.*
Kissinger *What methods should they desist from?*
Ecevit: *They say they are ready for a ceasefire. But they have already let us see the tricks they will use to violate the ceasefire.*
Kissinger *Are you telling me that you will not accept a ceasefire?*
Ecevit: *We will accept a ceasefire.*
Kissinger *Today?*
Ecevit: *We are still discussing the problem.* [1]

Kissinger may have found his remarks funny and noteworthy, for he published this dialogue in the third volume of his memoirs. Objectively, it is rather proof of Kissinger's cynicism, because for 56 sailors[2] of the destroyer Kocatepe this dialogue meant the death sentence, because the Turkish air force attacked the three destroyers and sank the Kocatepe.[3]

Around the same time, the Special Actions Group chaired by Kissinger met in Washington. It was decided to have a memorandum prepared on the possibilities of American policy on the Cyprus question and on the situation in Cyprus after a ceasefire. Kissinger complained about the Turks; he had phoned Ecevit five times, but chaos reigned there. Kissinger understood that Ecevit was trying to buy time. The ceasefire was urgently needed, but what should happen afterwards? The best thing to do was to put Ecevit under pressure again so that he would agree to a ceasefire. Kissinger then went on to talk about the time after the ceasefire: *"It is against our interests to have the Greeks in there. A strong Turkish presence would be highly desirable."* He wanted to know if the Kliridis option actually still existed. Kissinger then turned to developments in Greece. He heard from Callaghan that the government there would probably fall the next day. He feared that the new government would be

1 Kissinger, *Erneuerung*, p. 179f.
2 Erol Mütercimler, *Satilik Ada Kibris*. (Istanbul: Alfa, 2007). Figures in the appendix.
3 Details of the sinking of the Kotacetepe in Richter, *op. cit.*, IV, pp. 441f.

Soviet-friendly. It was therefore necessary to achieve a ceasefire quickly and he would therefore call Ecevit again.[1]

In his memoirs, Kissinger claims that he, together with Callaghan and the French Foreign Minister Jean Sauvagnargues, issued an ultimatum to the Turks and Greeks: *"If the ceasefire was not reached within twelve hours, the United States would withdraw its nuclear weapons on both sides of the Greek-Turkish border in Thrace."*[2] This is not confirmed by Callaghan, who reports that Kissinger alone made this threat to Ecevit.[3] Kissinger may have threatened to withdraw nuclear weapons, but this was at best an empty threat, for he himself was opposed to this idea, which in fact came from Defence Minister Schlesinger, as Kissinger himself reports. He himself, as he reports in his memoirs two pages earlier, had rejected Schlesinger's proposal to withdraw the nuclear weapons, but had agreed to the proposal that the warheads be removed from the delivery weapons and safely stored.[4] Sauvagnargues represented the EEC, which would certainly not have gone along with such a threat.

In the meantime, the Americans and the British were trying to persuade both sides to conclude an actual ceasefire. In a telephone conversation with Kissinger, Ecevit had agreed in principle to a ceasefire and a meeting with the Greeks somewhere in Europe, but only in principle. Kissinger wanted to know from Ecevit whether he would agree to a ceasefire at 5 pm (Turkish time). Ecevit replied that he could not stop the army until full security was achieved. Kissinger replied that the time was sufficient. *"Your bridgehead is strengthened, your reinforcements are about to land on the island, and can continue to do so after the cease-fire. In short, you have time to take all measures necessary for your security. If you do not agree to a cease-fire, the US will have to make a public announcement to that effect."* Ecevit promised to discuss the matter with the general staff.[5] Kissinger thus winkingly told Ecevit that he did not have to comply fully with the ceasefire.

In Washington, around noon on 22 July, the Special Actions Group presented its Briefing Memorandum on the Problems of Cyprus and Options for US Policy, which had been prepared under the chairmanship of Assistant Secretary of State for European Affairs Arthur A. Hartman. This document proved that its authors, unlike their boss, had a good grasp of the problems facing Cyprus, even if they, like their boss, had the misconception that upon his return Makarios would lean entirely on the communists. After a brief overview of the situation, the authors asked whether it was in the US interest for Turkey to consolidate its military position in Cyprus in such a way that the island was de facto divided and Turkey was put in a position to actually divide the island or to find another construction. There were two options: *"Double enosis is the more likely: it is a long-standing Turkish goal; once on Cyprus in force the mainland Turks are unlikely to withdraw and permit any other solution. At the same time, double enosis would mean NATO-ization of Cyprus and, coming*

---

1 *FRUS 1969-1976*, XXX, pp. 355-364; Callaghan, *op. cit.*, p. 345.

2 Kissinger, *Jahre der Erneuerung*, p. 180.

3 Callaghan, *op. cit.*, p. 345: *"Kissiger says he has told Ecevit that the United States will proceed to remove nuclear weapons from Thrace and Anatolia if there is no ceasefire."*

4 Kissinger, *Jahre der Erneuerung*, p. 178.

5 Birand, *30 Hot Days*, p. 45. The content of this telephone conversation was recounted by Ecevit Birand in one of his interviews. Henry Kissinger confirmed the accuracy in his interview with Birand. Birand in an e-mail to the author on 1 July 2008.

*on top of recent Soviet losses in the Mideast, would raise the issue of Soviet responses in its most acute form. - Substantial return to the 1960 constitutional arrangements is also a possibility: it would defuse adverse international reaction to Turkish military intervention, would preserve Cypriot independence, and would thereby be more acceptable to the Soviets. At the same time, it is a potentially less stable solution than double enosis, and would make the return of Makarios as a hostage of the left more likely."*Of course, combinations of the two models were conceivable. The memorandum looked at what the options were if the fighting continued in Cyprus, but these options were all quite theoretical. Should the ceasefire be respected, one should support the negotiations within the framework of the Zurich and London Agreements, which one was in fact already doing.[1]

Had Kissinger read this memorandum, he would not have asked a number of questions at the meeting of the Special Actions Group, which met on 22 July from 10:42 am to 11:25 am. Kissinger wanted to receive Makarios later in the day and face him in an informed manner: *"What exactly is the situation on the island? I've got to know for my talks with Makarios this afternoon. Isn't the Turkish position on the island weaker now than before?"* When one of his advisers pointed out to him that the Turks had taken his advice and sunk their own ships, he reacted with incomprehension and repeated that he had the impression that the Turkish position was weaker now than before the invasion. His subsequent remarks about the National Guard and Sampson did not reveal too much knowledge either. When his advisers tried to make him understand that the Turks were in the process of strengthening their position, he passed this over. Then Kissinger came to talk about Makarios: *"It seems to me that if Makarios were to go back, he would have to look around for additional support, and to my way of thinking that means the East Bloc and left-wing Cypriots. Well, that's okay, We'll know what to do then, although it is a very complex problem. I want to make it clear that we are not disassociating ourselves from Makarios, but by the same token, we have no incentive to push him. We'll wait to see what emerges from the negotiations."* The discussion turned to the Turkish enclaves, again showing that Kissinger had no idea of the problems of the enclaves. Finally, the discussion turned to the arms deliveries to Turkey and Greece, and Kissinger welcomed the fact that these had never been stopped. This could also be noted at the subsequent press conference. In conclusion, he summed up his impressions in a self-satisfied manner: *"I think this has been a well-coordinated and well-run crisis. I want to congratulate you all."*[2]

Shortly afterwards Kissinger and Callaghan spoke on the phone. Kissinger claimed that there was a coup in Greece and that the conference would have to be postponed until Thursday. He would see Makarios later. *"He would play it cool and would be non-committal though he would be friendly."* Callaghan advised Kissinger to treat Makarios with caution. *"He should not get himself isolated in not supporting Makarios."* Kissinger replied that he just did not want to commit himself definitively. In conclusion, it was agreed to work towards removing Sampson from the presidency as soon as possible.[3] The alleged coup in Greece was a return to democracy and the seizure of power by Karamanlis. In Cyprus, the ceasefire came into effect on that day and on 23 July, the coup regime under Sampson also

1 *FRUS 1969-1976*, XXX, pp. 366-374.
2 *Ibidem*, pp. 374-382.
3 *Ibidem*, pp. 382-386; *DocBritPol*, p. 120.

collapsed in Cyprus and Parliamentary Speaker Kliridis became Acting President, as provided for in the Constitution.

Kissinger's meeting with Makarios on the afternoon of 22 July was characterised as a private meeting. Kissinger did not want to receive Makarios officially as head of the Republic of Cyprus, as this could be prejudicial, which is why the State Department announced on 19 July that Kissinger would meet with Archbishop Makarios and not with President Makarios. The State Department press spokesman also let it be known that Makarios, and not the junta in Athens, was held responsible for the situation in Cyprus.[1] The meeting, which was also attended by Ambassador Dimitriou and McCloskey, lasted one hour and 20 minutes. Makarios showed Kissinger his six pages of handwritten proposals for a solution to the current Cyprus crisis, among which was the proposal for a return to the status quo ante. He expressed his agreement with Kliridis' conduct of official business. *"However, elections must be held within 45 days. Makarios said he understood the United States wants him to stay away from Cyprus for some time, but I [Kissinger] told him this was an unfair statement. We want the parties to work things out themselves. He is cold-blooded, and I told him we were looking at the situation in a cold-blooded way ourselves."* When Makarios told Kissinger that he would run again in the elections, Kissinger replied that he would not oppose it. Makarios replied that this was not enough, because he needed the support of the USA. *"I replied that that would depend on who else he asks."* Makarios noted that he had to make it clear to his people that enosis was no longer an option. Makarios rejected a federal solution.[2] Kissinger's claim in his memoirs that Makarios rejected a return to the status quo ante, i.e. the Zurich and London Agreements, and instead called for the establishment of a unitary state under Greek Cypriot control, to be enforced by the US through military pressure on Turkey,[3] does not sound very credible in the light of Makarios' remarks to Ambassador Ramsbotham shortly before, and besides, Makarios was just calling for a return to the 1960 state at their next meeting on 29 July.[4]

After this conversation with Makarios, Kissinger received Ramsbotham and reported to him. As far as the future government of Cyprus was concerned, he agreed to drop Sampson, but he rejected Makarios. The following dialogue ensued:

K: I object to him because he is ambitious, able and strong; with the present balance of forces in Cyprus he must get the Turks out, and this can only be done with Soviet help.

R.: I think you are wrong on that. I hold no brief for him; indeed, he has caused the UK a lot more difficulties than he has the United States, but he has handled that lot on Cyprus successfully for 14 years without outsiders like the Russians coming in.

K.: I enjoyed talking to Makarios. He is wily and clever and gets subtle points. But I now see a balance of forces which will drive him to the Soviet bloc. Clerides might be able to do it.

R.: Maybe the Turks don't feel so strongly now in view of their poor performance.

---

1 *IHT* (22 July 1974), p. 2.

2 *FRUS 1969-1976*, XXX, p. 385 Footnote 4, p. 387.

3 Kissinger, *Jahre der Erneuerung*, p. 182.

4 Facsimile of a State Department document dated 29 July 1974 in Makarios, *Apanta*, XV, p. 1.047.

K.: *We are trying to be cold-blooded about who takes over and have no objection if Makarios could structure it satisfactorily. [...] We would like to delay a bit and see how the balance of forces develops following the excellent British example of the 19th century.*[1]

So Kissinger had not corrected his ideas in the slightest. He continued to dislike Makarios and thought that the Kliridis solution was better. Out of his communist phobia, he did not realise that Makarios had largely tamed the Cypriot communists and that the Soviets preferred a neutral Cyprus to one that was a NATO member. He still maintained the policy of waiting and not committing himself until the last moment. He continued to be unwilling to delve into the specific problems of Cyprus, but assumed that the conflict between the two Cypriot communities and their mother countries functioned in a similar way to the Middle East conflict between Arabs and Israelis. He did not understand that Cyprus belonged to the European cultural area and this also in the field of political culture. In the Middle East there were indeed attempts to play the superpowers off against each other, but not in Cyprus. The role was played mutatis mutandis by the mother countries. The Americans' task would have been to remain neutral and to mediate from an equidistance. Kissinger let things take their course as long as they did not lead to a Greek-Turkish war. But he openly admits in his memoirs that Greece and Turkey were important to him as cornerstones of NATO for geostrategic reasons. Therefore, he was also prepared to tolerate the totalitarian regime of the colonels. Turkey, however, had an even greater geopolitical weight in his eyes than Greece. *"With its borders with the Middle East, Central Asia, the Soviet Union and Europe, it was indispensable for American policy in all these regions. Turkey was considered our firm and loyal ally during the Cold War. [...] For all these reasons, I was extremely reluctant when it came to sanctions."*[2] Therefore, Kissinger did not object in the slightest when Turkey reinforced its troops in Cyprus and "consolidated" its positions during the ceasefire.

On 28 July 1974, 27 members of the Senate Judiciary Committee voted yes and 11 voted no to impeach President Nixon for obstruction of justice in the Watergate trial. A second impeachment motion for abuse of power followed one day later.[3] Nixon's days were thus numbered - he resigned from office on 9 August - and Kissinger's attention was largely focused on domestic political developments in the USA. On 29 July, another memorandum was submitted by the Cyprus Task Force, which it had been decided to prepare on 25 July. After an overview of the situation, the memorandum stated that Turkey probably intended to remain in Cyprus permanently with considerable forces. Possible solution models followed, and then the authors of the memorandum stated that a federation was probably the best solution, but that it could fail because of the Greek Cypriots if too many concessions were made to the Turkish Cypriots.[4]

On 29 July, Kissinger received Makarios for a second meeting. Makarios again presented Kissinger with six proposals for a solution, which were strongly reminiscent of the proposals made on 22 July at their first meeting: The demands of UN Security Council Res-

---

1 *Ibidem*, p. 388.

2 Kissinger, *Jahre der Erneuerung*, p. 182. On the military relevance of Turkey: Alfred Joachim Fischer, "Die Bedeutung der Türkei für die NATO" *Wehrkunde* 8 (1975), p. 396.

3 *NZZ* (29. Juli 1974).

4 *FRUS 1969-1976*, XXX, pp. 406-409.

olution 353 should be applied. The guarantor powers should hold talks on a lasting solution, the basis of which should be the 1960 constitution. Should these talks fail to produce a result, the 1960 Constitution should be considered in force, with the proviso that the Cypriots could amend it by consensus. A committee of representatives of the guarantor powers and representatives of the Greek and Turkish Cypriots, together with the representative of the UN Secretary-General, should take practical steps to establish constitutional conditions. A mixed police force, in cooperation with the UN police, should disarm all those who possessed illegal weapons. Finally, Makarios proposed the total demilitarisation of the island.[1]

The version of this conversation published by the State Department omitted these points and the discussion about them. When the conversation turned to Turkey's behaviour, the following dialogue developed:

> M.: *I am not satisfied with the position of the United States. It is in your interest to stop the Turkish invasion. I don't say you should exercise pressure and in the process develop anti-U.S. attitudes. I don't know what you've conveyed to Turkey. But, despite this, Turkey is continuing its invasion without showing any respect for the Security Council Resolution.*
> K.: *Turkey is not advancing any further.*
> M.: *They are now seeking to impose themselves in Cyprus. Greece is weakened. I don't know whether Karamanlis can survive. The Turkish demands are unreasonable.*
> K.: *What ?*
> M.: *1) They won't go back to the lines called for in the Security Council Resolution. 2) They are calling for federation. 3) Ecevit is saying "our troops will stay." This is blackmail![...]*
> K.: *What concretely do you want us to do?*
> M.: *Take a more decisive role. You are in a position to play this role. You can make certain proposals. Turkey will accept. When you sent Sisco to Athens and Ankara I have read that you used strong language. And now you are very cautious.*

Kissinger said he could not interfere in the Geneva negotiations. Makarios wanted to know if this was not possible behind the scenes. Kissinger came to talk about the Turkish troops. Makarios expressed fears that Turkey intended to leave them in Cyprus until a final settlement was reached, and negotiations on this could take years. Kissinger agreed. Makarios wanted to know if the troops would stay there only until a settlement or forever. Kissinger said something between a settlement and forever. When Kissinger said he had the impression that Makarios would like the US to play a bigger role, Makarios agreed. The conversation ended with Kissinger taking refuge in non-commitment. When Makarios wanted to know if he could call Kissinger in an emergency, Kissinger replied in the affirmative.[2] But it was obvious that Kissinger had no interest in getting more deeply involved. He still wanted to let things take their course as long as they did not run counter to US interests.

---

1 Makarios, *Apanta*, XV, p. 1.047.
2 *FRUS 1969-1976*, XXX, pp. 410-415.

This policy of waiting was precisely recognised by the Turkish government and planned accordingly.[1]

His press release of 1 August 1974 shows how little he understood what was actually being played: *"The US position is as follows: we recognize the position of the Turkish community in Cyprus requires considerable improvement and protection. We have supported a greater degree of autonomy for them. The parties are negotiating on one or more Turkish autonomous areas. The avenues of diplomacy have not been exhausted and therefore the United States would consider a resort to military action unjustified. We have made this clear to all parties."*[2] This could only be interpreted by the Turkish side as approval of the implementation of their plans; the military intervention would admittedly not be considered justified by the Americans. But this was more of an encouragement than a warning to continue on the chosen course. When an American diplomat at the embassy in Ankara gave Makarios' six-point plan to Barutçu, the head of the department for Greek and Cypriot affairs, to read, the latter laughed several times on reading it and said it was all too late. A return to the 1960 constitution was out of the question for the Turkish government; now they would write a completely new constitution.[3]

Kissinger and the Geneva Negotiations - 22 July - 14 August 1974

When the acting president of Cyprus, Glafkos Kliridis, realised that he could expect no help from either the British or the Americans in the event of another Turkish advance, he turned in desperation to the representative of the Soviet Union, Ambassador Sergei Astavin, on 26 July: *"I [...] requested him to convey to his Government my appeal for Soviet intervention, stating at the same time that I was prepared to make available Cyprus territory for a Soviet base. I explained that even the presence of some Soviet troops in Cyprus would constitute sufficient deterrent for Turkey not to attempt to break out of the bridgehead. The Ambassador heard me in complete silence. He made no comment and did not ask for clarifications. He simply said that he would communicate my request to his Government and inform me of the reply."* The answer came shortly before Kliridis left for Geneva: *"The Soviet Union would be willing to intervene only if the intervention would be made jointly with the United States."*[4] History shows two things: first, the extent of Kliridis' desperation, which led him, the conservative, to seek help from the Soviet Union. Secondly, the great caution of Soviet foreign policy, which sounds plausible given the experience in Cuba. After all, Kliridis' push may have brought about the Soviet intervention in the Security Council on 28 July.

Through unknown channels, the Americans learned that Kliridis had met with the Soviet ambassador. Kissinger reacted immediately by asking US Ambassador Davies in Nicosia to see Kliridis immediately and to make it clear to him that contacting the Soviets was a serious mistake because it only complicated the situation. Soviet interference could force the USA into a position it would otherwise never take - which was probably meant to mean that it would back Turkey. They sympathised with the suffering of the Cypriots, but Soviet interference would in no way serve the interest of the Cypriots. Ambassador Davies did as

1 Facsimile of a letter from Hartman to Kissinger on 4 August 1974, in: Makarios, *Apanta*, XV, p. 1.049ff.
2 Nicolet, *op. cit.*, p. 440.
3 Asmussen, *op. cit.*, p. 150.
4 *Ibidem*, p. 38.

instructed and went to see Kliridis on 27 July and recited Kissinger's threats to him. Kliridis tried to make out that he had only asked the Soviets for diplomatic support to persuade Turkey to respect the ceasefire. Davies warned him that such actions could lead to renewed unrest by the far Right in both Nicosia and Athens. Moreover, one of the arguments put forward by the Turkish government to justify its intervention was the growing influence of the communists on the island, which threatened Turkey's national security. Davies also hinted that the British might close their bases. Pressed in this way, Kliridis rowed back: the British presence on the island was the best guarantee for the Greek Cypriots. He would not get involved with the Soviets.[1]

On 5 August, the deputy head of the European Department, Arthur Hartman, appeared at the Foreign Ministry in Ankara and delivered a message from Kissinger to Ecevit in which he explained that the USA accepted the legality of the Turkish intervention in Cyprus and the guarantee rights of the Turkish population group. But the new government in Athens should be given a chance and the conflict should be settled with sobriety and understanding through dialogue. In his meeting with Ecevit, Foreign Minister Güneş and Defence Minister Işik, the Turkish ideas became clear: within an independent federal Cyprus, there should be a large area for the autonomous Turkish Cypriot community. This, he said, was a necessary surgical operation. Ecevit assured that thereafter the reduction of Turkish forces could begin in phases. Hartman warned that the impression that this solution was being forced on the Greek government must be avoided, otherwise there was the threat of another upheaval either to the Left towards the Communists or again to the Right towards the military. Ecevit stressed that he wanted a permanent solution, based on the existing self-governments of both sides. The ethnic groups would have to live in a closed territory. The 1960 constitution and the Zurich and London treaties were dead, he said, with the exception of the guarantee treaty. Turkey was ready to negotiate with Greece on the size of the Turkish territory and the modalities of the future state construction. Hartman promised that Washington would examine these ideas sympathetically. They would take a position on the matter in all openness. In his report to Kissinger on this conversation, Hartman stated that the Turks expected the American side to sell these ideas to the Greeks.[2]

On the afternoon of 5 August, Hartman met with Kliridis. Hartman handed him a letter from Kissinger in which the latter praised him as the right man in the right place. Obviously Kissinger was still holding on to the Kliridis solution. Probably to let him emerge unscathed from the negotiations in Geneva, Hartman advised Kliridis not to go to Geneva himself. Although Hartman apparently gained the impression that Kliridis' thoughts were moving in the same direction, this must have been a misunderstanding, for staying away was ruled out by the matter in hand, especially since Denktaş would appear in Geneva. Be that as it may, Hartman warned Kliridis against flirting with the Soviets again, otherwise he would lose American support. The next day, Hartman flew on to Athens.[3]

---

1 Report by Davies on his conversation with Kliridis.Drousiotis, *Cyprus 1974*, p. 238f.

2 Drousiotis, *Cyprus 1974*, p. 248f. Drousiotis confuses the chronological order of the visits. The British ambassador reported that Ecevit had been completely intransigent. For him, compromises were only conceivable with corresponding concessions from the other side. *DocBritPol*, p. 170 Fußnote 12.

3 Drousiotis, *Cyprus 1974*, p. 246f.

Karamanlis also received a personal letter from Kissinger, which Hartman handed over on 6 August.[1] It said that it was necessary to return to close cooperation in NATO. He said he intended to support Greece in protecting its interests. This could be done all the more effectively if a realistic assessment of the interests of all parties was made. He did not yet have a crystal clear idea of the nature of such a solution, but he was convinced that a solution could only be found if all agreed. He asked Karamanlis to present his ideas for a solution through Hartman.[2] It was obvious that Hartman was trying to make a solution based on the status quo palatable to Karamanlis. This would have meant that the Greek government would have had to drop Makarios, accept the Turkish plans and impose them on the Cypriots. Such a solution would have been fatally reminiscent of Zurich and London.

Karamanlis was not prepared to do this and replied with dignity: the Turkish side had to understand that it was no longer negotiating with the colonels who had staged the coup of 15 July. Turkey was trying to take advantage of the situation that had arisen. He had always been in favour of an honourable and just solution, but no Greek government could accept such humiliation. Turkey, however, was striving for such a solution. If it continued, Greece would be forced to go to extremes. He intends to treat the matter seriously and avoid demagogy. Since his return, he had avoided anything to aggravate the situation, he had not even mentioned the word Cyprus. He said he expected the Americans to use their influence in Ankara because the solution depended on it. He was ready for a meeting with Ecevit, provided it was sure to be successful.[3]

The first round of negotiations in Geneva lasted from 8 to 13 August. On 9 August, Nixon had resigned and Gerald Ford had been sworn in as the new President of the USA. Kissinger had a telephone conversation with President Ford at 3:30 pm (10:30 pm Cypriot time) on 10 August. Kissinger did not yet know what exactly Ford thought about the Cyprus conflict and tried to influence him in his favour by using suitable arguments. He tersely informed Ford of the fact that negotiations were taking place in Geneva and that Hartmann was there to support him. To counteract possible direct demands by Callaghan for an armed confrontation, Kissinger said the following: *"The British Minister represents a government that will have to stand for election so they are looking for a quick success and they are a bit like a bull in a china shop. Callaghan is not too experienced. The Turks want a quick result leading to partition of the Island into Greek and Turkish parts with sort of a general federal Government which would however be very weak. They have about 15 percent of the island and want 30 percent. They might try to grab it. I have talked to the Prime Minister of Turkey. He was a student of mine and I have told him that we could not - really in the first 48 hours of your term of office - be very relaxed about unilateral military action. [...] If that happens we might have to dissociate from that which we have tried to avoid. Our danger in Turkey [sic] and why we must maneuver carefully. They might turn very nationalistic and the Russians have been trying to exploit that but we cannot let them act unilaterally."* He would write a personal letter to Ecevit in which he would explain his view of the negotiations. The Turks are proposing a division of the island into two parts. *"I think the Greeks*

1 *NZZ* (8. August 1974), p. 2.

2 Svolopoulos, Konstantinos (ed.), *Konstantinos Karamanlis. Archeio. Gegonota kai Keimena*, VIII (Athen: Ekdotiki Athinon, 1996), p. 53f.

3 *Ibidem*, p. 54f.

*we can push into a position where they would be willing to accept two or three autonomous Turkish areas but not one contiguous area. That would avoid a population transfer."*Ford agreed. Kissinger continued: *"This would give us an opportunity to stall military actions long enough to get it working on the foreign minister level to see if we can get a compromise."*

Ford wanted to know whether Kissinger's letter to Ecevit could dissuade him from military action and lead him to modify his demands. Kissinger replied: *Right. The British are all out backing the Greeks right now and are even threatening military action against the Turks which is one of the stupidest things I have heard. All they have there on Cyprus are a few Phantoms and 1,000 troops. It is purely a political thing. They could not pull it off. They want to get a crisis started and we would then have to settle it and they would claim credit."* This was a perfidious line of argument, but it worked, for Ford urged him to continue in his vein. Kissinger assured him that he was striving for a neutral position: *"It is to take a position which is between the British and the Greek position and the Turkish one so we can ameliorate the Turkish demand but not let the Turks claim that we were the ones that thwarted them and at the same time be tough against unilateral Turkish military moves."* Ford added: *"And calm down our British friends a bit."*[1]

Kissinger thus continued to favour the Turkish side. Since it was clear to him that the Greek side would not accept a division of the island into two parts and that this would threaten the collapse of the conference and a military conflict, he looked for a way out that was compatible with Turkish and American interests. In his eyes, this way out was the cantonal solution, which had already been discussed several times. This could be imposed on the Greeks and would satisfy the Turks. Kissinger did not understand that such a solution was similarly impracticable as the functional federation propagated earlier by Kliridis. This lack of understanding was not surprising, since he had not yet dealt with Cyprus in practice. The cantonal solution was a means to avoid an armed conflict and to induce the Turks to be a little more flexible.

Still on the afternoon of 10 August, Kissinger formulated a letter to Ecevit: the USA had viewed the Turkish position with sympathy from the beginning and supported it, but another unilateral military action would cause the USA the greatest difficulties, because such an action would not be understood in America. Should Turkey expand the territory it occupies through military action, he said, the US administration could not support Turkey in the Security Council. He also rejects any policy that uses pressure. After this rather mild admonition to exercise restraint, Kissinger came to talk about the cantonment solution. Turkey, he said, wanted a single autonomous zone, whereas the Greeks wanted a cantonal arrangement with several cantons. The latter assertion was objectively false. On this level, one could come closer. Ecevit should think about the creation of two or three clearly defined zones. The US was not committed to any formula, but would support any reasonable solution that would bring peace and stability to the island.[2] This was food for thought to encourage the Turkish leadership to be more flexible. At the same time, Kissinger instructed Ambassador Macomber in Ankara and Hartman in Geneva to ensure that the Turks did not

---

1 *FRUS 1969-1977*, XXX, p. 419f. Callaghan war Finanz- und Innenminister gewesen und war seit März 1974 Außenminister, H. Kissinger erst seit dem vergangenen September.

2 Asmussen, *op. cit.*, p. 196.

characterise his proposal as such. *"We have not made a proposal; we have only suggested that there may be other arrangements which could be looked at by the parties to find a compromise which all could support."*[1]

During the conversation between Ecevit and US Ambassador Macomber, the latter recited Kissinger's letter. Ecevit initially reacted completely dismissively to the Canton proposal, saying it was nothing but an extension of the status quo, and even wanted to end the conversation. With a lot of persuasion, Macomber managed to convince Ecevit that Kissinger was only looking for a way out of the diplomatic impasse. And there were several ways out, Macomber added. The Greek Cypriots rejected a partition of the island. But Kliridis is apparently willing to accept a cantonal arrangement, he said. *"I asked whether it was really out of the question for Turkey to achieve its objectives through a solution which left them with one or two major cantons and one or two smaller ones. The Prime Minister said that this was completely impractical."* Ecevit got a map of Cyprus and Macomber showed him on the map, following a map that had been published in a Milliyet article some time ago, how he imagined it. At one point in the discussion, Ecevit made a remark that showed what problems he was actually thinking about: *"Of course, if we had separate cantons, we would have to have Turkish troops in each of these cantons - at least at first. I [Macomber] let that pass without comment."*Ecevit promised to think about the proposal and inform Macomber of the outcome.[2] The whole thing was really just shadow boxing, because the decision for the military solution had already been made.

Around noon on 11 August, Callaghan wanted to know from Hartman what Kissinger thought of the situation. He replied that Kissinger had called Ecevit and also sent him a message asking Ecevit in the friendliest tone not to break off negotiations and not to take military action.[3] Ecevit's reply had completely satisfied Kissinger. A hard line would only have the opposite effect, namely a hardening of the Turkish position. Kissinger wanted the negotiations to continue. *"He thought there was a real possibility of moving the Turks off their idea of a single Turkish zone in Cyprus."* They just need to be shown a face-saving way. *"Kissinger would react very strongly against another public announcement of British military activities. It would have an adverse effect on his tactics with Mr. Ecevit."* Kissinger thus struck the harsh tone towards Callaghan that would have been necessary towards Ecevit.

Callaghan replied that Kissinger seemed to be oblivious to the real situation. He would like to know how the USA planned to react in the event of another Turkish advance. Hartman evaded the question: Kissinger would show Ecevit the consequences of military action so that he would see them for himself and his country. Callaghan said he hoped that Kissinger had nevertheless considered this eventuality, even if he did not talk about it. *"Hartman said that Dr. Kissinger was afraid that even to focus on this eventuality would influence events to move on to a military plane. If the focus moved from the diplomatic negotiations then they could not advance."*These were strange remarks, reminiscent of ideas from the

---

1 *Ibidem*, p. 198.

2 Asmussen, *op. cit.*, p. 197f.

3 According to British information, Kissinger's admonition had been more than gentle: *"Kissinger's letter to Mr. Ecevit had spoken in the 'friendliest possible way' of the serious consequences of military action." DocBritPol*, p. 193 Footnote 4.

realm of magic, of conjuring, but which had nothing to do with reality. Callaghan said matter-of-factly that one haootto prepare for all eventualities in view of the real threat.

The conversation continued at this level for some time. Kissinger's ideas bordered in effect on the well-known policy of appeasement at all costs, as Chamberlain had practised in Munich in 1938. Finally, Hartman said Callaghan should listen and wait. Callaghan replied: *"He was prepared to listen. He had shown no impatience in the meetings, but he also had a responsibility to take military precautions. The tougher you were with the Turks the more they would listen to you. He thought that Dr. Kissinger was mistaken about this. The last time the Turks had backed off was at Nicosia airport when he had said to Ecevit that he was putting British troops in blue berets but that he was not prepared to see British troops shot up. He believed that the Americans were not yet handling the Turks in a way which would have an effect. He wishes to work with the United States on this and would not make an announcement today about his intention to order in more Phantoms and further troops at once. He would wait to see what came out of the Turkish Council of Ministers but thereafter he would see if he wished to make any publicity for the reinforcement. Mr. Hartman urged him to inform Dr. Kissinger beforehand he intended to make such an announcement."* Callaghan agreed but reserved its freedom of action.[1]

On the morning of 12 August, Hartman reported to the British delegation that Ecevit had promised Kissinger not to take military action before the end of the negotiations in Geneva. Kissinger had then told Ecevit that Turkey could not count on American support in the UN Security Council if it went ahead. On the contrary, the USA would then support the British in their diplomatic efforts to stop the advance. *"But the United States could not themselves consider taking military action, particularly so soon after the inauguration of President Ford, nor did they consider that the threats of military action were helpful or appropriate in these circumstances. The United States Government considered that talk of military action distracted concentration from the political options."*[2] It was thus clear that the British would have to face the Turks alone if in doubt.

Callaghan, however, wanted final clarity. He instructed the British ambassador in Washington, Ramsbotham, to tell Kissinger the following: the Turks had to be confronted in two ways, diplomatically and militarily. Although he had been in constant contact with Güneş for 11 days, he did not know what he really thought. His assurance not to advance further was never clear. Even if the Americans did not realise it, the military threat was real. He admitted that he should have informed Kissinger about his military measures in advance, but Kissinger was also discussing a cantonal solution with the Turks and claimed that he had not proposed any solutions, although the Turks were talking about an American plan. If he was to cooperate with the Americans, he would have to know exactly what Kissinger intended.[3]

Kissinger replied in the afternoon via Ramsbotham: *"[He] explained that he had been totally preoccupied during the past week with the change of Presidency, and that during 6-10 August he had been 'virtually out of touch with the Cyprus problem'. He had, he said, thought it right, besides warning Mr. Ecevit against a military move, to also offer him a*

1 *DocBritPol*, pp. 192-196.
2 *Ibidem*, p. 201f.
3 *Ibidem*, p. 206f. Callaghan, *op. cit.*, p. 352f.

way out by encouraging him to put forward his own proposal at Geneva. [...] He was [...] determined to avoid the United States incurring the hostility of both Greek and Turkish Governments, as this could only weaken NATO. He would be frank in saying that he perhaps cared less about events in Cyprus itself."[1]

When the negotiations in Geneva came to a head on 12 August, Hartman informed Kissinger in Washington. Kissinger realised that Güneş had effectively issued an ultimatum ("take it or leave it"), but did not really know what to do and tried to call Ecevit, who could not be reached. Kissinger wanted to know if the Turks had submitted their cantonment proposal. One of his aides told him that the Turks were striving for a large autonomous zone in the north. Whether they had proposed that, Kissinger wanted to know. Yes, to Callaghan, was the reply of the Deputy Assistant Secretary of State, Wells Stabler, who headed the European Department. Kissinger stated: *"There is nothing we can do until we hear from Callaghan. I will talk to Ecevit and tell him to put the proposed forward."* Stabler said it was necessary to find out from Ecevit whether he had really issued an ultimatum. Kissinger said: *"What exactly have the Turks done? Assuming it is an ultimatum, what do we do? Use the 12 F-4s? After my call to Ecevit has failed, what do we do?" Stabler: "If he is determined to go, there is not much we can do." Kissinger: "We would not support him in the Security Council and we would probably have to support a resolution against the Government of Turkey. Then what do we do?"* MacCloskey said that US military aid could be cut. Kissinger replied in the negative.[2] It was obvious that Kissinger had already reached the end of his Latin. His strategy of a free hand led to the disaster of Cyprus.

A little later, however, Kissinger reached Ecevit, who told him that the Greeks wanted to make counter-proposals. Therefore, he said, another meeting of the conference should be scheduled for 13 August. He assured Kissinger that if the Cypriot National Guard withdrew from the area claimed by Turkey, the Turkish army would not occupy it.[3] Kissinger then called Callaghan and informed him of his conversation with Ecevit. He then suggested to Callaghan that he go to Ankara to influence the course of events on the ground. Callaghan promised to think about it.[4]

In a conversation with President Ford, Kissinger expressed self-satisfaction with the outcome of his negotiating skills. *"The Turks have accepted that they will settle for general commitment rather than specific, but the total is sizeable. They will put it in Geneva as their proposal but maybe Callaghan should. He is trying to hit a home run and take sides. I learned to stay out and let all the parties jockey. Turkish military intervention becomes less likely as time goes on and we are dragging things out. (...) The longer Callaghan is tough, the better our position with the Turks becomes. The Turks have already favorably compared the US with the UK. This is interesting because we have been cutting back Turkey's options."* Kissinger apparently simply relied on the reports of Macomber, whom Ecevit wrapped around his finger with flattery.[5]

---

1 *DocBritPol*, p. 207 Footnote 6.
2 *FRUS 1969-1976*, XXX, p. 421f.
3 *DocBritPol*, p. 216 Footnote 3.
4 *Ibidem.*
5 Jan Asmussen, *Cyprus at War. Diplomacy and Conflict during the 1974 Crisis* (London: Tauris, 2008), p. 204.

Around 9 a.m. (4 p.m. Cypriot time) on 13 August, Kissinger and President Ford talked about the Cyprus problem, and it became clear that Kissinger still had great sympathy for the Turks: the longer the negotiations in Geneva lasted, the more difficult it would be for the Turks to act unilaterally militarily. That is why they also rejected the 36-hour postponement. Ford wanted to know what would happen if the Turks went ahead. Kissinger replied that they would probably have to vote against them in the Security Council and that they would have their hands full to keep the Greeks from going to war. *"If the Turks run loose on Cyprus, the Greeks could come unglued. We certainly do not want a war between the two, but if it came to that, Turkey is more important to us [...] We have been trying to bail the Cyprus situation out after it got out of control. The British have made a mess of it. [...] There is no American reason why the Turks should not have one-third of Cyprus."*[1] Kissinger thus again played the realpolitik politician of the 19th century, for whom no ethical problems but only questions of power were important, and in his eyes the British were to blame for the situation.

The British had originally been determined to oppose the Turks if they advanced further. The well-informed Dutch ambassador to Athens at the time, and later to NATO, Carl Barkman, recalls in his memoirs: *"Callaghan wanted to tell the Turks that they would be facing British troops wearing blue helmets, if they should move beyond the agreed cease-fire line. He was convinced that if the United States supported his plan, this would effectively stop the Turks in the same way as they had backed down over the issue of Nicosia airport. The UN Secretary-General, Waldheim, had given his agreement in principle. However, Mr Callaghan naturally felt that since the events of 1956, it should be a principle of British policy not to intervene militarily in the Middle East or Eastern Mediterranean unless the United States agreed."* When Callaghan began to row back afterwards, it was clearly because of Kissinger's attitude. On 12 August Kissinger had given him to understand that at best he was prepared to take diplomatic action. *"Hartman made it clear, moreover, that the US did not want the UK to oppose Turkey militarily, not even under the aegis of the United Nations."* In the meantime, Kissinger had also bought Waldheim's thunder: *"In the meantime, Dr. Waldheim withdrew his agreement. His staff (or more likely the US Government?) had persuaded him that Callaghan's UNFICYP plan was not feasible. Without US backing, nothing came of it anyway."*[2] On their own, the British government did not want to do anything, because the memory of American behaviour during the Suez crisis, when the Americans had actively prevented the British attack on the Egyptian fleet, was also ever present in the minds of Labour politicians.[3] So the Turks had a free hand and an easy game.

The reasons for Kissinger's behaviour were still the same. Ambassador Barkman noted in his diary on 29 July 1974: *"We are [...] critical of the fact that our American allies are not exercising more pressure on Ankara and of Kissinger's extreme reluctance to intervene in any way; his only concern being that the Soviets do not increase their influence in the region."*[4] This was followed on 15 September 1974 by another entry about a conversation

---

1 *FRUS 1969-1976*, XXX, p. 423f.

2 Barkman, *op. cit.*, p. 267f; Waldheim, *op. cit.*, p. 140.

3 Chris P. Ioannides, *Realpolitik in the Eastern Mediterranean. From Kissinger and the Cyprus Crisis to Carter and the Lifting of the Turkish Arms Embargo* (New York: Pella, 2001), pp. 122f, 135.

4 Barkman, *op. cit.*, p. 193.

with US Ambassador Henry Tasca: *"[Tasca] rather bitterly commented on the 'cool power politics' of his Secretary of State, who looked first and last at the relationship between the US and the Soviet Union. In talks with various American colleagues I have heard this same criticism. They say that Dr. K. considers the countries in between the two superpowers as so many 'pieces of real estate'. Who were in power there, he did not care much as long as American strategic interests were not affected. [...] They also say that another important consideration for Kissinger had been the fact that Turkey in his view, was even more important to NATO than Greece. He had assumed, they say, that 'he could keep those Greeks under control'. He had made the great mistake [...] of thinking that in the twentieth century one could play power politics without taking into account certain moral principles and psychological factors."* The American demarches in Ankara were always extremely mild, and US Ambassador Macomber made sure that they were further defused. For Kissinger, strategic considerations had priority and therefore he refrained from anything that could even remotely resemble an intervention; and finally, in the background, there was his dislike of Makarios. For Henry Kissinger, the Turkish action that was now beginning was the sword stroke that cut the Gordian knot of the Cyprus problem in two. In fact, however, it was now finally pulled tight and inextricable. In the early hours of 14 August 1974, the two-week ceasefire ended and the Turks continued their advance.

Kissinger and the Turkish Invasion (Attila II) - 14-16 August 1974

In the early hours of 14 August, the Turkish Foreign Minister Güneş broke off the negotiations in Geneva. Precisely half an hour later at 5 a.m. Cypriot time (3 a.m. CET), the renewed attack by Turkish forces in Cyprus began.[1] In Washington that morning, Helmut Sonnenfeld, a senior member of the US National Security Council, wrote a memorandum outlining the current options for American policy on Cyprus: the partition of the island was probably a fact. It was now necessary to restrain the Greeks from hasty action and to make it clear to the Turks that they would have to stop their action the next day at the latest. But by then they would have achieved their aims. The Turks must be told confidentially that *"we will get them solution involving one third of the island, with some kind of federal arrangement; assure Greeks we will contain Turkish demands and allow additional enclaves etc."*[2] So, according to Sonnenfeld's ideas, US policy should allow the Turks to create a fait accompli and stall the Greeks with empty promises.

Kissinger sent a message to Ecevit mildly criticising him for breaking off the negotiations and renewing the military action, but then offered that the US would intervene directly in the negotiations if Turkey and the other parties so wished. *"We would also be prepared to use our influence toward developing the consensus that would be necessary to obtain a lasting solution."*For this, however, it was necessary to end the military action as soon as possible. He was waiting for his answer.[3]

At about 3 p.m. (10 p.m. Cypriot time), the Special Actions Group chaired by Henry Kissinger met in Washington. CIA chief William Colby gave an overview of the situation in Cyprus and the region. It was clear from Kissinger's questions that he was still not quite

1 Richter, *op. cit.*, IV, pp. 507-512.
2 Asmussen, *op. cit.*, p. 231f.
3 *Ibidem*, p. 232f.

up to the mark and was trying to stick to his previous course: *"I think that it is in our interest now to keep all avenues of negotiation open. Our major strategy now is not to get ourselves in a position that would give vent to righteous indignation on the part of either the Greeks or the Turks. I think this development has its own logic for solution. We don't want to contribute to the Greek humiliation, and we don't want the Turks to feel that we have turned against them. The British are out in front on this thing, and as long as the British are out in front, it is better from our point of view."* The British would be massively attacked in Greece, but the American side would also experience this later. But *"if we play our cards right, and with some skill, we will come out of this thing on the good side, with both governments."* No decisions could be made at the moment, the reports of the embassies had to be available first.

Then Kissinger became agitated that a State Department press release had said that US military aid would be cut: *"That is total nonsense. I want them to keep going as if nothing is happening. I don't want to escalate this thing into a big deal. Our object is to keep NATO together and to keep peace between the two parties.*" It was decided to revive the disbanded Cyprus working group and to meet again the next morning.[1] So Kissinger still saw no need for action, because things were still going on, in his opinion, in such a way that American interests would not be affected. A few weeks later, the report of the Senate Committee on Refugees on this kind of policy said: *"Although flatly denied in all quarters of the Administration, to many observers there has been a perceptible 'tilt' toward Turkey in the American approach to Cyprus. [...] United States policy [...] seems to have been one of hasty improvisation, coldly calculated to minimize disturbances within NATO, more than anything else. This has not only achieved the opposite result in the end, but more importantly in human terms, it has failed the defenseless people of Cyprus and, for many observers, has confirmed a Turkish 'tilt' in United States policy toward Cyprus."*[2]

Late in the morning of 15 August, the Special Actions Group, chaired by Kissinger, met again. After getting excited about the imminent return of Andreas Papandreou to Athens, Kissinger said that Ecevit had informed him that the Turkish forces would stop at the planned division line. He said the operation would go according to plan by the next day. CIA chief Colby warned that the Turks might advance further in the northwest. Sisco confirmed this: *"[The Turks] said they were going to keep their military operation going until they get what they want."* When further concerns were raised, Kissinger said: *"Well, I think that once this Turkish operation runs its course, they won't go any further. We won't stand for it. We just can't stand for any more Turk operations. They have already stretched us to the limit."* Kissinger complained that the reply to his message to Karamanlis was not yet available. In conclusion, Kissinger made one of his customarily witty remarks: *"Well, [...] if this situation leads to double enosis, Makarios will become a Greek politician. There is no joy in that."*[3]

---

1 *FRUS 1969-1976*, XXX, pp. 432-437. "US Threatens to Cut Aid if 2 Allies War" *IHT* (15 August 1974), p. 1.

2 US Senate, Committee on the Judiciary, Subcommittee to Investigate Problems with Refugees and Escapees, *Crisis on Cyprus. A Report* (Washington: US Govt. Printing Office, 1974), p. 44. Ab hier zitiert als *Crisis on Cyprus*.

3 *FRUS 1969-1976*, XXX, pp. 438-441.

Kissinger and Callaghan spoke on the phone around noon. Kissinger complained that Mavros had not yet replied to his invitation to Washington. Then Callaghan wanted to know from Kissinger what he intended to do if the Turks became active in the Aegean. Kissinger replied that he would take tough action in that case. *"I [Callaghan] told him that I was not sure that we could wait until the Turks acted. If for instance they created a situation where the de facto partition of the island resulted in enosis, whether double or otherwise, the consequences could only be unfortunate. Among other things Makarios would become a Greek politician. An alliance between Makarios and [Andreas] Papandreou would result in a neutralist government in Greece."*Kissinger promised to think about it.[1]

In the afternoon, a round of specialists met at the State Department. Callaghan's arguments had obviously made Kissinger uneasy. Realising that things were not going as he imagined, he reacted frantically and demanded 'action': Another letter would have to be written to Karamanlis; he himself would telephone Ecevit to urge him to end the military operation. This letter to Karamanlis would have to go out that day and the next would have to be followed by a request in the form of a letter from President Ford to Karamanlis and Ecevit urging them to have a three-way meeting with Kissinger. Kissinger repeated himself and pressured. Sisco said this time to take their time. It would all be over by the evening of the next day, then they should send the letters. Kissinger agreed, since such a meeting could not take place for several days. The Greeks would give in sooner or later. The best solution would be for the Turks to give up 10 per cent of the territory they had conquered.

Kissinger instructed one of his staff to draft the letter to Karamanlis. He was to list everything America had done for Greece. Karamanlis could count on America's goodwill. Kissinger thus wanted a letter that would put moral pressure on Karamanlis to act as Kissinger imagined. As far as Turkey was concerned, Kissinger continued, one had to be very careful, because one needed it in the next Middle East war. So one should not move too far away from it. *"If we can get agreement for a meeting in Washington, then President Ford can join Ecevit, Karamanlis and myself. At this meeting we can establish guidelines for a reconvened Geneva conference."* Callaghan had not been able to do that. More disparaging remarks about Callaghan followed. Kissinger let slip that the failure of the Geneva conference would not have happened to him.[2] Callaghan's comments do indeed seem to have hit Kissinger's self-confidence hard, for these increasingly negative remarks can hardly be explained otherwise.

Later, Kissinger had Ecevit on the phone. Ecevit said that military operations would end on 16 August at 12 noon New York time. After that he would be available for talks. He agreed for Kissinger to tell Waldheim and Karamanlis, but asked that he wait until the early hours of the morning, Turkish time, on 16 August. Kissinger agreed and, for his part, promised to prevent a vote on a resolution submitted to the Security Council by the French government. Ecevit was highly satisfied.[3]

Kissinger kept to the agreement and called Karamanlis at 7:22 p.m. New York time, which is around 1:22 a.m. Greek time. He informed him that the Turks would cease their operation at noon. He said he was ready to play an active role in the negotiations from now

---

1 *DocBritPol*, pp. 251-253.
2 *FRUS 1969-1976*, XXX, pp. 442-445.
3 *Ibidem*, p. 445f.

on. Karamanlis replied that he would think about it, but after this Turkish fait accompli, negotiations would be somewhat difficult. Kissinger said that a statement had been issued condemning the Turkish action. Everything was being done, *"to strengthen your position and show our friendship for Greece."* Karamanlis repeated himself: *"I appreciate it but I am afraid it is a little late. As I said the Turks have created a fait accompli."* Karamanlis refused to negotiate under military pressure. Kissinger wanted to know if Karamanlis would be willing to travel to America. Karamanlis refused: *"It is difficult for me to leave the country. We have many problems. The people are very bitter, angry, the armies are upset. It is difficult to leave the country. Maybe a little later, but just now it is impossible."* In conclusion, Karamanlis said that Kissinger must do more than give good advice to the Turks.[1]

On the afternoon of 16 August, the usual round of State Department meetings resumed in Washington. Sisco said that it would probably be necessary to wait a while until the situation in Greece calmed down. In a while, the Greeks would have to be reminded that we had common interests. Kissinger said that one should not overdo the attention to Greece, otherwise one would lose the Turks. Hartman suspected that Karamanlis was faking the difficulties because he did not want to come to the conference table. Kissinger suspected that Karamanlis was acting so tough in order to get ahead of the Left. If one wanted to get Karamanlis to negotiate, the Turks would have to offer a reduction in area or a reduction in troops. He thought Ecevit was capable of doing this, but was not sure that he could convince his military leaders to do so. Decisions would probably have to wait until after the weekend, i.e. until 19 August. On the same day, the Turkish advance on Cyprus ended.

On 17 August, Henry Kissinger discussed with the State Department's Cyprus specialists. Kissinger admitted that the Greeks had to be appeased. But one should not give the impression that one would accept everything. If the Greeks continued in this way, a change of course would have to be considered. *"We have no interest in supporting a country which follows a professional anti-US position."* Kissinger alluded here to negative press reports about him in Greece, but obviously Kissinger had a guilty conscience towards the Greeks, so he rumbled on. He would not allow the USA to be pushed around. *"Greece is in NATO not for US interests but for Greece's own interests. [...] I don't think we are going to get anywhere by being too soft or gentle."* But then he had to admit that he had misjudged the situation in Geneva. He sent the following message to Ecevit via US Ambassador Macomber: *"We have received disturbing reports that despite your assurances Turkish forces are continuing to occupy more territory and that fighting is still in progress. I cannot emphasize strongly enough my earlier warning that the domestic situation in the United States has now reached a point where further Turkish military operations will put the USG in an impossible position. If they continue, we will be obliged to take public steps which would threaten our ability to work together toward a just solution on Cyprus and result in a further deterioration of the Western security position in the area. I therefore ask that the GOT take all steps necessary to see that the ceasefire is strictly observed."* Ecevit had to make a generous gesture towards the Greeks, otherwise the Greeks would not return to the conference table. In the meantime, the Soviet Union was also beginning to interfere. But then Kissinger, in typical fashion, softened his exhortation again: *"The United States has not changed position with regard to Cyprus nor its sympathy for an acceptable and lasting res-*

---

1 *Ibidem*, pp. 446-448; slightly different wording Woodhouse, *Karamanlis*, p. 218.

olution of the problems the Turkish Cypriots have so long faced." Ecevit's response showed that Kissinger's call to accommodate the Greeks did not impress him in the least: he recommended breaking off cooperation with the Greeks.[1]

When the American ambassador was killed in Nicosia on 19 August in connection with an anti-American demonstration, Kliridis made a formal apology. Kissinger accepted the apology but took the opportunity to put pressure on Kliridis: *"But the only thing I would ask is that the deliberate effort to blame the United States for what has happened is one of the contributing causes to this situation, and if we are to play a useful role, which we are eager to do, we cannot do it under this sort of pressure. And so we are asking all responsible Greek leaders to stop the anti-American agitation or we will withdraw completely from the negotiations, and leave it to be settled directly between Greeks and Turks. [...] There has to be an end to agitation."* By this, of course, he wanted to express that if the agitation in Athens and Cyprus continued, he would wash his hands of it.[2] This can justifiably be described as an open threat to a weaker party; it was the well-known arrogance of power. Kliridis was not intimidated by Kissinger's arrogant behaviour. At a press conference, he criticised the American attitude: the Americans could have exerted more determined pressure on Turkey to stop it from invading Cyprus. After the invasion, however, the Americans had worked to prevent a further Turkish advance. He said his government was seeking a peaceful negotiated settlement, but was not prepared to give way to ultimate pressure and go to Geneva. It would be a mistake to believe that the Cyprus problem could be solved by a military victory.[3]

Kissinger's attitude towards Ecevit, however, was quite different when he called him a little later. He told him that he had to make a statement in view of the public protest in Washington. He intended to say that they were in favour of resuming negotiations, which would have to result in a reduction of Turkish troops. In addition, the Turkish side should vacate parts of the occupied territory; it must show flexibility. He asked if he could say in this statement that Ecevit agreed. Ecevit evaded and invoked the Geneva Agreement. Kissinger wanted to know if he could at least say this. Ecevit promised to get back to him after consultations. About two hours later, Ecevit got back in touch with a fully formulated statement. It said, as in the Geneva declaration of 30 July, that Turkey was ready for a "timely and phased reduction of forces", provided conditions allowed. He was also prepared, under certain circumstances, to negotiate the demarcation line. Obviously, Ecevit was not prepared to make any concessions, Kissinger was satisfied with vague phrases, no pressure was exerted.[4]

Kissinger then claimed to the press that Ecevit had assured him that Turkey was ready for a partial withdrawal in Cyprus and for negotiations on the demarcation line, and that it would respect the Geneva Declaration on troop reduction. He then read out a statement, agreed with President Ford, according to which it would be necessary for Turkey, as the

1 *Ibidem*, pp. 454f, 678.
2 *Ibidem*, p. 456.
3 *NZZ* (21. August 1974), p. 2.
4 *FRUS 1969-1976*, XXX, pp. 458-460.

stronger power, to be flexible and take into account Greek sensitivities both in terms of the territory occupied and the size of the forces in Cyprus. He had also said this to Ecevit.[1]

In the meantime, the Greek lobby in the USA began to agitate against Kissinger and Greek-born congressmen even went so far as to call Kissinger a murderer. As the attacks on Kissinger continued in Greece and Cyprus, he sent retired ambassador William Tyler to Athens on 9 September. When Karamanlis wanted to know what the American position was on the Cyprus issue, Tyler said that the US would be happy to help provided the Greek government took a constructive stance. Just like Greece, the US rejected any outside pressure. Karamanlis wanted to know what pressure Tyler meant. Tyler replied: *"If the atmosphere is poisoned by anti-Americanism [...] then we will have no choice but to stand aside until another opportunity arises, if it ever does."* Then he submitted new ideas to Kissinger: *"If the Aegean question were included, a package settlement might be achieved in which Greece would obtain compensations to offset whatever concessions the Greeks might have to make on Cyprus."*[2]

Karamanlis rejected the accusation of anti-Americanism: *"These sentiments were generated both by popular disappointment with American policy on Cyprus and by a general feeling that the US Government had supported the Greek military regime. Popular bitterness increased as the Turks continued their military operations on Cyprus and there was still no effective American reaction. [...] If the US was genuinely concerned about anti-Americanism in Greece, Washington should admit that it had followed the wrong policy and help to find a solution to the Cyprus crisis."* This was the only way to reduce anti-Americanism. Ambassador Tyler said he would report everything to Kissinger. But *"the PM should not deceive himself into believing that the US was laboring under a sense of guilt. The President and the Secretary believed that they had done everything that we could do to avert the crisis. We had no intention of admitting 'mistakes' because we did not accept that we had made mistakes."* If Karamanlis believed that the USA had supported the junta, he was wrong. He repeated this several times and concluded that he had not come to Athens as a pleader. Karamanlis said he understood this and saw that the US denied any blame.[3]

Tyler's remarks showed two things, the arrogance of power and the typical ignorance of certain Americans. Tyler's tone was that of a typical American proconsul in a client state, demanding obedience with threats. Disobedience would be punished by being left out. The proposal to solve the Cyprus conflict together with the Aegean conflict in one package betrayed absolute ignorance of the actual problem. The Aegean conflict was about Greek positions under international law regarding territorial waters, delimitation of the shelf, air sovereignty and air control (FIR), where the Turkish government made unfounded demands. There was also another area of conflict between Turkey and Greece, namely that of the minorities in Istanbul and Western Thrace. To link these bilateral Greek-Turkish conflicts with the conflict of the independent state of Cyprus showed that Washington had apparently not understood that Greece's politically objectifiable relationship with Cyprus existed only in the form of the Treaty of Guarantee. The idea that Greece would make concessions in the

1 *IHT* (20 August 1974), p. 2.
2 *FRUS 1969-1976*, XXX, pp. 491-486.
3 *Ibidem*, pp. 495-500.

Aegean in order to obtain Turkish concessions in Cyprus - or vice versa - was more than unreal.[1]

Kissinger and the arms embargo

On 15 August, the second day of the Attila II operation, Kissinger had received some congressmen led by John Brademas (Democrat from Indiana). After some self-critical remarks and some evasions to defuse the forthcoming criticism, he accused Callaghan of having mismanaged the Geneva conference, which was why it had collapsed. He then claimed that he had made every diplomatic effort to stop the Turkish advance. If there were any positive developments in Cyprus, he said, they were due to his initiative. Brademas was not impressed by this, but accused Kissinger of being to blame for the defeat of American policy in Greece and Cyprus. Kissinger's policy of confidential personal diplomacy had failed. His silence on the events in Cyprus was intolerable. American arms deliveries to Turkey must be stopped until Turkey withdraws its troops from the island.[2]

A clause in the Foreign Military Assistance Act allowed the use of American-supplied weapons only for defence and prohibited their use in civil wars or wars of aggression. At his press conference on 19 August, Kissinger also commented on this issue. When a reporter wanted to know whether American military aid to Turkey should be stopped, Kissinger replied that such a thing would only come into question under extreme circumstances, and these were not present.[3] The reporter was alluding to the position taken by US Secretary of Defence James Schlesinger. Schlesinger had demanded the cessation of US aid. Kissinger assured that he would have this question legally examined. This was indeed done, but the legal opinion was so unfavourable that he preferred not to make it public.[4]

On 19 August, the Subcommittee on Europe of the Committee on Foreign Affairs of the House of Representatives met. It was chaired by Benjamin Rosenthal from New York and invited by the Secretary of State for European Affairs, Arthur Hartman. After a detailed overview by Hartman of developments in recent months, Congressman Pierre du Pont of Delaware wanted to know whether American aid to Turkey was continuing and whether it would not be wise to suspend it until the fighting was over. Hartman answered entirely along Kissinger's lines: *"It was not wise at this time to cut off assistance to either side; that this would be an assumption by the United States of a responsibility for the situation which we do not believe that for us to assume."* It had been decided not to take such a decision while efforts were being made to bring the two sides back to the negotiating table. Du Pont followed suit: *"I take it you would oppose an amendment that tied military aid to both a Turkish and Greek observation of UN resolutions?"* Hartman agreed: *"We would feel that the executive branch should have the flexibility to use all the means at its disposal to try and bring these parties together."* Du Pont countered dryly: *"Somehow there has to be a little less flexibility and also somewhat fewer bullets."*[5]

---

1 Richter, *Friede in der Ägäis*, passim.
2 Stern, *Wrong Horse*, p. 141f.
3 US Senat, *Crisis on Cyprus*, pp. 78, 81.
4 Stern, *Wrong Horse*, p. 143; US Senat, *Crisis on Cyprus*, p.78.
5 US Congress, House of Representatives, Committee on Foreign Affairs, Subcommittee on Europe, *Cyprus 1974 Hearings* (Washington: US Govt. Printing Office, 1974), p. 18f.

Another MP (Peter Kyros) took up this issue again after some time: *"I think we should have had a firmer policy in dealing with the Turkish Government, and it is for you to carry this out. It should be done."* Hartman admitted that they had miscalculated: In fact, the Turks could not have been persuaded to do anything. However, it was questionable whether the threat of an arms embargo would have worked.[1] At the end of the hearing, Chairman Rosenthal stated, *"that your efforts of imploring the Turkish Government to cease and desist have not worked. I see nothing down the road in the future why that should change, particularly when they have achieved their military objectives. The responsibility is now with the Congress."* There was no alternative but to stop all military aid to Turkey by means of an amendment.[2] At the continuation of the hearing the next day, the main witness was former Secretary of State George Ball, who was very critical of Kissinger's Cyprus policy. He reminded those present that a war over Cyprus had been avoided in 1964 by taking the necessary tough measures. He considered the embargo to be an appropriate measure: *"I would think this would be a very useful thing. It seems to me that really this is the kind of role that the Congress can play in the whole area of foreign relations, [...] It signals something to the Greeks, it signals something to the Turks, and it signals something to the Secretary of State and the President."*[3]

Ultimately, the issue was whether the executive could override laws in its foreign policy. Kissinger saw it this way: *"The Congressional representatives' concern was to justify a single act of legislation, mine, on the other hand, to steer an ongoing process. The congressmen were thinking in absolute terms; I was pursuing the same aim by working with nuance."*[4] Apparently Kissinger did not want to realise that he was about to break the law and the Constitution. He regarded the Congressmen's attitude as bossiness. The implementation of foreign policy aims was his priority. That he was aware of this was demonstrated a few days later when a young State Department staffer confidentially approached Senator Thomas Eagleton (Democrat-Missouri) and told him that the State Department's legal department had concluded that the continuation of arms shipments to Turkey was against the law, but that pressure was being exerted from above to modify the opinion to suit Kissinger's tactical demands. Senator Eagleton maintained confidentiality, but publicly stated, alluding to the Watergate affair, that violations of the law led to failure. *"It is my belief that [President Ford] is ill advised or being kept uninformed of the legal ramification of his inaction in the Cyprus matter in order to protect erroneous policy judgements made by the foreign affairs bureaucracy."*[5]

The following months Kissinger waged a protracted struggle against the embargo, and when it was enforced by Congress, he fought to have it lifted. The belated embargo failed to have its effect, for it now only led to a hardening of the Turkish position. Here, for once, Kissinger had been right in thinking that threatening the embargo would be more effective than imposing it. - But he himself had always rejected an effective threat during the period when it could have been effective. After further negotiations, Kissinger realised in the sum-

1 *Ibidem*, p. 28f.
2 *Ibidem*, p. 30.
3 *Ibidem*, p. 50f.
4 Kissinger, *Jahre der Erneuerung*, p. 190.
5 Stern, *Wrong Horse*, p. 143f.

mer of 1975 that he had reached the end of his Latin with regard to Cyprus and asked the Europeans for help.[1] But this is another story.

These elaborations would not be complete if one did not register Henry Kissinger's behaviour towards Warner Boyatt, who was a nuisance to him. Kissinger removed Boyatt from his post and put him on leave. A few days later, Boyatt received a phone call in which his superior informed him that he was scheduled for the highest qualifying advanced training (Senior Seminar). Boyatt did not want to believe this, but his supervisor insisted and so it happened. Boyatt attended this institution for a year. About six months later, the Chairman of the House Committee of Inquiry on Intelligence, Pike, contacted him and asked him to testify before the Committee. Boyatt referred to the official channels, saying he could only testify if the State Department approved it. After some back and forth, during which Kissinger tried to block the testimony, he finally accepted that Boyatt be allowed to testify about classified, but not top secret, matters. Boyatt then became head of mission in Santiago. This was the reward for Boyatt's failure to blacken Kissinger's name in Congress.[2]

But Kissinger did not limit himself to keeping his subordinates silent, he even tried his best to obstruct the House investigating committee. *"The Pike committee report accuses Kissinger of putting forth 'a new doctrine that can best be characterized as secretarial privilege'. He defied Congressional subpoenas, prevented State Department witnesses from testifying, and leaked stories to embarrass the committee."*[3] Added to this was the CIA's attempt to influence the final report editorially. When Pike did not give in, he was threatened. But Pike remained unbending, and therefore attempts were made to block the publication of the report by the Republican majority in the House of Representatives: The report endangered national security and should therefore not be published without the president's approval. Pike backed down: *"The House just voted not to release a document it had not read. Our committee voted to release a document it had read."* Er werde den Bericht überhaupt nicht veröffentlichen, denn *"a report on the CIA in which the CIA would do the final rewrite would be a lie."* In fact, the report was never officially published, but it famously found its way to Daniel Schorr, a reporter for the Village Voice magazine, which printed it almost in its entirety in a special edition under the bar headline on the outside cover *"The Report on the CIA President Ford doesn't Want You to Read"*.[4] Schorr immediately came under pressure and lost his job at CBS News, and the House Ethics Committee tried to force him to reveal his source, but by a narrow majority this attempt was defeated. It was a stellar moment of investigative journalism and provided the historian with a valuable source for which to be grateful, just as the ADST interviews did some 20 years later.

At the end of these considerations, it can be clearly stated that there was no continuous line of American Cyprus policy, as the supporters of the conspiratorial view of history claim, not even on the question of the bases. Democratic and Republican US administrations pursued quite different policies and even under Kissinger there were different posi-

---

1 Richter, *op. cit.*, IV, 2, p. 642f.

2 *Ibidem*, p. 7f: *"Kissinger didn't want me to testify, because I was right about Cyprus and he was wrong."* Boyatt in ADST-Interview.

3 Aaron Latham, "Introduction to the Pike Papers" *The Village Voice* 21:7 (16 February 1976), p. 79.

4 http://www.spartacus.schoolnet.co.uk/JFKpikeO.htm. See also footnote 75.

tions in the administration. What was decisive was that Kissinger took over the decision--making process and, unfortunately, did nothing, but let things take their course, observing the Turkish actions with a sympathetic eye, because for him Turkey was more important than Greece for strategic reasons; a policy that basically still applies today. For Kissinger, Cyprus was a kind of annoying mosquito whose buzzing disturbed his world political circles; therefore, he did not mind its removal. The result was the disaster of 1974, the consequences of which are still present today.

THE HIGH LEVEL AGREEMENT OF 1977[1]

Between 14 and 16 August 1974, the Turkish army continued the invasion it had begun on 20 July 1974, occupying 36.3 per cent of the island. 70 per cent of the agricultural land was lost. The loss of industrial capacity was just as great. Most of the tourist centres were also lost. About 100,000 Greek Cypriots were refugees. The acting president Glafkos Kliridis (Makarios had been abroad since the junta coup) had to try to salvage what could still be salvaged on the diplomatic level with regard to the Cyprus problem. This was made more difficult by the fact that he had Henry Kissinger against him. Kissinger was furious because he had been called a murderer at demonstrations in Athens and Nicosia. When the US ambassador was killed in the wake of a demonstration on 18 August, Kissinger told Kliridis that he would wash his hands of further developments if the agitation against him continued in Athens and Nicosia.

In the following days, efforts were made to resume negotiations in Geneva. Denktaş interfered in this international exchange of views on 20 August when he appeared before the press in Ankara: he self-consciously threatened to found an independent Turkish-Cypriot state if negotiations did not begin soon. One day later he was more precise: If the Greek side did not give in and agree to negotiations, only two solutions remained: Federation with the greatest possible autonomy or complete division of the island with the formation of a separate state. There would be a population exchange. Greek land in the north would be sold or leased for compensation. A start had been made on setting up a separate administration. They would issue their own passports, found their own bank and introduce the Turkish lira as currency. He was prepared to talk with Kliridis about current humanitarian problems, but the guarantor powers would have to participate in peace talks. Obviously, the Turkish side was striving for a loose confederation.

On 22 August, in an interview in London, Makarios stressed that there could be no negotiations until Turkish troops had withdrawn to the ceasefire line agreed in Geneva on 9 August. The new negotiations should be held in New York under the auspices of the UN, and representatives of the permanent members of the Security Council should take part. A partition of the island would destroy Cyprus as a state. A federal solution was out of the question, as it was the precursor to partition. Makarios obviously did not understand the real situation, but his attitude considerably limited Kliridis' room for manoeuvre.

During a discussion with the Greek government in Athens, Kliridis stated that militarily they were in a hopeless situation. The discussion turned to the question of whether or not to negotiate with Turkey and what conditions to set. It became clear that the only one who correctly assessed the situation was Kliridis. He was convinced that Turkey would never withdraw its troops to the ceasefire line of 9 August. Therefore, this should not be made a precondition for negotiations. It was necessary to act quickly because there was a danger that the Turks would establish their own government in the occupied part of Cyprus. Foreign Minister Mavros was under illusions: The pressure exerted by the UN, the FRG and the Soviet Union would cause the Turks to back down, so one should wait and see. Karamanlis thought this was unrealistic. Kliridis said that no diplomatic manoeuvre would prevent federalisation on the basis of geographical separation, whereby he was prepared to give the Turks 24 per cent of the area of Cyprus. If the geographical division had been accepted dur-

---

1 The presentation is based on Heinz A. Richter, *Geschichte der Insel Zypern* Band IV *1965-1977* Teil 2 (Mainz & Ruhpolding: Rutzen, 2009), pp. 546-708, resp. Idem, *Kurze Geschichte des modernen Zypern 1878-2009* (Mainz & Ruhpolding: Rutzen, 2010), pp. 235-253.

ing the negotiations in Geneva in July and August, Cyprus would be in a better position today. He was afraid of public opinion, but he should have accepted the division in Geneva. There would be no solution except a federation with geographical division. Prime Minister Karamanlis agreed.

Nevertheless, for domestic and foreign policy reasons, Karamanlis imposed unfulfillable preconditions for the opening of negotiations by demanding the return of the refugees and the withdrawal of the Turkish armed forces to the ceasefire line of 8 August. Only after that did he consider a federal solution based on geographical separation possible, but without population displacement. Karamanlis did not yet see himself in a position to steer a more realistic course, mainly for domestic political reasons.

Kliridis, on the other hand, named three conditions for opening negotiations with the Turks on 25 August: The Turks would have to be prepared to make serious territorial concessions; the Turkish troops would have to be completely withdrawn in stages ("a phased total withdrawal"); the refugees would have to be allowed to return. A release of Varoşa would greatly ease the situation of the refugees and improve the climate overall. So Kliridis tried to build a golden bridge for the other side. If they had gone along with it, the population exchange would also have become a fact, but it would ultimately have been on a voluntary basis and thus legitimised, and the accusation of expulsion would have been eliminated. The territorial concession in the Varoşa area was not a big price for the Turkish side. The demand for a total withdrawal of Turkish troops in stages accompanied by a demilitarisation of the island was by no means illusory. Kliridis' proposal was based on the do-ut-des principle and was quite realistic. He believed that if he and Denktaş could negotiate alone, they would quickly reach a solution. He was undoubtedly right about that, but from now until the recent present, all decisions were made in Ankara.

When UN Secretary General Waldheim tried to convene a conference at the end of August, it became clear that Turkish Prime Minister Ecevit only wanted the Geneva negotiations to continue and rejected any internationalisation. He and Denktaş sought to secure the status quo under international law. Kissinger, on the other hand, was not prepared to put pressure on Ankara to participate in an international conference because he had been angry with the Greeks since the demonstrations. There were direct negotiations between Kliridis and Denktaş about pending humanitarian problems, which were also regularly solved, but this did not bring them any closer to the conference.

Kissinger's proposal to Karamanlis in mid-September to combine the Cyprus conflict with the bilateral Greek-Turkish Aegean conflict and to settle it through a package solution shows once again abundantly clearly that Kissinger had still not grasped the complexity of the conflicts. Karamanlis rejected the proposal: he was prepared to accept a federal solution, but he rejected a solution that was humiliating for Greece or unacceptable for the Greek Cypriots. It was thus clear that there would be no Geneva III. Movement in the deadlock could only come if Makarios accepted a solution based on a bi-zonal federation. But Makarios tried to turn back the clock with the help of the UN by bringing the Cyprus problem before the UN General Assembly.

Makarios hoped that the latter would issue an unequivocal condemnation of Turkey, because there could be no veto in the General Assembly. Moreover, the non-aligned states and the members of the Warsaw Pact had a large majority. He even thought it possible to achieve a clear condemnation of Turkey as an aggressor, which could lead the Security

Council to take a tougher line, perhaps even sanctions against Turkey. Finally, a General Assembly resolution would also rebuild the morale of the Greek Cypriots. In order to prepare this action in the best possible way, Makarios gave a large number of interviews and undertook a publicity tour of the non-aligned states in the Mediterranean.

The outcome of the debate in the General Assembly at the end of October was sobering: Resolution 3212 (XXIX) called on all states to respect the sovereignty, independence, territorial integrity and non-alignment of Cyprus and to refrain from any act or intervention against it. It urged a speedy withdrawal of all foreign troops. The future constitutional order, it said, was exclusively a matter for the Greek and Turkish Cypriots. Negotiations between the representatives of the two communities should continue under the aegis of the UN Secretary General. The refugees should return. All parties should cooperate with UNFICYP. This resolution demanded less in substance than the previous Security Council resolutions, but it sounded good, impressed the Cypriots, but did not commit anyone to anything, so even Turkey agreed to it. The adoption of such resolutions developed in the following years into a kind of meaningless ritual that was carried out again and again and, as we know, achieved nothing.

In Cyprus, the acting president Kliridis came under increasing pressure from Makarios' supporters and those of the junta in these weeks. The first suspected Kliridis of trying to prevent the return of Makarios in order to stay in power. But only Makarios would achieve the return of the refugees to their homes. Kliridis wanted the division of the island and only Makarios could prevent this. The junta supporters hoped that Makarios would amnesty them on his return and save them from court and punishment. The leaders of both camps began to agitate for Makarios' return in an unholy alliance with the church leaders who had been ousted in 1973 and who had worked against Makarios and for the junta.

The real reason for these nasty manoeuvres was progress in the talks between Kliridis and Denktaş. Political issues had already come up at the beginning of September. Denktaş had hinted that in the event of a possible withdrawal of the demarcation line, Morphou could become Greek again and Varoşa could be opened for the return of refugees. On 20 September, he asked Kliridis if he was authorised to sign a possible agreement. Denktaş thus signalled concrete willingness to negotiate, and proposed a seven-point solution plan. Kliridis thus needed a free hand for the negotiations, but now Makarios announced his imminent return. Kliridis knew that in this case the new negotiations would fail, because Denktaş had clearly indicated that he would not negotiate with Makarios.

Kliridis informed Karamanlis of this situation and announced his resignation from all offices in the event of Makarios' return. Karamanlis was horrified. He had by now agreed to a bizonal solution, provided the Cypriots agreed and the Turks made territorial concessions. In a public statement, he rejected a resignation by Kliridis. At the same time, he called on Makarios to publicly declare that he supported Kliridis unconditionally. If Makarios refused, he would publicly distance himself from him.

Makarios took his time with his answer and only called Kliridis on 2 October and asked him to stay in office. A day later, he declared in a message to his people that he alone would decide when to return. He would make the decision on this after attending the debate in the UN General Assembly. In the meantime, he said, the people of Cyprus should support Kliridis, who enjoyed his full confidence. Kliridis then agreed to remain in office. On 6 November, Kliridis accepted the situation and moved forward.In a speech, he stated that a return to the status quo ante was unrealistic, as Turkey would never accept such a move. The only possible solution, he said, would take a federal form. Anyone who believed that the UN could achieve a solution to the Cyprus problem was, in his opinion, politically naïve. When his opponents attacked him for this, Kliridis followed up: He said that anyone who claimed that negotiations could achieve a result other than a federal solution based on territorial separation was lying to the people. The Turkish Cypriot press praised Kliridis, and Denktaş called Kliridis' attitude realistic and constructive.

Kliridis understood that a return of Makarios would undermine his position as a negotiator with Turkey. He therefore sought a document that would have to be signed by Makarios and the Greek government. This should set out the framework for a solution. He refused to negotiate further if in the end Makarios refused to sign the solution found.

On 20 November, Kliridis flew to London for talks with Makarios. There, the British government had meanwhile made Makarios understand that it considered a bi-zonal federation to be the only solution. But Makarios was still under illusions. He believed that Kissinger would put pressure on Turkey to impose a multicantonal solution. Such a solution would be acceptable, he said, provided the central government had real power, a Greek Cypriot majority and Turkish Cypriots no longer had veto power, either in the legislature or the executive. Kliridis disagreed: Kissinger had already wanted a bi-zonal federation at the Geneva negotiations and nothing had changed. Makarios was not impressed by Kliridis' arguments and stood by his opinion.

On 22 November, Makarios told Foreign Minister Callaghan that he was ready to accept a multi-regional federation. The refugees would have to return and the Turkish troops would have to withdraw. Callaghan was sure that the Turkish side would only agree to a bi-zonal federation. He did not even address Makarios' demand for the withdrawal of Turkish troops. There was a danger that Turkey would see the status quo as a solution. Makarios indicated that he would return to Cyprus in early December.

On 29 November 1974, Makarios, Kliridis and Karamanlis and representatives of both governments discussed possible solutions. Kliridis emphasised that the Turks would only accept a bi-zonal federation, which would even have the character of a confederation, and nothing else. The Güneş plan of Geneva with its cantons was dead. Denktaş had said that the Turks were ready to reduce their share of the total area to 25 per cent. The UN could not help. The Americans, he said, were in favour of a bi-zonal federation and were not ready for a cantonal solution. Great Britain as well as the Eastern Bloc states and also the European states were in favour of a bi-zonal federation. Makarios, however, clung to Kissinger's vague statements.

As the conference continued on the evening of 30 November, it became apparent that the Greek government was in favour of negotiations on the basis of a geographically separate federation, whether with two or four cantons. This was the view of Kliridis and Foreign Minister Christofidis on the Cypriot side. Tassos Papadopoulos indulged in wishful thinking and Kyprianou leaned towards Makarios' opinion. So the crucial thing now was whether Makarios moved or not. But Makarios remained stubborn in his demands for a multi-regional federation with many cantons. Karamanlis then distanced himself: the dialogue had to take place between the Greek Cypriots and the Turkish Cypriots. Kliridis warned that the negotiations would get stuck. Moreover, he had information that the Turks would soon start bringing mainland Turks to the island. Makarios, however, did not want to understand that it was not possible to haggle over a fait accompli.

Kliridis knew Makarios and therefore did not rely on the verbal agreements from the end of the Athens negotiations, but demanded written instructions that would also bind Makarios in case of doubt. The Greek Foreign Ministry submitted a written draft to this effect, which was given to Makarios. Makarios found so many passages with which he disagreed that the draft had to be revised twice. In his opinion, one should haggle over every iota.

Kliridis received the following instructions for his negotiations with Denktaş, which began again on 19 December: The aim of the negotiations should be the creation of a multi-regional federation on a bi-communal basis with a strong central government. The area of the Turkish share should be proportional to the share of the population, but should not exceed 25 per cent. Refugees should be allowed to return analogous to the percentage difference between 18 and 25 per cent. The cantons should be established where Turkish villages were already concentrated. The canton between Nicosia and Kyrenia should extend to the sea. Meanwhile, the other conditions were also completely unrealistic.

Makarios had thus largely pushed through his ideas. Kliridis was sent into the negotiations with his hands tied, so to speak, by these instructions. The question remains, why did Kliridis get involved in this game? He knew that Denktaş trusted him to a certain extent and that no one else but him was a match for Denktaş's negotiating skills. Furthermore, he knew that the Turks would never negotiate with Makarios because of their mistrust. If anyone could extract concessions from the Turks, it was he. At the same time, Kliridis presumably thought it possible that Makarios would after all come to the necessary understanding and give in on specific issues in the negotiations. Moreover, Kliridis' sense of duty was great enough to prompt him to save what could be saved, even on this mission impossible. Makarios returned to Cyprus on 7 December 1974. The population gave him an enthusiastic welcome.

In December, Kliridis and Denktaş negotiated the modalities for the new round of negotiations, which were to begin in January. Makarios, however, still did not think of giving Kliridis much leeway in the negotiations. To this end, he set up a so-called National Council, which included all the leading figures in Cypriot politics. The Council was to have a purely consultative function, but because of its high-profile composition it would nevertheless carry great weight. Kliridis was to inform the Council of the results of his negotiations with Denktaş at 14-day intervals. In January 1975, Makarios reshuffled the cabinet. With only two exceptions, all the ministers Kliridis had appointed were dismissed. This clarified the balance of power: Makarios again largely controlled the situation.

Negotiations between Kliridis and Denktaş continued over the next few months, but they did not stop the latter from pushing developments in his favour. His proposals for a constitution, presented on 13 February, clearly indicated that he was striving for confederation: the constitution would have to provide for a bicommunal and biregional federal state. Laws enacted by the central government should not interfere in the internal affairs of the two federated states. The central government should have only enough powers to enable the state to function. All other competences should remain with the federal states. All common institutions should have equal representation, so that de facto as well as de jure equality prevails and domination of the other side was prevented.

On the same day, Denktaş created a fait accompli: he had the Council of Ministers and the Parliamentary Assembly of Turkish Cypriots meet in the morning in Northern Nicosia and passed a resolution stating that the ultimate objective of the Turkish Cypriots was to unite with the Greek Cypriots in a bi-regional federation. But until then, the autonomous Turkish Cypriot government (administration) would restructure and organise itself on the basis of a secular, federated state. The legislature of the autonomous state would be transformed into a constituent state. Rauf Denktaş was appointed president of the federated state in a second resolution. Thus, a separate state was proclaimed in Northern Cyprus. While this move was condemned by all parties except Turkey, nothing else happened.

The use of the term federation by Denktaş and Ankara should not deceive. They did not want a federal solution at all, but aspired to a kind of confederation, a loose confederation with a weak central government and largely autonomous constituent states. From now on, when the Turkish side spoke of a federal solution or federation, they really meant a solution based on a confederation. Denktaş' step was a separation under state law. However, from the outside, i.e. from the point of view of international law, Cyprus still remained a common state. The step towards full secession was not taken until 1983, when Denktaş proclaimed the "Turkish Republic of Northern Cyprus", which, however, has so far not been recognised by any other state except Turkey.

Nevertheless, negotiations between Kliridis and Denktaş began in Vienna in April 1975 under the auspices of UN Secretary General Waldheim. It soon became apparent that Denktaş, on Ankara's orders, was not negotiating seriously but only giving the appearance of doing so: two states were to be established which would merge into a federation. They were to cede to the central government only those rights that were absolutely necessary for its functioning. The two federated states were to be equal in every respect, forming a condominium. The central government would only be responsible for foreign policy, defence, federal banking, the stock exchange, currency, the federal budget, the federal court, post and telecommunications, health services, and the like. These statements described a loose confederation of states and by no means a federal state. Such a confederation would have made the status quo the solution to the Cyprus problem. How intransigent the Turkish side had become in the meantime was shown on 8 June, when the referendum on the constitution of the Turkish-Cypriot federal state was held. So the second round of the Vienna talks did not produce any results either. Makarios wanted to break off the talks, but Athens wanted them to continue.

At the talks in August and September 1975, it became apparent that Denktaş had come empty-handed. International efforts now began to relaunch the Cyprus talks and fill them with substance, which continued into the autumn. Especially the French Foreign Minister Sauvanargues and his German colleague Hans Dietrich Genscher put pressure on Ankara to resume negotiations. Prolonged diplomatic back and forth finally led to the objective. On the sidelines of the NATO summit on 11 and 12 December 1975, the foreign ministers of Greece and Turkey, Çağlayangil and Bitsios, began talking to each other. Çağlayangil dropped all preconditions for the resumption of negotiations that he and Denktaş had raised in the previous months. He accepted that the territorial issue should be discussed first, because the number of refugees who could return to their homes depended on it. The territorial issue and the return of the refugees were known to be Makarios' priority and to this end he was prepared to cede 25 per cent of the territory.

A package solution was agreed upon: the three topics of territory, federal structure and competences of the central government would be discussed. None of the issues would be allowed to be concluded separately, they would have to be adopted together as a package. Both governments would influence Denktaş and Kliridis to promote their goodwill. The Turkish side would not present territorial proposals, instead the Greek side should first say which territories it demanded to be vacated by the Turkish army. This was agreed with Makarios. The negotiations were not to last two or three days as before, but a longer period. At an advanced stage, mixed committees of lawyers could be brought in as advisers, provided the negotiators accepted this. Strictest silence was to be maintained to ensure the success of the negotiations. Makarios was kept informed by Bitsios throughout these negotiations.

The Brussels Agreement opened a way to a solution, especially since Makarios had declared his agreement. To interpret it as some kind of NATO solution, as has been done in the past, is misleading. The concept had indeed been developed by the NATO powers France and Germany, and it was turned into reality in a NATO meeting, but it was not a NATO plan. Only once had a NATO solution been sought, when a peace-keeping force of NATO troops was to be sent to Cyprus in 1964. In terms of realpolitik, the Brussels Agreement had a real chance of resolving the Cyprus conflict.

On 14 December, the Director General of the Greek Foreign Ministry, Ioannis Tzounis, came to Nicosia on behalf of Karamanlis to brief Makarios on the negotiations and the Brussels Agreement. Greek Ambassador Michalis Dountas and Foreign Minister Christofidis attended the meeting with Makarios. Kliridis had not been invited, which made him suspicious. Indeed, there was reason enough for Kliridis to be suspicious, because Dountas asked him if he would mind if Tassos Papadopoulos and Michalakis Triantafyllidis were appointed as advisors. The term advisor was a euphemism in this context; they were supposed to be overseers or watchdogs of the nationalist hardliners with whom Dountas sympathised.

The "militant camp" (machitiki parataxi) of the hardliners was led by Vassos Lyssaridis, who was far more influential than his EDEK's electoral strength would suggest. He advocated a "militant realism" based on a "triptych of national salvation", the elements of which were internationalisation, harnessing all foreign aid and popular struggle. His ideas about the realisation of the latter were sometimes quite adventurous. Concessions were out of the question for him, because they would only sanction the injustice that the Turks had done.

The other members of the National Council Takis Evdokas, Spyros Kyprianou and Tassos Papadopoulos had a similar intransigent view. For them, the only solution was a return to a modified status quo ante. Kliridis' realpolitik was already bordering on treason in their eyes, and Makarios' slow approach to reality due to his insight into the necessity was also rejected by them. What is really astonishing about the whole manoeuvre is that Makarios did not make any attempt to bring the hardliners under control; he probably shied away from direct confrontation, because it would have shown how weak his own position now was.

The appointment of the two "advisers" was also absolutely counterproductive. A few months earlier, Kliridis had managed with some difficulty to reject Denktaş' "foreign minister" Çelik as his advisor, firstly in order to prevent the upgrading of the Turkish federated state and secondly in order not to release Denktaş from responsibility for the negotiations. If the Greek advisers were to take an active part in the negotiations, Çelik would also have to be admitted and Denktaş would be given the chance to withdraw from the negotiations and to shift the negotiations to a lower level without decision-making competence and to let them drag on. On whose initiative Waldheim refused the direct participation of the "advisors" in the negotiations to Makarios, and the latter accepted this, is not known. The fact was that they were not allowed to be present at the actual negotiations.

On 28 January 1976, Makarios informed the National Council of the Brussels agreement, which he knew in detail and had accepted: he considered it right that the Greek side should be the first to submit its territorial proposals, provided that the Turkish side undertook to submit its counter-proposals within a reasonable period of time. The National Council, however, maintained its position that the Turks had to move first. Finally, they agreed on Kliridis' compromise proposal: he would suggest to Denktaş to present his proposals simultaneously. The National Council further decided that Kliridis should refuse to talk about the structure of the republic and the competences of the future government if there was no prior agreement on the territorial issue. This decision was completely contrary to the Brussels Agreement, which sought a package solution.

Unfortunately, the Greek Cypriot hardliners had thus successfully torpedoed the Brussels package solution. If the package was unravelled again, Denktaş could again pick apart or block the individual elements at will. In fact, they undermined Kliridis' negotiating position and ruined - once again - a realistic chance to solve the Cyprus problem with their demands. In the following days it became clear that now Denktaş was stonewalling. Finally, it was agreed that negotiations would resume in Vienna on 17 February 1976. What is actually astonishing is that Makarios did not take a clear position.

On the way to Vienna, Kliridis and his " watchdogs" went to see Karamanlis. He made it clear to them that the negotiations were a matter for the Cypriots. The Greek government had opened the way in Brussels with the support of the Europeans, especially the French and the Germans. He had no intention of imposing his opinion on the Cypriots, but time was working against them. Kliridis hinted that Karamanlis should put pressure on Makarios. Since the latter was not prepared to do so, it was clear that the negotiations in Vienna would fail. The National Security Council had forced Kliridis to take a course that was bound to lead to failure. Whether it would have been possible for Karamanlis to force a change of course by putting his foot down the day before the negotiations began in Vienna is doubtful. He had done his duty and opened the way to a package solution through the Brussels Agreement. If the Cypriot leadership did not want to take this path and stuck to its old proposals, it was itself responsible for the failure. Actually, Kliridis should have resigned here.

The negotiations in Vienna, which began on 17 February 1976, quickly reached an impasse because Denktaş was intransigent due to Turkey's demands and Kliridis could not move due to the decisions of the Cypriot National Council. On 19 February, the end of the talks was imminent. In this situation, Kliridis addressed Makarios by telex. He recalled his instructions and noted that Denktaş was referring to the Brussels agreement, according to which the Greek side had to be the first to present proposals on the territorial question. The multiregionality demanded by the Council had already been rejected at the last round of negotiations. It had been decided in Brussels that the territorial proposals should have a regional character and a bi-zonal basis. In Waldheim's opinion, now was the time for the Greek Cypriots to present their proposals. Should this not happen, he could not blame the Turks for the failure of the talks.

Since his advisers continued to adhere to the course set by the National Council, they called Makarios. Makarios evaded a decision: Kliridis should decide himself in consultation with his advisers. He would accept their decision. Since they stubbornly stuck to their course, the negotiations had actually failed. But Kliridis knew that Makarios actually agreed with him, as his behaviour in the National Council at the end of January and in his telephone call had shown. But Makarios did not have the stamina necessary for a head of state and government to push through the course he had recognised as correct in the face of opposition. He had backed down in the National Council and when Kliridis' "advisers" pressed him, he backed down again and delegated decision-making to the three in Vienna, even though he knew that two of them were radically opposed to the Brussels agreement. He probably secretly hoped that Kliridis would react as he did.

In fact, Kliridis made a lonely decision. At the next meeting with Denktaş on 20 February 1976, he proposed that the exchange of territorial ideas take place within 6 weeks. He himself would present his proposals first and Denktaş 10 days later. Denktaş accepted. Absolute confidentiality was agreed. The communiqué released afterwards spoke of substantive talks on territorial and constitutional issues. It said they had agreed to exchange written proposals over the next six weeks through Javier de Cuellar, who had been appointed Special Representative of the UN Secretary-General in Cyprus in September 1975. The next round of talks would take place in May. It was through the civil courage of Kliridis that the 5th round of talks had been saved from failure.

This gentleman's agreement meant that Denktaş or Ankara would have had to show their colours at the end of March and clearly state what territorial concessions they were prepared to make. But that was exactly what Denktaş and certain forces in Turkey did not intend to do. However, if no proposal had been put forward, there would have been no 6th Vienna Round of Talks and the blame would clearly have been on the Turkish side. Therefore, Denktaş, in consultation with Ankara, developed a plan to prevent this from happening and at the same time to delay the negotiations for months: An indiscretion was committed in mid-March and the Turkish Cypriot press was given not too concrete information about the confidential agreement from Vienna. Almost the entire Greek Cypriot press picked up on this "news" and spoke of a secret agreement between Kliridis and Denktaş, of which Makarios knew nothing. It was clear that here the hardliners of every colour were trying hard to harm Kliridis and torpedo the negotiations. Kliridis denied having concluded a secret agreement.

In order to compromise Kliridis once and for all, Denktaş claimed in an interview with the correspondent of the London Times that he had the future proposals of the Greek Cypriots in his possession. These had been handed over to him by Kliridis on 24 March. The journalist took this story unchecked, did not realise that Denktaş was using him to compromise Kliridis, and innocently told it to the government spokesman in the South. In fact, Kliridis had handed over nothing. But this fabricated story was the hardliners' chance. At a joint meeting of the National Council and the Cabinet, Kliridis was confronted. The latter reacted indignantly and refused to defend himself against such absurd accusations.

On 7 April, Kliridis resigned as chief negotiator for the Greek Cypriot side. The National Council and the cabinet accepted Kliridis' resignation on 8 April. Tassos Papadopoulos was appointed in his place. This eliminated the only moderate Greek Cypriot politician who had led the intercommunal negotiations for nine long years. From now on, the hardliners set the course. Denktaş reacted immediately. He refused to negotiate with the former EOKA man Papadopoulos and appointed Umit Süleyman Onan, who until then had been deputy speaker of the Turkish Cypriot parliamentary assembly, as the new negotiator on the Turkish Cypriot side. One day later, Denktaş let it be known that he did not consider Papadopoulos to represent the Greek ethnic group. However, he was prepared to negotiate with Makarios. The intercommunal negotiations had thus been successfully downgraded by Denktaş and could be dragged out at will from then on. Progress would only be made again when Makarios was ready to accept Denktaş as a negotiating partner on an equal footing and to negotiate with him.

Denktaş's intrigue would never have been crowned with success without the "support" of Greek Cypriot hardliners. Kliridis had been a match for him in the negotiations, often far superior. The hardliners won a Pyrrhic victory with Kliridis' resignation, because only the realpolitik course pursued by Kliridis offered the chance of a solution to the Cyprus conflict. In the end, the hardliners supported and cemented Denktaş's separatist policy. It is an irony of history that eleven months later Makarios arrived at something like the solution policy that Kliridis had repeatedly proposed. But by then it was too late. Had Makarios sided with Kliridis in the attacks on him in the National Council and the Cabinet, the history of Cyprus would have taken a happier turn. But it is not even impossible that Makarios was not unhappy about Kliridis' resignation, because from now on he was again controlling things on the Greek side.

In contrast to the Greek Cypriot leadership, Denktaş was a realist politician of the purest water, who was not afraid to fight even with indecent means if this enabled him to assert his interests and, if necessary, to do so vis-à-vis Ankara. His intrigue against Kliridis also torpedoed the Brussels Agreement. Meanwhile, Denktaş wanted his own state. The only possible solution for him was a loose confederation of states. He could only achieve this goal if Kliridis was no longer in business. An unnatural coalition of hardliners from both sides had successfully torpedoed the Brussels package solution.

In April 1976, both sides submitted their proposals for a solution in written form. The Greek proposals represented a major step backwards from the beginning of the Vienna negotiations. All the progress and concessions that Kliridis and Waldheim had laboriously negotiated and wrested from Denktaş were wiped away. The hardliners tried to impose their own ideas. It was clear that Denktaş would not accept these demands. Denktaş' counter-proposals showed that he still wanted a confederation. On 22 April, T. Papadopoulos complained to UN representative de Cuellar that Denktaş had signed as president of the Turkish federated state of Cyprus. This state was not recognised by anyone. With the proposal to establish an interim government, he merely wanted to undermine the internationally recognised government of Cyprus. The proposals are incompatible with UN resolutions. It was obvious that the Turkish side was not interested in constructive negotiations and was trying to delay them in order to gain time to consolidate the situation created by violence. On 5 May, Umit S. Onan replied in the same unqualified manner, and this kind of exchange of views continued until the beginning of June. The first meeting between Papadopoulos and Onan on 27 May was therefore only about humanitarian issues such as missing persons. The intercommunal negotiations were de facto interrupted.

In mid-December 1976, Makarios said in an interview that he was prepared to accept a federal solution under certain conditions. But such a federation would have to ensure the unity of the state. He would not accept any solution that would lead to a division of Cyprus. The fundamental condition for the acceptance of a separate Turkish Cypriot administration was the freedom of movement and settlement and the right to property. Denktaş used this statement as an opportunity to write a letter to Makarios on 9 January 1977, in which he declared his willingness to meet with the Archbishop in the presence of de Cuellar to discuss the problems at hand.

On Kliridis' advice, Makarios accepted the proposal, because otherwise Denktaş would certainly have accused him of torpedoing the negotiations, which would have had nasty international consequences. On 27 January, the first meeting between Makarios and Denktaş since Christmas 1963 took place in the presence of de Cuellar.

Makarios then made it clear that he was speaking to Denktaş in his capacity as an ethnic representative and not as President of the federated Turkish state. Denktaş countered that he did not recognise Makarios as President of Cyprus either. Both agreed that a package solution would probably be best. Makarios criticised that Denktaş was talking about federation but meant confederation, which Denktaş strongly denied. On the territorial aspect, Denktaş was talking about territories and Makarios about a 20 per cent share. Denktaş demanded 32.8 per cent, which would correspond to the land ownership of the Turkish Cypriots. Makarios hinted that he would go as high as 25 per cent. Denktaş stuck to his percentage figure. The discussion turned to freedoms. Denktaş was willing to grant the Greek Cypriots freedom of movement, but avoided being specific. He also accepted the right of settlement, but not to the extent that the federation was questioned. A limited number of refugees could return to their homes, but by no means all. It was clear from Denktaş' answers that he wanted two loosely connected states and as much separation as possible.

Makarios and Denktaş agreed that the inter-communal talks should continue. Denktaş stressed that they could both intervene if they faltered. Makarios agreed. De Cuellar proposed another meeting on 13 February in the presence of Waldheim, in which the two negotiators could also participate, which Makarios and Denktaş accepted.

Makarios informed the National Council of this outcome on 27 January. At two further meetings on 2 and 8 February, it became apparent that hardliners were still against a resumption of the talks if Denktaş did not fulfil their preconditions. The discussion took on features reminiscent of those Kliridis had experienced before he left for the last Vienna round. But Makarios was not impressed this time and decided that the negotiations had to continue.

On 12 February 1977, Makarios and Denktaş met with Waldheim. After four hours of talks, they agreed on the following formula, which went down in Cypriot history as the High Level Agreement of 1977:

1. an independent, non-aligned, bicommunal federal republic should be sought.

2. the territory administered by each community should be discussed from the point of view of economic suitability or productivity and land ownership.
3. questions such as the principles of freedom of movement, freedom of establishment, the right to property and other specific questions should be discussed, taking into account the elementary basis of a bicommunal federal order and certain practical difficulties which might arise for the Turkish community.
4. the power and functions of the central federal government should be such as to secure the unity of the country while respecting the bi-communal character of the state.

With this agreement, Makarios took a cautious step towards recognising reality. The first sentence of the agreement said goodbye to the unitary state as provided for in the 1959 constitution and accepted a future bi-communal federation. The bi-communal character of the state was nothing new, because the old constitution had also provided for it, as had independence. At most, the statement that the future republic was to be non-aligned was new, but strictly speaking this was no more than the codification of a practice that had been applied for a long time. The only really new thing in this first sentence was the specification of a federation.

In the second sentence, the principle of proportionality with regard to the population share in the territorial distribution of the area was abandoned in favour of economic considerations, thus moving closer to the principle of regions, which had been under discussion for a long time. The reference to land ownership was a concession to the Turkish side and at the same time formed the percentage upper limit of the Turkish share of the area. It was the starting point of the negotiations.

The principles of freedom of movement and settlement as well as the right to property were recognised in point 3 on the one hand, but on the other hand their possible modification and restriction was conceded depending on the federal system and constraints on the Turkish Cypriot side. Point 4 stipulated that the competences of the future central government had to be shaped in such a way that the unity of the country was guaranteed. This meant that the future republic would be federal and not confederal in character. Makarios' concessions meant no more than that, out of an understanding of necessity, he conceded positions that were no longer tenable. His agreement to the establishment of a federation was one such manoeuvre.

The republic established under this agreement would thus have been independent, non-aligned and bi-communal. Bizonality is nowhere mentioned expressis verbis. Nevertheless, almost everyone in Cyprus was and is convinced that the agreement provided for a bi-communal and bizonal federation. The explanation is quite simple: as Denktaş later reported, Makarios did not want to provoke a major reaction from the hardliners and therefore asked for Denktaş' agreement to omit this irritant word from the published text. Denktaş agreed. It was therefore a verbal agreement, a gentleman's agreement. This version is also supported by the wording of the text itself, because the text of paragraph 2 speaks of the territory (singular) of each ethnic group and not of territories (plural). If cantons had still been at issue, the plural would have been used. Waldheim is said to have said at a press conference in Vienna on 16 February 1977 that both sides meant a bizonal federation, even though the agreement spoke of a bi-communal federation. Kliridis confirms that Makarios accepted bizonality in his talks with Denktaş, and admitted that the Greek side would be the first to present its territorial proposals together with a map, but concealed this in his report to the National Council and the Council of Ministers.

The High Level Agreement was a reasonable step towards a solution based on a bi-communal and bi-zonal federation. The only thing that could be criticised about the agreement is the fact that it came about a year too late. It still forms the basis of all subsequent proposals for a solution.

On 23 February 1977, former US Secretary of Defence Clark Clifford arrived in Nicosia as President Carter's personal emissary. He had previously visited Athens and Ankara. Makarios informed him about the gentlemen's agreement with Denktaş. Clifford suggested that the Greek side should be the first to present its proposals on all aspects of the problem, including territorial ideas, accompanied by a map. Makarios accepted this. This brought Makarios to the substance of the Brussels Agreement after more than a year. Negotiations would continue and the Greek side would present its proposals first.

At the meeting of the National Council and the Council of Ministers on 9 March 1977, Makarios pushed through his new course in the face of fierce opposition from the hardliners. As the debate continued in the National Council on 17 March 1977, the same arguments were repeated stereotypically by the hardliners. Makarios paid no attention to their concerns and ordered that the proposals of the Greek Cypriot side be elaborated and a map drawn delimiting an area in the north of the island, which had about 20 per cent of the surface area. On 16 March 1977, Makarios informed Waldheim in a letter that the Greek Cypriot side would present its entire proposals, including a map, at the next meeting in Vienna. Waldheim in turn informed Makarios that Denktaş was also ready for substantial negotiations. He would not present a map, but was prepared to discuss the Greek one.

Thus, in March 1977, they had returned to exactly where Kliridis had left off almost exactly a year before. The discussion in the council had shown that the hardliners were still in the majority. Their motives ranged from stubborn principle riding and fixation on fears to hatred of the Turks, from lack of civil courage to opportunism. The only one who still had a clear view was Kliridis, and it was almost tragic that he was no longer the Greek side's negotiator, because T. Papadopoulos was ultimately also a hardliner and, on the other hand, not as skilful a negotiator as Kliridis. Makarios had finally come round to a realistic position. But the question was whether he would remain in control in the upcoming negotiations.

The sixth round of talks in Vienna differed fundamentally from all the previous rounds in that it was no longer a discussion between the two representatives of the two ethnic groups in the presence of the UN Secretary-General, but was attended by two advisors in addition to the negotiators. Gentlemen's agreements, such as Denktaş and Kliridis had occasionally concluded, were thus impossible. Although Papadopoulos presented a bizonal map at the first meeting on 31 March, his written proposals for solutions already fell short of the High Level Agreement. The meetings themselves were an unproductive exchange of blows with long-known arguments. After a total of eleven meetings, Waldheim gave up in exasperation and adjourned the talks until mid-May 1977.

If the High Level Agreement had ever had a chance of realisation, it was lost in the negotiations in the spring of 1977. From the beginning of April, Makarios was ailing and increasingly lost control of the National Council and the Council of Ministers. From then on, the hardliners and Spyros Kyprianou determined the course, and the latter set his sights on a solution within the framework of the UN. When Makarios died on 2 August 1977, the High Level Agreement became obsolete. In terms of content, however, it remained the necessary core of any kind of solution to the Cyprus problem.

VAROŞA VERSUS NICOSIA AIRPORT

A NEW ROUND IN THE POKER GAME OVER CYPRUS

When Glafkos Kliridis was elected as the new President of the Republic of Cyprus in February 1993, hope was once again raised that the Cyprus conflict might yet find a solution, especially since Glafkos Kliridis and Rauf Denktash the head of the so-called Turkish Republic of Northern Cyprus, which is only recognised by Turkey, have known each other well since their schooldays and especially from the time of the inter-communal negotiations in the 1960s and 1970s and have a certain degree of trust in each other.[1]

A few days after Kliridis' election victory, UN Secretary-General Boutros Boutros-Ghali approached Kliridis and Denktash as part of his mandate and invited them to a joint meeting in New York on 30 March 1993. There, the timing, modalities and preparations for the resumption of talks were to be negotiated. Both sides accepted the invitation. On 26 March, the UN Security Council, which Boutros-Ghali had in the meantime informed on 18 March, stated that the status quo in Cyprus was unacceptable and that a mutually acceptable overall framework agreement should be reached without delay on the basis of the *Set of Ideas*[2] approved by the Security Council in 1972. Both sides should demonstrate their goodwill and cooperate with the Secretary General so that meaningful progress could be made in direct negotiations between the two sides. In conclusion, the Security Council asked Boutros-Ghali to report back to it after the meeting.[3]

On the morning of 30 March, Boutros-Ghali first held individual talks with Kliridis and Denktash. Joint meetings took place in the afternoon of that day and the following day. Kliridis and Denktash agreed that direct negotiations be resumed on 24 May at UN headquarters in New York. The basis for the negotiations was to be the *Set of Ideas;* the aim of the negotiations was to conclude a *"mutually acceptable overall framework agreement"*. In addition, both sides agreed that in the meantime the representative of the Secretary-General in Nicosia should hold talks with them on, among other things, the implementation of confidence-building measures in order to create a climate of trust that would contribute to the success of the negotiations.[4]

Indeed, during the negotiations between President Vasileiou and Denktash on the Set of Ideas in late October/early November 1992, Boutros-Ghali had recognised that there was an abysmal mistrust between the two sides. He concluded that the chances for progress in the negotiations would increase considerably if both sides initiated a series of confidence-building measures. This would lead to an improvement in the climate, which would bring the aim of concluding a framework agreement on the basis of the Set of Ideas closer.[5] The Security Council, to which Boutros-Ghali presented these ideas on 19 November 1992, supported the Secretary General's proposal by appealing to the parties to initiate such confidence-building measures.[6]

---

1 In Cyprus and Greece, the rumour persists that Kliridis and Denktash even married cousins. This belongs to the realm of mythology.

2 S. Annex of S/24.472 of 21 August 1992.

3 S/26.026 of 1 July 1993: Report of the Secretary-General on His Mission of Good Offices in Cyprus, p. 3.

4 S/25.517 of 2 April 1993: Letter from the Secretary-General Addressed to the President of the Security Council.

5 S/24.830 of 19 November 1992: Report of the Secretary-General on His Mission of Good Offices in Cyprus.

6 Resolution of the Security Council 789 (1992) of 25 November 1992.

Between 15 April and 5 May and from 14 to 19 May, Boutros-Ghali's representative, Gustav Feissel, tried to pave the way in 34 meetings with Kliridis and Denktash, which together lasted almost 50 hours. The talks dealt with two sets of issues: confidence-building measures and resolving differences over the Set of Ideas. Feissel asked Kliridis and Denktash to identify those issues in the Set of Ideas that were important and whose resolution would be beneficial to both sides. Both politicians agreed to this proposal, and at the meetings encouraging progress and convergence of positions was then achieved on three sets of issues: *"(a) displaced persons/territorial adjustments, (b) security and guarantee, and, (c) the workability of the federal Government."*[1] But it turned out that both Klridis and Denktash preferred to put the main emphasis of the preparatory discussions on the issue of confidence-building measures. The starting point for the discussions were the proposals made by Boutros-Ghali in his report in November 1992.[2] In the course of the discussions, a significant number of measures emerged that both sides were willing to apply.

At the request of both sides, efforts were made to reach agreement on the part of Varoşa that has been a ghost town since the Turkish invasion of 1974.[3] In the past, there had already been various efforts to solve this thorny problem. In 1977, there was speculation that the Turkish side intended to release Varoşa for settlement. Following UN intervention, Denktash refrained from doing so. In the so-called High Level Agreement, signed in May 1979 by the then President Spyros Kyprianou and Denktash, it was stipulated that high priority would be given to reaching an agreement on the resettlement of the city under the auspices of the United Nations.[4] In 1984, the UN Security Council had passed a resolution[5] stating that if Varoşa became accessible again, it should be settled exclusively by its original inhabitants, mainly Greek Cypriots.

During the discussions in Northern and Southern Nicosia it quickly became apparent that the effect of a consensual agreement on the Varoşa issue would have a signalling effect, but at the same time it became clear that such an agreement could only be reached if both sides would derive substantial benefits from it. A lively discussion now began about the concretisation of this benefit, as Denktash kept putting forward new proposals.

---

1 S/26.026

2 S/24.830.

3 Varosha is the south-eastern new town of Famagousta, where almost exclusively Greeks lived until 1974. Most of the island's hotels were located along the coast. Actually, the Turkish army had not wanted to occupy Varosha in 1974, but when the invading army advanced on Famagousta in the second phase of the occupation of the north of the island, the 40,000 Greek Cypriot and European inhabitants fled in panic to the British base of Dhekelia. It was only three days after the ceasefire that a Turkish patrol 'captured' the empty town. The Swedish UN force looked on. As the Turks had no intention of settling there permanently, the town remained closed to civilians and was not repopulated. They wanted a pledge for later negotiations, as the then general and later president Evren wrote; see Ralph Raymond Braun, Zypern (Erlangen: Müller, 1993), pp. 379, 394. Since then, this part of the city has been separated from the rest of the city by barbed wire and is practically empty.

4 Article 5 of the agreement had stated: *"Priority will be given to reaching agreement on the resettlement of Varosha under United Nations auspices simultaneously with the beginning of the consideration by the interlocutors of the constitutional and territorial aspects of a comprehensive settlement, after agreement on Varosha has been reached; it will be implemented without awaiting the outcome of the discussion on other aspects of the Cyprus problem."* Quoted from Heinz A. Richter, *Friede in der Ägäis? Zypern - Ägäis - Minderheiten* (Köln: Romiosini, 1989), p. 137.

5 Security Council Resolution 550 (1984) of 11 May 1984.

The original UN proposal was for a substantial part of Varoşa to be placed under UN administration to create opportunities for contact and trade between the two communities.[1] Denktash, who in the past had always been keen to prevent or at least hinder grass roots contacts between Greek and Turkish Cypriots at the checkpoint between the north and south of the island at the Ledra Palace Hotel under UN auspices, was less than enthusiastic about the idea but believed he could extract major concessions. Thus, he felt that the above proposals constituted insufficient compensation for the fact that he was releasing this part of Varoşas from his control. Adequate compensation for such a concession would be if the embargo imposed on his part of the island were lifted. In particular, Northern Cyprus should be allowed direct flights to and from Europe.[2] Furthermore, the restrictions on the ports of Northern Cyprus should be lifted.

Feissel immediately recognised that Denktash was obviously trying to impose some recognition of his pseudo-state as part of the confidence-building measures, and therefore pointed out to him that neither side should try to extract political concessions from the other. The practical benefits of the measures should be substantial, but no measures should be demanded that would oblige the other side to change its political status. Nevertheless, the UN wanted to try to have most of the trade barriers for the Turkish Cypriot side lifted as part of an overall agreement. Denktash then proposed the reopening of Nicosia airport, which had been closed since 1974 and was now only used by UN planes. Both sides would benefit from this.

In the second phase of the negotiations, it became apparent that Kliridis and Denktash were prepared to put together a package that included Varoşa and Nicosia airport. A classic case of *do ut des* was emerging.

In the case of Varoşa, the package agreement provided for the following: The fenced-in part of the city was to be placed under UN administration as of a certain mutually agreed date. This state of affairs would last until a final settlement of the Cyprus problem. The area under UN administration was to be a special zone for contact and trade between the two communities, i.e. a kind of free trade zone. The UN would be responsible for the security of the area. The costs of administration and security were to be raised locally. The area would be opened up in two phases, during which the former owners could assert their ownership claims. In accordance with the special character of the area, the chambers of commerce and industry of both sides were to be involved in the administration. The UN would also select other organisations on both sides to help develop and implement the inter-communal contacts.

Greek and Turkish Cypriots were to be allowed to enter the area freely without any formality. Trade and exchange of goods with both sides would be completely free. The establishment of new enterprises would be encouraged. The two chambers would encourage the establishment of joint ventures by Greek and Turkish Cypriots through loans. Tourists wishing to visit the north from the south would be able to travel unhindered through this area.[3] In

1 S/26.026, p. 5.

2 Tymbou (Erçan) Airport, 25 km west of Nicosia, is served only by the Turkish airline THY (Türk Hava Yollari) and its associated Cyprus Turkish Airlines KTHY (Kībrīs Türk Hava Yollari) and by Istanbul Airlines. KTHY only has landing rights in Turkey. There are no scheduled flights without a stopover in Turkey.

3 So far, the only crossing point from the south to the north is the checkpoint at Ledra Palace Hotel, which involves the usual formalities at borders. The stay in the north is limited to daytime hours for tourists. Entry from the north

the Varoşa area, the laws that were in force on 1 December 1963 would apply. In the event of disputes involving members of both ethnic groups, the investigative bodies were to have equal representation. Changes to these provisions could only be made by joint decision together with the local UN authority. In the event of conflict, the UN would make recommendations for peaceful settlement. These measures should not have any prejudicial effect, either on the positions of the two sides or on the solution of the Cyprus problem as a whole.[1]

These proposals seemed very reasonable and acceptable to both sides, especially since they would both benefit and would not have to make any sacrifices. This is because the fenced-in area is uninhabited and under the military control of the Turkish army. The main benefit for the Greek Cypriot side would have been primarily the recovery of lost property. The Turkish Cypriot side would have benefited primarily from trade; but the reconstruction of the city would also create jobs for a long time, which would be quite important for Northern Cyprus with its high unemployment. Varoşa's proximity to the tourist centres of Agia Napa and Paralimni in the south, which attract over a million tourists every year, on the one hand, and the attractive sights of the old town of Famagousta and the ancient sites of Salamis in the north, on the other, would certainly contribute to the economic upswing of this region.

With regard to Nicosia airport, the agreement provided for the following: From a certain date, the airport was to be opened to civil passengers and cargo traffic under the administration of the UN in cooperation with the International Civil Aviation Organisation (ICAO).[2] Only those foreign airlines granted landing permits in Cyprus would have landing rights. This would also apply to airlines registered in Turkey.[3] Thus, the airlines of the South (Cyprus Airways) would still have had to fly to Larnaca, whereas the airline of the North (KTHY) registered in Turkey would have been allowed to land at Nicosia Airport. Both sides should have free access to the airport. Foreign visitors entering Cyprus through Nicosia Airport should be given the right to travel freely between the two sides during their stay on the island. The UN or ICAO, in consultation with both sides, should be responsible for the operation and security of the airport. The costs incurred should be borne jointly. Both sides should undertake not to interfere in any way with the movement of people and goods at the airport. In case of conflict, the UN should decide. This agreement should also not have any precedent effect on the overall solution of the Cyprus problem.

The main beneficiary of the reopening of Nicosia International Airport would of course have been the north. The airport would have given the north direct access to international markets. Imports and exports would no longer have had to go via Turkey. In this way, tourism in the north would probably even have increased, since until now any foreign tour operator offering trips to the north automatically lost the right to organise trips to the south of the island. Furthermore, Turkish Cypriots would have been able to travel abroad directly from Nicosia.[4]

---

to the south is not possible.

1 S/26.026, p. 12f.

2 The ICAO is responsible for the safety of international civil aviation. Among other things, it also defines the Flight Information Regions (FIR).

3 S/26.026, p. 14.

4 But this would also have meant that the Turkish side would no longer have been able to control the foreign travel of Turkish Cypriot opposition politicians.

According to an international team of experts, the direct economic benefits for both sides would have been considerable. The reopening of Varoşa's hotels would have increased the South's hotel capacity by about 15 %, but would have required an investment of $1 billion in reconstruction over a period of time. The cost of restarting Nicosia airport was estimated at around $37 million. Acceptance of the package would have meant a 20 % increase in gross national product for the Turkish Cypriot side. It was expected that about half of the 9,000 new jobs in Varoşa would have benefited the Turkish Cypriot side. The reopening of the airport would have increased the occupancy rate of hotels in both the north and the south from 31 to 55 per cent. It was expected that the airport could resume full operations within a year. The time needed to rebuild Varoşa was estimated at five years. Moreover, the package could become the catalyst for an overall solution.[1]

The package put together from the two agreements as a first confidence-building measure was reasonable. Both sides had moved; the Greek Cypriots more, the Turkish Cypriots less, but the compromise found on this issue seemed so attractive that there was even hope that an overall solution might be in sight. When Kliridis and Denktash agreed that this package should be the first item on the agenda at their meeting with Boutros-Ghali in New York on 24 May 1993, the UN Secretary-General got the impression that there was a will on both sides to conclude an agreement.[2]

The talks began as scheduled on 24 May under the chairmanship of Boutros-Ghali. Six plenary sessions were held until 1 June. Joe Clark, Boutros-Ghali's newly appointed Canadian representative, chaired another joint working session and numerous meetings were held with the respective delegations. During the negotiations, it appeared that the Greek Cypriot side was ready to conclude an agreement on the package as proposed, provided that no clauses were added which meant direct or indirect recognition of the so-called "Turkish Republic of Northern Cyprus".

Denktash was of the opinion that the opening of Varoşa was a very big concession, which would be inadequately compensated by the opening of Nicosia airport. A proportional compensation would be the lifting of the overall embargo on all airports and seaports. In addition, KTHY would have to be allowed to fly directly from Tymbou to Europe.

Boutros-Ghali approached the ICAO President, Dr Assad Kotaite, with this problem. ICAO's answer was clear: international flights take place within the framework of treaties concluded between states. KTHY's participation in international air transport is not possible without recognition of the "TRNC". Flights from northern Cypriot airports, as Denktash demanded, were therefore not possible. Denktash then tried to find another way to achieve his aim by citing a precedent. When the details of this case were investigated and he was presented with the conditions attached to it, he withdrew his request, as they would have meant concessions.[3] However, during the research it then turned out that KTHY is indeed a Turkish airline, as it is registered in Turkey. Kliridis was flexible and said that he had no

1 *The Cyprus Weekly* (17.-23 Devember 1993), p. 8.

2 S/26.026, p. 6.

3 *"Mr. Denktash put forward ... an arrangement that had been made earlier in 1993 concerning flights to and from Taiwan by a British-registered airline. However, when the details of this arrangement were examined it became evident that the Turkish Cypriot side would be unwilling to accept such an arrangement mutatis mutandis in the case of Cyprus."* S/26.026, p. 7.

objection to Turkish planes landing at Nicosia airport, as the agreement allowed foreign airlines to land. Denktash then raised no further objections.

With regard to Varoşa itself, Denktash again had doubts. He wanted to establish a kind of buffer zone in the northern part of the city between the port of Famagousta and the UN-controlled district of Varoşa for security reasons. This zone was to be settled by Turkish Cypriots, as a kind of territorial anticipation of the future overall solution of the Cyprus problem. Kliridis was again sympathetic to the security needs of the other side and suggested that the opening could proceed in stages.[1]

On the evening of 27 May 1993, Boutros-Ghali had the impression that *"the time had come when the two leaders could be asked to confirm their agreement to the basic principles concerning Varoşa and Nicosia International Airport."* As soon as both sides agreed, a detailed agreement on its application could be worked out in Nicosia in close cooperation with both sides at a certain point in time. At the plenary session on 28 May, Boutros-Ghali asked both politicians if they agreed. Boutros-Ghali reports on the rest: *"Mr. Denktash indicated that before he could give his response he would have to consult with his `Government' and `Parliament' as well as with the Government of Turkey. He said that he would wish to leave New York for Cyprus and Turkey and that, because of the imminent Bayram festival, he could not return to United Nations Headquarters before 21 June."*[2]

Boutros-Ghali reproached Denktash for the fact that all the details had been known before his trip to New York and that all the changes had been made at his request, so it was not clear to him *"why further prolonged consultations elsewhere were necessary"*. In view of the UN Secretary General's harsh reaction, Denktash suggested that he return on 15 June. Boutros-Ghali said that Denktash could be expected to finish his consultations in Nicosia and Ankara within a week and then return to the negotiating table and give a definite answer. Denktash should come back by 4 June 1993. When Denktash insisted that the consultations would take several weeks, Boutros-Ghali replied that this necessitated a meeting in the presence of the President of the Security Council and the representatives of the permanent members.

This meeting took place on 1 June 1993 under the chairmanship of Joe Clark. He summarised the development so far: The package was extremely fair and was of great benefit to both sides. Neither side had to make any unwanted political concessions; it contained no new elements. Therefore, both sides should have been able to complete the work in New York and reach an agreement. If further consultations were deemed necessary, it would still be possible to conclude them within a week. Denktash was expected to give assurances that he would work for the adoption of the package. Both sides owe it to their communities and to the international community to demonstrate their goodwill by taking this modest step forward. There was no risk involved, but it could have a dramatic effect on overcoming the mistrust between the two communities and clear the way for a solution.[3] The permanent members of the Security Council called for a speedy adoption of these proposals.

Denktash promised to be back in New York by 12 June so that meetings could start again by 14 June at the latest. He also gave assurances that he would work for the adoption

1 *Ibidem*, p. 8.
2 *Ibidem*, p. 8.
3 *Ibidem*, p. 9.

of the package in Nicosia and Ankara. After those present had taken note of this clear assurance, they adjourned until Monday, 14 June 1993.

The well-known Turkish journalist Mehmet Ali Birand said in the Sabah newspaper on 3 June 1993 that Denktash could actually be quite satisfied with the result achieved; the crucial problem, however, was who would take responsibility for implementing the package. If Denktash agreed, the 'head of government' of the "TRNC", Derviş Eroğlu, would fall upon him. That is why Denktash intends to let Turkey decide. But Ankara was afraid to take responsibility. Birand commented that a rejection of the proposals would be a pity, as the package was actually very positive for the Turkish side.[1] In fact, there were two camps in Turkey with fundamentally different views. President Suleyman Demirel and the current Prime Minister, Erdal Inönü, were in favour of the agreement, whereas the former Foreign Minister and current head of the Motherland Party, Mesut Yilmaz, was in favour of a hard line.[2] Demirel said it made little sense to be intransigent. It is not acceptable to say no to every proposal. This was neither in the interest of Turkey nor of Cyprus.[3]

On the same day, Denktash gave an interview during a stopover in Istanbul. When a reporter asked him about his opinion on certain statements made by Demirel, he replied that he, Denktash, would probably be called stubborn and intransigent, but that he feared that if an agreement was reached after three years, we would again be faced with a situation like that of 1974. After his arrival in Northern Cyprus on 3 June, he announced that he would discuss the matter with the "government", the "parliament" and Turkey. Overall, however, one got the impression that he was actually not disinclined to agree to the package, provided he did not have to bear the responsibility alone.

In the next few days, opposition to the package began to form. On 6 June, in a radio interview, Eroğlu sharply rejected the package: there could only be an overall solution to the Cyprus problem. The next day he claimed that ceding Varoşa to the UN would contradict the constitution of the "TRNC", which guarantees the territorial integrity of the country. He then claimed that the opening of Nicosia airport would only benefit the island Greeks. While airlines registered in Turkey were also allowed to land there, this could be stopped with a single bullet, whereas it would be impossible to regain Varoşa once it was handed over to the UN. If Varoşa were returned, the Greeks would next demand the return of Morfou. Otherwise, he was in favour of not making a decision until Turkey had a new prime minister.[4]

Probably in order to push Eroğlu's views through in Ankara, a six-member delegation from the "government camp", consisting of representatives of the conservative to right-wing parties of the "parliament", set off for Ankara on 7 June.[5] Before their departure, Göktuğ stated in a radio interview that the majority of the "parliament" rejected the package. She said that one should not give in to the pressure of the UN. Parliament had so decided and they would fight for it together with the motherland. The representatives of the other parties

---

1 *Turkish Press on Cyprus*, 6:2 (April - June 1993), p. 23.
2 *Turkish Press and Other Media*, Nr. 100/93 (29.-31. 5. 1993), p. 1f.
3 *Ibidem*, Nr. 104/93 (4 June 1993), p. 2.
4 *Ibidem*, Nr. 105/93 (5.-6. 6. 1993), p. 4f.
5 From the National Unity Party (NUP) these were Güner Göktuğ, Zaim Necatigil and Aydemir Erdoğan; from the Democratic Party Serdar Denktash (Rauf Denktash's son) and Kenan Akīn. The Free Democratic Party was represented by its leader Ismet Kotak.

also expressed grave concerns. Kotak suspected the UN of trying to take advantage of the fact that there was only an interim government in Turkey. After arriving in Ankara, Göktug said that the Varoşa handover was unacceptable as a confidence-building measure. It would only trigger a flood of similar demands. The President of the Turkish Parliament, Hüssamettin Cindoruk, promised that the Parliament would not accept any agreement that had not been approved by the "TRNC Parliament". A resolution to this effect would be passed.[1]

In the meantime, a letter from US Secretary of State Warren Christopher had arrived at the Turkish Foreign Ministry demanding that the proposed confidence-building measures be accepted. Ankara spoke of pressure: Washington obviously wanted the Cyprus problem to be solved and Ankara to persuade Denktash to accept.[2] Nevertheless, the Turkish Foreign Ministry reacted positively; the UN proposals were a step forward. It was clear that the Turkish Foreign Ministry still had an open ear for Washington's wishes. In contrast, Yilmaz Demirel criticised: he suspected that the President was prepared to make unilateral concessions.

On 7 June, Denktash briefed the leaders of the opposition parties Özker Özgür (Republican Turkish Party, RTP), Mustafa Akinçi (Communal Liberation Party, CLP) and Alpay Durduran (New Cyprus Party). Özgür got the impression that Denktash was not negative towards the UN proposals. He himself regarded the confidence-building measures as very positive. The population is fed up with the eternal tensions, he explained. The former mayor of Northern Nicosia, Akinçi, looked forward with warmth to the opening of Varoşa, and Durduran hoped that Denktash's meeting in Ankara would bear fruit.[3]

The RTP newspaper Yenidüzen published this party's statement on the confidence--building measures on the same day. The package was a balanced proposal. Nevertheless, in Northern Cyprus, attention was only focused on Varoşa. Efforts were being made to give the impression that Northern Cyprus was being forced to give away the Varoşa area without receiving anything in return. The discussion would have to look at the actual facts. The current proposals are based on the decisions taken by Denktash and Kyprianou in 1979. Those who play down the economic and political benefits of the package are indifferent to the problems of the Turkish Cypriots. If the package were accepted, 80-95% of the embargo would be lifted, as Denktash himself had witnessed.

Demirel had said that the Turkish Cypriot side had "an image problem". Moreover, this would harm Turkey. If the Turkish Cypriot side agreed to the package, they would be rid of the "image problem". If Turkey and the Turkish Cypriot side agreed, they could no longer be accused of wanting to maintain the situation created by the military intervention. It would also send a signal to the world that they were ready to solve the Cyprus problem through a do ut des policy. However, if the Turkish Cypriot side of the package refused, this would certainly have serious consequences.

"The officials, who have preferred to ignore the people's problems, have claimed that the Community can resist any move to intensify the embargo or increase the pressure on the Turkish Cypriot side. But nothing is gained through such resistance. The Turkish Cypriots are frustrated by the economic, political, and social problems. None of the sectors in the

1 *Turkish Press and Other Media*, Nr. 105/93, p. 6f.
2 *Ibidem*, p. 8.
3 *Ibidem*, p. 10.

Turkish Cypriot Community, including the political domain, is able to survive without Turkey's economic and political support...The Turkish Cypriots also rely on Turkey to deal with political developments. But the question of 'resistance' has now been raised. This approach also threatens Turkey's interests. It is a fact that the political structure in northern Cyprus needs Turkey's support to stand on its feet."[1]

A rejection of the package by the Northern Parliament would also increase the pressure on Turkey. The parliament itself does not represent the whole "TRNC". Akinçi's party expressed a similar view. But this did not impress Denktash in the least.

When he gave a radio interview at Tymbou airport on 8 June, accompanied by "Prime Minister" Eroğlu and "Foreign Minister" Kenan Atakol, before his departure for Ankara, he already announced that he would reject the package. He said he had been confronted in New York with a pro-Greek programme aimed only at diminishing the rights of Turkish Cypriots. The package offers nothing to Turkish Cypriots. Only those who do not know anything about Cyprus and the Greek Cypriots think it is positive. In fact, it will destroy the economy of the Turkish Cypriots. After his arrival in Ankara, Denktash said that he would reject the package and expected Turkey to support him. If he was forced to accept it, he would resign as a negotiator. The Security Council insisted on the adoption of mini-packages, but nothing would be achieved in this way. He would inform the Turkish parliament. He would not be able to move further in a direction he did not believe in. He would resign as a negotiator. But he hoped that Ankara would support the Turkish Cypriot cause.[2] He made similar comments to the English-language *Cyprus Today*. His son backed him in a statement to the semi-official Anatolia news agency, saying negotiations should be postponed until new elections in the north. Opposition politician Bulent Ecevit, during whose prime ministership the invasion had taken place in 1974, rejected a cession of Varoşa in the newspaper Milliyet and accused the government of a stab-in-the-back policy towards Denktash. Yilmaz saw the future of Cyprus in danger if Varoşa were to be ceded.

The acting Turkish Prime Minister Inönü, on the other hand, said that he would warmly welcome it if Varoşa were handed over to the UN. If an agreement is reached, the embargo will be largely lifted. Addressing his parliamentary group, he said that most of the confidence-building measures proposed by the UN had originally been proposed by the Turkish Cypriots. The measures concerning Nicosia airport had been proposed by Denktash himself.[3] President Demirel was uneasy. He had the impression that Denktash was behaving intransigently. The commentator of the Hürriyet newspaper Ertuğrul Özkök asked why Denktash had come to Ankara if he had already decided.

It was an open secret in Ankara that Denktash's behaviour divided the country's political class. Demirel, Inönü and the Foreign Ministry were in favour of accepting the package, whereas Yilmaz, Ecevit and Parliament Speaker Cindoruk sided with Denktash. According to the Hürriyet newspaper, the meeting between Denktash and Eroğlus and Demirel must have been quite heated. In a press conference Denktash claimed the opposite, but then he

1 *Ibidem*, Nr. 108/93 (11. 6. 1993), p. 7.
2 *Ibidem*, Nr. 106/93 (9. 6. 1993), pp. 1-4.
3 *Ibidem*, p. 11.

stated that pressure was being exerted on him by certain circles. But this did not bother him much, he was used to it. He would take a clear stand before the Turkish parliament.[1]

In the Turkish media, the waves were running high. Demirel also took a stand. In a statement to the *Hürriyet* newspaper, he rejected the criticism levelled against him and stated that Turkey had a problem, namely the Cyprus problem. He was of the opinion that reconciliation would be useful. If the Turkish Cypriot side could decide to accept the confidence-building measures, he would welcome such a decision. Opposition leader Yilmaz, on the other hand, said after talking to Denktash that the UN proposals did not offer any advantages to the Turkish Cypriots. The leader of the extreme right, Necmettin Erbakan, claimed that there was no such thing as a Cyprus problem. It is only about the worldwide recognition of the "TRNC" as a state.[2]

Probably to put pressure on Denktash, Inönü leaked to the newspaper Kibris a letter Denktash had written to Inönü on 29 May. In it, Denktash had described the UN proposals as acceptable. In his reply, Inönü had informed Denktash that Turkey also wanted the proposals to be accepted.[3] It was obvious that Demirel and Inönü were extremely angry about Denktash's current behaviour.

On 10 June came Denktash's big appearance before the parliament in Ankara. His speech was a masterpiece of demagogy full of half-truths and appeals to Turkish national sentiment. He claimed that in all his years as a negotiator he had never been so threatened. The Turkish Cypriot delegation had been treated like schoolboys. In New York he was given an ultimatum: Acceptance or rejection. Negotiations were out of the question. Should Boutros-Ghali's Set of Ideas be applied, Denktash said, Ankara would have to intervene again. The Cyprus problem was only unsolvable because the Greek Cypriot side would not give up its claim to sole representation. The package proposed by the UN would give one-sided advantages to the Greek side. It was clear that Denktash was speculating on the uninformedness of the MPs. When his appeals to emotion and national pride met with a positive response, he announced that he would not go to New York on 14 June, but would send "Foreign Minister" Atakol.

Faced with the enthusiasm of the MPs, the government backed down. Minister of State Orhan Killercioğlu, who was responsible for the Cyprus problem, announced that a Cyprus solution that caused difficulties for the Turkish Cypriot people could never be accepted. All governments in Turkey had understood the Cyprus problem as a national issue. Of course, the UN proposals still needed clarification. The Turkish government would never accept negotiations under pressure. A representative of the Motherland Party (Kamran Inan) said that this package was an attempt to give the Greeks what they could not win before 1974. The package was only to achieve enosis (the annexation of Cyprus to Greece). It had to be made clear to the world that they were not prepared to betray a national issue for the sake of joining the EC. There was no point in making concessions to please the West. He then called on all parties in parliament to pass a joint resolution showing the world that the Cyprus problem was a national issue and that nothing would be achieved by pressuring the Turkish nation and that no concessions would be made. Indeed, the parliament passed such a resolu-

1 *Ibidem*, Nr. 107/93 (10. 6. 1993), p. 2f.
2 *Ibidem*, pp. 4-6.
3 *Ibidem*, p. 6.

tion, which concluded that Boutros-Ghali had disregarded the basic principles observed so far in the negotiations by using pressure in the negotiations. As long as pressure is applied, the Turkish parliament sees no benefit in further negotiations.[1]

With his demagogic talent and his appeals to national pride, Denktash had won over the Turkish National Assembly. The weak interim government of Inönü had to bow to this vote. Whether Denktash had the approval of the Turkish General Staff for his course of action is unknown, but those who know Denktash's close connections to this decisive body in Turkey do not rule out approval from this side. Denktash had been the military's man since the late 1950s and after 1974 had given many top officers beautifully situated villas that had belonged to Greek Cypriots before 1974. Denktash had once again successfully blocked even the very first steps towards a solution. Boutros-Ghali noted indignantly that Denktash had even broken his promise made in New York that he would work for the acceptance of the package.[2] But had Denktash ever actually negotiated seriously in the past 19 years? For a while he was lucky that the Greek Cypriot side under Kyprianou was quite inflexible and he could therefore pose as the conciliatory one. Kliridis' willingness to compromise proved that Denktash had only ever thought of partition. In a recent statement he said very clearly what his real aim was: *"If we ensure separate Turkish Cypriot sovereignty, beyond that of a federation, then even if all Turkish Cypriots are killed, the territory will remain Turkish."*[3] In other words, Denktash wants at least Northern Cyprus to join Turkey at some point. Since a rapprochement between the north and the south would jeopardise the achievement of this goal, any pretext is justified to hinder a rapprochement. On 11 June, the Turkish foreign minister apologised in a letter to Boutros-Ghali on behalf of Demirel, saying that they had worked for an acceptance of the package.[4]

In a commentary in the Sabah newspaper of the same day, journalist Sedat Sertoğlu said that the course taken by Demirel, Inönü and Çettin had been correct. One could not call for a solution in Bosnia and Karabakh on the one hand and support a "non-solution" in Cyprus on the other. Denktash's behaviour was imposing the consequences on Turkey. Denktash shamelessly exploited the fact that there was a weak transitional government in Ankara. The Turkish Cypriots and the settlers wanted a solution to the problem. Denktash was ruining his image.[5]

On 11 June, Denktash returned to Northern Cyprus and informed Boutros-Ghali that he would not come to New York on 14 June. Instead, he would send "Foreign Minister" Atakol, who would explain the situation and ask some important questions on Denktash's behalf.[6] Boutros-Ghali informed Kliridis of Denktash's unilateral action. On 12 June, Atakol left for New York. On the same day, Boutros-Ghali issued a statement expressing regret that Denktash had broken the agreement of 1 June. He would inform the Security Council about this regrettable development. In Northern Cyprus, the opposition newspaper Yenidüzen was upset that Denktash and Eroğlu were misleading the population by telling the untruth. They were clearly in favour of a "non-solution" of the Cyprus problem, and the proposals Denk-

1 *Ibidem*, p. 4f.
2 S/26.026, p. 10.
3 Quoted from *Cyprus Weekly* (31 December 1993 - 6 January 1994), p. 13.
4 *Ibidem*.
5 *Turkish Press and Other Media*, Nr. 108/93 (11. 6. 1993), p. 11.
6 S/26.026, p. 11.

tash was now rejecting were precisely those he himself had put forward in 1984.[1] One of Sabah's commentators said that in view of Denktash's behaviour he now understood why foreign diplomats hated Denktash. Ankara was paying a lot of money for Cyprus. Denktash should use his cunning against foreigners and not against Turkey, the only place where he is considered a hero. Another said that as long as the UN could not get its way in Bosnia, no dramatic steps would be taken in Cyprus.[2]

1 *Turkish Press and Other Media*, Nr. 109/93 (12.-14. 6. 1993), p. 6.
2 *Ibidem*, p. 9.

HISTORICAL BACKGROUND OF THE CYPRUS CONFLICT

Until the summer of 1996, the Cyprus conflict was one of those forgotten, repressed conflicts in Europe that were considered insoluble. Since no shots were fired in Cyprus for years, the conflict had no news value, and the European public had become accustomed to the status quo, which was almost considered a solution; an attitude that was considered good, at least by the Turkish side. But in Greece, too, interest in the Cyprus conflict had declined sharply: In an opinion poll in 1994, 81 per cent of Greeks considered the Macedonian problem, 38 per cent the population decline, 37 per cent the shadow economy and only 30 per cent the Cyprus conflict an important problem. This changed abruptly in mid-August 1996 when two young Greek Cypriots were killed in connection with demonstrations in the UN-controlled buffer zone. The background to the events is of a complicated nature and goes far back in history.

The older generation of Greek Cypriots, especially the politicians, keep talking about the fact that there will and must be a solution in Cyprus, but one can get the impression that many have resigned themselves to the status quo. The country is prospering economically and there are hardly any risks involved in the course taken. A part of the younger generation is increasingly frustrated by this policy of non-solution. A rally of 200 motorcyclists from Berlin across Europe to Cyprus wanted to draw attention in their own way to the fact that the human right of free movement does not apply in Cyprus. This was to be documented by a demonstration at the demarcation line, in which other young Cypriots would also participate. Since a peaceful demonstration at the demarcation line would not be newsworthy, the organisers decided to do something similar to what the "Women Walk Home" movement did a few years ago: They would enter the UN-controlled buffer zone in order to provoke media reactions from the other side. The Cypriot government and the UN would try to prevent the incursion into the buffer zone, as in the past, but this would be impossible given the length of the demarcation line. The intrusion into the buffer zone would provoke the Turkish side and there would be some incidents, but as in the past, they would end relatively harmlessly, but would provide media-rich images and draw the world's attention back to Cyprus.

The organisers did not realise that the Turkish side had learned from the past and was steering a harder course. Whereas the clashes with the women had been organised by Denktash supporters and had been limited to scuffles, this time the new Turkish Foreign Minister, Tansu Çiller, ensured that a large number of Grey Wolves activists were transported to northern Cyprus, as she was accused of doing in the Turkish parliament.[1] When the motorcyclists arrived in Cyprus, the planned demonstration at the demarcation line in Nicosia was called off at the behest of the Cypriot government. This prompted other like-minded demonstrators to carry out the plan elsewhere. The protesters entered the buffer zone near Derynia in eastern Cyprus, where the unarmed demonstrators were met by Grey Wolves thugs. These had not come to scuffle, but proceeded tactically as a cohesive unit, beating to kill. A 24-year-old Greek Cypriot was beaten to death like a mad dog in front of the lenses of international media representatives. According to UN representatives who had witnessed the riot themselves, even the Turkish Cypriot police took part in the action.[2] The purpose of the ac-

1 Gerd Höhler, "Wer bezahlte die Grauen Wölfe auf Zypern?", *Frankfurter Rundschau* (29. August 1996).
2 *The Cyprus Weekly* (30 August 1996), p. 5.

tion was clear: to prove to the world public once again that Greek and Turkish Cypriots cannot live together peacefully.

The international reaction prompted the Turkish side to take the Grey Wolves thugs out of circulation. When clashes broke out again in the buffer zone two days later after the funeral of the first victim, it was the Turkish army that intervened. The UN report on the incidents later stated that Turkish or Turkish Cypriot troops had used force completely unjustifiably. When a young Cypriot in exuberance tried to take a Turkish flag from a pole, he was literally executed. One of the perpetrators, a Turkish settler, was shortly afterwards appointed "Minister of Agriculture" of the "TRNC". The other perpetrator, also a settler, was the commander of a special unit of the Turkish Cypriot police. Both are now wanted by Interpol. The soldiers then fired indiscriminately into the unarmed crowd. Two British UN soldiers were lightly wounded and one Cypriot woman was seriously injured; it was a miracle that more people were not injured or killed in the wild shootout.[1] The deployment of the Grey Wolves thugs in Cyprus means that the conflict in Cyprus has taken on a new quality. Now the terrorism that has long been prevalent in Turkish politics has also been brought to Cyprus. Commenting on the excessive overreaction of Turkish soldiers against a hotheaded young man who wanted to take down the Turkish flag, the Turkish Foreign Minister said that Turkey would not hesitate to smash the hands of those who dare to touch the Turkish flag.[2] This is exactly the tone that provokes wars. Denktash noted that events had proved that Greek and Turkish Cypriots could not live together

The murderous events of August 1996 suddenly brought Cyprus back to the forefront of international public interest. But it became clear that many media commentators were hardly familiar with the facts. In Britain, most of the press took an anti-Greek position, and many newspapers expressed the opinion that Greek and Turkish Cypriots could not live together. In many letters to the editor, also in the German press, it became clear that the PR work on the Turkish side, which had been quite efficient for years, had not failed to have an effect, because the arguments put forward were often full of half-truths, which, as we know, are worse than untruths. In view of this situation, it seems useful to take a look at the origins and development of the conflict.[3]

The British Colonial Period 1878 - 1959

"Whoever wishes to become and remain a great power in the Middle East must have Cyprus under his control," wrote the British historian Sir John Hill in his History of Cyprus. Indeed, Cyprus controlled the Anatolian peninsula, the Middle East and parts of North Africa because of its geostrategic position. This fact caused Cyprus to experience one invasion and foreign domination after another for the past three and a half thousand years. Cyprus became the bone of contention of the respective regional powers.

1 *The Cyprus Weekly* (23 August 1996).

2 *Rheinische Post* (17. August 1996).

3 At the same time, the following preliminary remark seems necessary: The text will always refer to the north or south of Cyprus or to northern and southern Nicosia. This is primarily for stylistic reasons, because the constant reference to the "occupied territory" seems somewhat formulaic, even if it is the correct description of the state of Northern Cyprus under international law. The terms south and north are understood as geographical indications.

In the second half of the 16th century, the Ottomans seized Cyprus from the Venetians. Cyprus remained under Turkish rule until the Congress of Berlin in 1878, i.e. for about 300 years. During this time, Turkish immigrants came to Cyprus and settled there. While earlier immigrants had been assimilated by the majority, in this case there was only ethnic coexistence, as Muslim Turks and Orthodox Greeks as well as other minorities did not mix. However, the two ethnic groups lived peacefully side by side. Although they adhered to different religions, they celebrated their respective religious festivals together. Both ethnic groups led a rural life and had the same worries when the rain failed to come. For about 300 years, Greek and Turkish Cypriots proved that they had enough tolerance to live together peacefully. The Greek liberation struggle from 1821 to 1830 did little to change this, for it was only registered by the Greek upper class. They showed sympathy, but the spark of the Greek uprising did not spread to Cyprus.

In 1878, Cyprus became a kind of British protectorate. In 1914, Great Britain annexed the island. In the Lausanne Peace Treaty at the end of the Greek-Turkish War of 1919 to 1922, Ankara recognised the British annexation and formally renounced Cyprus. Cyprus became a crown colony in 1925.

Two aspects of British colonial policy need to be highlighted in our context. The colonial authority built up a rather efficient administration with modern structures on Cyprus, which enabled Cyprus to successfully govern itself when it finally became independent. Special British measures allowed the clientelistic structures from the Ottoman period, which were also present in Cyprus in rudimentary form, to stagnate and wither away, giving rise to political structures that were far more European than those of the two mother countries. This created the preconditions for the emergence of a separate political culture. If the balance of British colonial policy in the administrative sector was positive overall, British cultural policy had an ambivalent character. On the one hand, it ensured the literacy of the population, but on the other hand, it divided both ethnic groups. This was because the teachers came from the mother countries or were trained there and brought curricula, values and – enemy images – from there, i.e. the nationalisms of the mother countries were brought to Cyprus via the schools. School socialisation reinforced the tendency of parallel identities. Until the early 1950s, however, the formation of different identities did not yet lead to conflicts. Nevertheless, it was clear that this type of education system had interrupted the emergence of a Cypriot identity and created starting points for a policy of divide et impera.

Since the turn of the century, the desire for union (enosis) with Greece has been growing among the Greek Cypriots. It was hoped that London, in an act of magnanimity – similar to the case of the Ionian Islands in 1864 – would cede Cyprus to the mother country.[1] But London believed it could not give up Cyprus for military reasons (securing the Life Line through the Mediterranean). In 1931, the Enosis desire became visible for the first time when there were major riots. The colonial power suppressed these and ruled the island dictatorially until the outbreak of the Second World War. Athens showed extreme restraint towards the Greek Cypriot desire for Enosis, as it did not want to anger the British protecting power. The Second World War then once again demonstrated the overriding strategic importance of Cyprus as an unsinkable aircraft carrier. This importance increased even more

1 Michael Pratt, *Britain's Greek Empire* (London: Rex Collings, 1978).

after the outbreak of the Cold War and the founding of NATO. From this logic, it was clear to London that Cyprus had to remain British.

The Fight for Independence 1955 - 1959

In 1950, the Orthodox Church of Cyprus made a push by organising an unofficial plebiscite on Enosis. Although the overwhelming majority of Greek Cypriots voted for union, London took no notice of the vote. The newly elected Archbishop of Cyprus Makarios III, however, was not satisfied with this and forced the Athens government under Prime Minister Papagos to act by threatening to take the Cyprus case to the UN. Papagos initially tried to settle the problem bilaterally with the Eden government (Enosis in exchange for bases), but the British prime minister haughtily rejected the Athenian offers. When Papagos indicated that he intended to take the Cyprus question to the UN, Eden countered by stating that Cyprus was also a matter for Turkey.[1] It was quite obvious that London was trying to neutralise Greek ambitions with Turkish ones, that is, to play the mother countries off against each other. Ankara reacted immediately to the British offer: if there was any change in the status of Cyprus, the Lausanne Peace Treaty would be null and void.[2] The British tactical manoeuvre thus made Ankara a player in the poker game over Cyprus. But London not only pursued its divide et impera policy vis-à-vis Athens and Ankara, but also began to play the ethnic groups on Cyprus off against each other.

In 1955, the struggle of the Greek Cypriot underground organisation EOKA began under the former Greek officer G. Grivas, who was born in Cyprus; the political leader of EOKA was Makarios. The Turkish Cypriots had always followed the Enosis efforts with suspicion, because they were worried that the union with Greece could lead to discrimination. They wanted to maintain the status quo and therefore turned more to the British. This gave the British the opportunity to play off island Greeks against island Turks in two ways. In order to save British forces, a special police unit was set up to fight the EOKA, which was almost entirely recruited from Turkish Cypriots. The deployment of this unit inevitably led to the first confrontation with the EOKA. With British acquiescence, the Turkish General Staff also built up an armed underground organisation (initially VOLKAN, later TMT). The military leader was always a Turkish officer; the political leader was Rauf Denktash, who has since been the representative of the Turkish military in Cyprus. The political aims of the Turkish side changed during the conflict; in the beginning, they had propagated the maintenance of the status quo, but now, with Ankara's approval, they demanded the division of the island, Taksim in Turkish.

The first clashes between the TMT and the EOKA took place in 1958. At the same time, both organisations sought to destroy functioning models of cooperation between the two ethnic groups. Thus TMT supporters murdered two Turkish Cypriot leaders of the left trade unions and terrorised members of the left trade union federation. An attack on the press office of the Turkish consulate in Nicosia, orchestrated by Ankara itself, served as the occasion for the start of unrest. The unrest quickly escalated to such an extent that one can speak

---

1 Anthony Eden, *Full Circle* (London: Cassell, 1960), p. 315.
2 Ludwig Dischler, *Die Zypernfrage* (Frankfurt: Metzner, 1960), p. 31.

of civil war-like conditions.[1] At the same time, a struggle against "deviants" began within the ethnic groups.

The playing off of the mother countries triggered the Greek-Turkish minority conflict in 1956, of which the Istanbul Greeks became the victims. While Istanbul's Greeks numbered over 100,000 at the time of the outbreak of the conflict, the state-directed riots caused a mass exodus. Today, at the end of this, Istanbul is home to just over 2,000 Greeks.[2] In 1956, something came into being that could be characterised as a system of communicating tubes: Whenever unrest broke out in Cyprus, repressive measures were taken against the Greeks of Istanbul and the islands of Imbros and Tenedos, where no Greeks live today. The British colonial policy of divide et impera thus ultimately gave birth to those other two conflicts that still plague the region today.

The failed Suez adventure of the British in 1956 caused the strategic value of Cyprus to shrink. The change in prime minister from Eden to Macmillan made British policy more agile. Added to this was American pressure – Washington saw NATO's south-eastern flank threatened by the constant squabbling between NATO allies Greece and Turkey. This and the high costs of military operations caused London to relent. It was realised that military bases would be sufficient for the presence in the eastern Mediterranean. In 1959, Greeks and Turks were persuaded to sit down at the Round Table in Zurich and negotiate a solution, which was subsequently imposed on the Cypriots.

The solution found in Zurich and a little later in London was a sham. It served mainly to settle the conflict between NATO allies and NATO interests. The British could continue to maintain a presence through their bases. Athens and Ankara, together with London, became guarantor powers of the newly independent state of Cyprus. They were allowed to maintain troop contingents on the island. De facto, Cyprus was thus an indirect member of NATO. However, the Zurich and London agreements had some serious flaws. The Cypriots had not participated in the negotiations; they were confronted with the results. There had been a failure to resolve the intra-Cypriot conflicts. In fact, the situation had been aggravated. If unrest broke out again, the Greek and Turkish troop contingents stationed on the ground would immediately be drawn into it. Any ethnic conflict on Cyprus now threatened an immediate clash between the mother countries.

The deepening of the conflict 1960 - 1964

The Republic of Cyprus, proclaimed in 1960, suffered from a similar flaw as the Republic of Weimar: the leadership of the ethnic groups and a large part of the population rejected the new state. Makarios still wanted union with Greece (Enosis) and the leader of the Turkish ethnic group, Küçük, wanted partition (Taksim). Both sides therefore inwardly refused genuine cooperation and headed for confrontation. The highly complicated constitution, which was worked out after great efforts, was not workable because it lacked the decisive prerequisite, the good neighbourly understanding of the ethnic groups.

The unwillingness of both sides to compromise was already evident in 1963, when Makarios wanted to push through certain constitutional amendments. The way in which Maka-

---

1 Niels Kadritzke & Wolf Wagner, *Im Fadenkreuz der Nato. Ermittlungen am Beispiel Cypern* (Berlin: Rotbuch Verlag, 1976), p. 29.

2 Today less than 1.000.

rios tried to push through these 13 amendments, which included as a decisive point the abolition of the absolute veto right of the Turkish vice-president, without offering compensation to the other side, was a major political mistake. However, to call this proposal a breach of the constitution or a denunciation of the state community, as is repeatedly heard from the Turkish side,[1] is completely exaggerated and only serves as an ex post argument to justify one's own intransigent attitude. The opinion that the constitution should be revised was also held by various British bodies, only they would probably have sought a different, more diplomatic way to enforce it. Makarios' move was a fatal political blunder, for it plunged Cyprus into a serious state crisis.

Ankara brusquely rejected Makarios' proposals for revision, thus setting the course for the Turkish Cypriot leadership around Küçük, although the latter had probably wanted to react in a more conciliatory manner. This led to an escalation process of provocations and counter-provocations in which extremists on both sides did their best to fuel the conflict. Plans were made in extremist circles on both sides to destroy the other. Kliridis confirmed in his memoirs that there was the so-called Akritas plan on the Greek side, but he also published the Turkish Cypriot counterpart.[2] The riots escalated rapidly and took on such proportions[3] that they must be characterised as an internal Cypriot civil war. The bloody confrontation gave new impetus to the idea of partition. In the beginning, the Turkish Cypriots spontaneously left the mixed settlements out of fear of attacks by the Greek extremists. But soon this exodus became a systematic policy by the leadership of the Turkish ethnic group. Hesitant people were taught by the TMT what the right way was by the appropriate means. In retrospect, it is clear that a political course was being steered here that aimed at the partition of the island in the longer term. The politically unwise reaction of the Greek Cypriot leadership exacerbated the tendency towards partition by placing blockade rings around the Turkish Cypriot enclaves and cutting off the inhabitants from many vital resources. About half of the island's Turks lived in these enclaves, and of these, about half were refugees. During the riots, various terrorist groups acted on the Greek side, some of which had emerged from the old EOKA. Among these, the terrorist group of Nikos Sampson was particularly notorious, who acquired the dubious reputation of a particularly evil Turk killer during this period.

The events of 1963 were a taboo subject on the Greek side for many years. In the meantime, a process of rethinking has begun on the Greek side. A former senior EOKA leader spoke of blindness at the time.[4] For many Turkish Cypriots, the attacks of that time are traumatic experiences. Based on their experiences in 1963, some Turkish Cypriots assert that living together with their Greek compatriots is out of the question. Denktash uses his experiences of that time as the main justification for his constant refusals to agree to a solution

1 The last time on 9 April 1997 by Denktasch in the FAZ.

2 No data for format specified. Glafkos Clirides, *My Deposition*, I, (Nicosia: Alithia, 1989), pp. 206ff.

3 Patrick estimates that between December 1963 and August 1964, about 350 Turkish Cypriots and about 200 Greek Cypriots were killed; R. Patrick, *Political Geography and the Cyprus Conflict: 1963-1971* (Waterloo, 1976); Faustmann assumes at least 191 Turkish and 133 Greek dead. Hubert Faustmann, "Menschenrechtsverletzung auf Zypern seit der Unabhängigkeit", in: Franz Josef Hutter/Heidrun Speer/Carsten Tessmer (Hg.), *Das "gemeinsame Haus Europa". Menschenrechte zwischen Atlantik und Ural* (Arbeitstitel). (Baden-Baden: Nomos Verlag, 1998).

4 In a conversation with the author.

based on a return to the status quo ante. It may be that Denktash cannot overcome the deep-seated fear, but at the same time the existence of this fear gives an indication of an important aspect for any solution: it must take into account the fear syndromes of both Cypriot communities, because the Greek Cypriots have also been suffering from them since the Turkish invasion in 1974. This can be done, for example, through a policy of confidence--building measures and through a total demilitarisation of the island.[1]

The years 1963-64 became decisive for the development of the Cyprus problem. The inner-Cypriot confrontation spilled over to the mother countries. In Istanbul, riots again broke out against the Greek minority. When a direct Greek-Turkish clash threatened in December 1963, US President Johnson, who had long been annoyed by the destabilisation of NATO's south-eastern flank, intervened directly and prevented the outbreak of war between Greece and Turkey. A little later, Washington, in coordination with London, proposed the deployment of a peacekeeping force of NATO troops. The size of the proposed contingent made it clear that the aim was to occupy the island permanently.[2] Makarios knew that a NATO presence would also have brought militant anti-communism to the island. This could have led to a ban on the communist party, just as in Greece, and it was this party that Makarios had been relying on for some time. He therefore refused the offer and turned to the Soviets. Khrushchev, for whom a NATO-affiliated Cyprus would have been a thorn in the flesh, readily intervened. The result was the deployment of a UN peacekeeping force, the UNFICYP, which has been stationed on the island ever since.

Before the UNFICYP troops arrived in larger numbers, the crisis in Cyprus escalated again. At the end of May 1964, President Inönü ordered a military invasion of Cyprus for the beginning of June. Only through massive pressure in the form of a threatening letter was Johnson able to avert the invasion at the last moment. The harsh tone of this letter had far-reaching consequences.[3] Inönü was so angered that he set Turkish foreign policy on a course of greater independence from Washington. From now on, Turkey, a NATO ally, was only conditionally loyal, a fact that was not fully understood either in the US or in Europe. The extent of the alienation process is shown by the fact that Ankara began a kind of flirtation with Moscow. The new friendship had - during the Cold War - incredible consequences. Ankara interpreted the 1936 Montreux Straits Agreement in such an extremely liberal way that it allowed the Soviets to bring a fleet into the Mediterranean, where it caused NATO strategists headaches for years as the so-called Eskadra.[4]

---

1 In recent discussions in Germany, the Turkish side has repeatedly made the claim that a holocaust was organised by the Greek side on Cyprus in 1963-64 against the Turkish Cypriots. On the one hand, this is completely exaggerated - as the figures mentioned above show - but on the other hand, this allegation is part of a rather interesting tactic: one is aware of the German sensitivity on the question of the violation of human rights, especially of minorities, and tries to instrumentalise this by presenting the Turkish victims of the riots of that time as the sole victims to the mostly poorly informed audience. They conceal the fact that they were victims of a civil war, i.e. that there were also Greek victims.

2 Vangelis Koufoudakis, "I Kypros kai i yperdynameis 1960 - 1979", in: G. Tenekidis & G. Kranidiotis, *Kypros. Istoria, provlimata kai agones tou laou tis* (Athen, 1981), p. 110f.

3 Public Information Office, *Cyprus: The Problem in Perspective* (Nicosia, 1969); Jacob M. Landau, "Johnson's 1964 Letter to Inönü and Greek Lobbying of the White House", (Jerusalem: The Leonard Davis Institute for International Relations, 1979) = Jerusalem Papers on Peace Problems.

4 Heinz A. Richter, *Der griechisch-türkische Konflikt und die Haltung der Sowjetunion* (Köln: Bundesinstitut für ostwissenschaftliche und internationale Studien, Nr. 8, 1987).

The trouble with Makarios prompted the Americans, in close cooperation with the British, to develop various plans for the solution of the Cyprus problem, all of which had one thing in common: The state existence of Cyprus was to be eliminated. Cyprus was to be annexed to Greece and the Turks were to receive territorial compensation from Greece. In a later version, which bore the name of the former US Secretary of State Acheson, even the division of Cyprus and the union of the respective parts with the mother countries (double enosis) was considered. Ankara agreed in principle, but the then Greek Prime Minister Georgios Papandreou had qualms about imposing such a solution on Cyprus, which displeased Washington and had far-reaching consequences for Greek domestic policy.[1]

Although Ankara had renounced the invasion, it allowed the Turkish air force to intervene in the renewed flare-up of fighting at Kokkina. When the Soviet Union intervened and urged restraint, Athens reacted quite hysterically, as recently published British files show: In talks with Americans and British, the concept was developed that went down in history as "enosis by coup". Greece was to organise a coup d'état in Cyprus and remove Makarios. Afterwards, the annexation of Cyprus to Greece was to be proclaimed immediately. The Americans and the British were to take on the task of preventing Ankara from reacting hastily. As soon as the situation had calmed down, Athens would come to an agreement with Ankara on compensation. Although this plan was not carried out in 1964 for various reasons, it was the blueprint that the Greek military tried to implement in 1974 under completely different foreign policy circumstances.[2]

The 1974 invasion

There is little doubt that G. Papandreou's vacillating policy on the Cyprus question was one reason why the Americans turned against him. This ultimately facilitated the coup of the military junta on 21 April 1967. The establishment of the dictatorship in Greece had two weighty consequences for Cyprus. First, the foreign policy dilettantism of the military weakened Greece's diplomatic position and its military presence in Cyprus. Secondly, a process of alienation began between Athens and Nicosia: the idea that the island's annexation to Greece would import dictatorship led to a strong cooling of the desire for enosis among many Cypriots. Makarios took this into account by strengthening his policy of non-alignment of Cyprus. Cyprus began to develop into an independent republic. This policy was certainly right for Cyprus, but Makarios nevertheless made a capital mistake by not normalising relations with the Turkish Cypriots and, for example, abandoning the blockade policy.

Makarios' policy of non-alignment provoked the Athens military junta and the Americans. The military realised that this policy made Enosis a distant prospect and removed Nicosia from the control of the Athens "national centre". To stop Makarios, the junta gave orders to undermine his position. Grivas supporters of the most radical kind provoked the Turkish Cypriots and made several plots against Makarios. Their aim was the overthrow of Makarios, even by assassination. The Americans had long been annoyed by Makarios' course of non-alignment. When the Communist Party of Cyprus (AKEL) made massive electoral gains in the 1970 Cypriot parliamentary elections, there were irrational reactions in Washington. Cyprus was compared to Cuba and Makarios was described as a Castro in a

1 Andreas Papandreou, *Democracy at Gunpoint: The Greek Front* (New York: Doubleday, 1979), p. 137.
2 Heinz A. Richter, "Zypern: Das Krisenjahr 1964", *THETIS* 2 (1995), pp. 281-94.

priest's robe. The secret services of Greece and the USA began to coordinate their efforts to overthrow Makarios.[1]

The Yom Kippur War of October 1973 once again made the strategic importance of Cyprus abundantly clear. One month later, the annual Mediterranean Seminar organised by the USA took place in Rome. On the fringes of this seminar, US Secretary of State Cyrus Vance is said to have indirectly given Ankara the green light to intervene in Cyprus if there were to be renewed unrest there. Around the same time, the students of the Athens Polytechnic revolted, dictator Papadopoulos fell and the head of the military police Ioannidis became the new dictator of Greece. The student uprising had shown that the days of the junta were counted. In order to consolidate his position, Ioannidis urgently needed a success, which he believed he could achieve in the field of Cyprus policy. He decided to carry out the "Enosis by Coup" plan of 1964.

Ioannidis' mad scheme was facilitated and made possible by several factors. Grivas died in February 1974. Grivas was a hardliner who never shied away from the use of violence, but at the same time he had a certain rationality. If he had not died, he would certainly have stopped the development that now followed, which was becoming more and more irrational. The Athens secret service received the order from Ioannidis to prepare the coup d'état against Makarios, and the terrorist group, the so-called EOKA B, which had still been set up by Grivas during the dictatorship, increased its activity. On 15 July, the coup began with a failed assassination attempt on Makarios. With this, the coup had actually already failed, but the coup plotters continued. As they could not find a presentable collaborator, they appointed Nikos Sampson, notorious as a Turk-killer, as president. This was bound to provoke the Turkish side to the utmost, but the excitement about Sampson was, on closer examination, only a convenient pretext. It can be assumed that the invasion would have been carried out even with a different politician; after all, it had been prepared long in advance.

Ankara proceeded with the greatest caution. Prime Minister Ecevit knew that US President Nixon was practically unable to act because of the Watergate scandal and that Secretary of State Kissinger had no objection to the elimination of a trouble spot. In order not to get into trouble with the British, Ecevit informed London, where he was told that they had nothing against unilateral action. In the meantime, the Turkish landing preparations had also been registered by the Soviets via satellite.[2] But they too did not seem to object to the imminent invasion, for they did nothing to stop Ankara. On 20 July, Turkish forces landed at Kyrencia. A bridgehead was formed and this was expanded in the following days. On 23 July, the military junta fell in Athens. One day later, Karamanlis returned to Greece and took over as Prime Minister. In order to be able to dispose of the Greek armed forces in the event of a possible war with Turkey, Greece withdrew from the military part of NATO on that day. This was a serious mistake because, as can be read in the memoirs of the Dutch ambassador Barkmann, NATO was ready to intervene in a mediatory way. On 25 July, negotiations between the parties began in Geneva. These negotiations were also necessary for the Turkish military, because Turkish military logistics had not been able to meet military requirements.

---

1 Kadritzke, *op. cit.*, p. 66f; Christopher Hitchens, *Cyprus* (London: Quartet Books, 1984), p. 70f.

2 Martin Lagasse, "Die militärische Intervention der Türkei im Rahmen der Zypernkrise im Sommer 1974", Magisterarbeit (Mannheim, 1996).

There are voices that consider this first phase of unilateral military intervention by means of an invasion by Turkish forces to be justified by the right of intervention to restore the status quo ante, since the other guarantor power was not prepared to fulfil its obligations; even Makarios saw it that way at the time. Indeed, one can debate whether the invasion was justified. Had Ecevit been content with restoring the status quo ante, he would have shown himself to be a great statesman. Through moderation, he would have brought his country closer to Europe; instead, he piled up obstacles on Turkey's path to Europe. Instead, however, he and the military in Ankara could not resist the temptation and on 14 August ordered the invasion to continue. By 16 August, the Turkish army occupied a third of the island. It deliberately advanced slowly in order to give the Greek Cypriots the opportunity to flee. Where they did not leave voluntarily, force was used. There were mass executions of hundreds of civilians and prisoners of war, rapes and maltreatment. The figures for Greek and Greek Cypriot deaths vary between 2,000 and 4,000. In total, just over 170,000 Greek Cypriots were expelled. The expulsion by the Turkish army in the north of the island also provoked violent reactions in the south of the island. Bloody riots broke out in the cities, causing many Turkish Cypriots to flee to the British bases. In the countryside, many Turkish Cypriots left their homes on the advice of compatriots and headed north. Many were lured north by promises that they would be compensated by Greek property. It should be noted in this context that there was no official expulsion policy in the south of the island; rather, the fear of Greek terror and the Turkish call to flee to the north played together. The motives for the population movement are therefore not the same. The British, who were not unwelcome to this development, willingly supported the population exchange. In the end, the island was divided and the ethnic reorganisation of the land was completed.

When the balance was taken after some time, it turned out that just over 1,600 Greek Cypriots were missing. Their relatives learned that they had fallen alive into the hands of the Turkish forces. For the next 23 years, the families of the disappeared tried in vain to find out about their whereabouts. Ankara allegedly knew nothing. In the spring of 1996, Rauf Denktash revealed half the truth in an interview: in 1974, the Turkish army had handed over the prisoners who were hindering the advance to Turkish Cypriot paramilitary units, and these had killed the prisoners. However, this claim is probably not correct, because there were still signs of life from many of the missing prisoners some time later; Denktash was obviously trying to exculpate Ankara.[1]

---

1 Faustmann, *op. cit.*: *"Seit den Wochen der Invasion von 1974 werden auf griechisch-zypriotischer Seite offiziell 1.619 Menschen vermißt (992 Soldaten und 627 Zivilisten, darunter 116 Frauen sowie 27 Kinder unter 16 Jahren). Nachweislich haben sich viele der Verschwundenen in türkischem Gewahrsam und einige auch auf dem türkischen Festland befunden. Die türkische Seite behauptet, daß es sich in vielen Fällen um Tote aus den innergriechischen Auseinandersetzungen während des Coups gegen Makarios handele. Dem widersprechen die Inselgriechen, stehen dabei aber vor dem Dilemma, daß die Ereignisse während des Coups aus innenpolitischen Gründen bis heute tabuisiert werden und daher keine verläßlichen Angaben über die Zahl und Identität der Opfer existieren. Die wenigen Angaben schwanken zwischen 400 und 600 Toten und 30 bis 40 Vermißten. Die griechische Seite besteht aber darauf, daß diese Opfer nicht bei den Angaben über die Toten und Vermißten der Invasion mit eingerechnet worden seien. Die türkische Seite verweist ihrerseits auf die türkisch-zypriotischen Opfer, die es bei Racheakten und Massakern von griechischen Zyprioten während der Invasion gegeben hat. Nach inseltürkischen Angaben starben 286 türkische Zyprioten, 560 weitere werden vermißt.*
1981 wurde von beiden Volksgruppen mit Unterstützung der Vereinten Nationen eine Kommission für Vermisste Personen aus den Jahren 1963-1974 eingerichtet. Für den Zeitraum der türkischen Invasion wurden von

My former doctoral student Hubert Fausmann and now history professor in Nikosia wrote on this topic: *"Since the weeks of the 1974 invasion, 1,619 people have officially gone missing on the Greek Cypriot side (992 soldiers and 627 civilians, including 116 women and 27 children under 16). Evidence shows that many of the disappeared were in Turkish custody and some were also on the Turkish mainland. The Turkish side claims that in many cases the dead are from the internal Greek conflicts during the coup against Makarios. The island Greeks contradict this, but are faced with the dilemma that the events during the coup have been tabooed to this day for domestic political reasons and therefore no reliable information exists about the number and identity of the victims. The few figures vary between 400 and 600 dead and 30 to 40 missing. The Greek side, however, insists that these victims were not included in the figures on the dead and missing from the invasion. The Turkish side, for its part, refers to the Turkish Cypriot victims who died in acts of revenge and massacres of Greek Cypriots during the invasion. According to island Turkish sources, 286 Turkish Cypriots died and 560 others are missing.*

In 1981, a Commission on Missing Persons from 1963-1974 was established by both communities with the support of the United Nations. For the period of the Turkish invasion, the files of 1,493 persons were submitted by the island Greek side, a figure closer to the true number of people abducted and probably murdered by Turks than the inflated 1,619. In October 1996, the President of the Republic of Cyprus Glafkos Clerides was quoted as saying that, based on the latest research, the fate of 96 missing persons who had died in combat could be determined. For their part, the Turkish Cypriots, who also exaggerate the figures and speak of 560 missing Turkish Cypriots during the invasion, handed over to the Commission the names of 272 people who have disappeared since 1974.

If the figures of the Commission on Missing Persons are taken as a basis, 1,534 Greek Cypriots and 500 Turkish Cypriots disappeared between 1963 and 1974 in the course of the disputes between the two ethnic groups, without either side having made more than fruitless token efforts to clarify their fate since then."

When the second phase of the invasion began, the British were prepared to place their troops stationed in Cyprus under UNFICYP in order to stop the advancing Turkish forces. London informed Kissinger of this, but he rejected the British proposal: The Cyprus problem should be eliminated.[1] Nothing, not even legal quibbles, could justify the second phase

inselgriechischer Seite die Akten von 1. 493 Personen eingereicht, eine Zahl, die der wahren Anzahl der von Türken verschleppten und wohl ermordeten Menschen näher kommt, als die überhöhten 1.619. Im Oktober 1996 wurde der Präsident der Republik Zypern Glafkos Clerides mit den Worten zitiert, dass aufgrund juengster Nachforschungen das Schicksal von 96 vermissten Personen ermittelt werden konnte, die im Kampfeinsatz umgekommen seien. Die türkischen Zyperioten, die ebenfalls überhöhte Angaben machen und von 560 vermißten türkischen Zyprioten während der Invasion sprechen, übergaben ihrerseits der Kommission die Namen von 272 Menschen, die seit 1974 verschwunden sind.

Legt man die Zahlen der Vermisstenkommission zugrunde, so sind zwischen 1963 bis 1974 im Rahmen der Auseinandersetzungen zwischen beiden Volksgruppen 1.534 griechische Zyprioten und 500 türkische Zyprioten verschwunden, ohne daß beide Seiten seither mehr als fruchtlose Alibianstrengungen unternommen haetten, ihr Schicksal zu klären.

1 C. D. Barkman, *Ambassadeur in Athene. 1969 - 1975 van Dictatuur tot Demokratie* (Gravenhage, 1984), p. 160f. The negative role of the USA in the two crises of 1963 and 1974 led the American special emissary Richard Holbrooke to say in 1997 that things had happened in those years for which one should be ashamed. *Athener Zeitung* 195 (14. November 1997), p. 4.

of the Turkish invasion, since the causes that had led to the first phase had been removed: the military dictatorship in Greece had collapsed, a democratic government had been installed, and in Cyprus the coup had collapsed; the second phase was an act of violent expansion.

Summarising the essential results of this first part of the explanations, one must conclude the following: The Cyprus conflict arose as a conflict provoked by the colonial power Great Britain. The Cold War and its main actors, the Soviets and the Americans, intensified it. The irredentist aspirations of Athenian nationalist politicians fuelled it, and the expansionist aspirations of Ankara and the Greek junta brought it to a negative climax. Extremist Cypriots in both ethnic groups got involved and plunged their country into disaster. International organisations proved too weak to stop the conflict. One-sided apportionment of blame is out of place. The causes of the disaster are more complex. The victims were the ordinary people of both ethnic groups who lived peacefully together.

Elements of a solution

Cyprus has been a divided and one-third occupied country since 1974. For 23 years, international institutions and individual states have been trying to find a solution. It would go far beyond the scope of this essay to attempt to trace these efforts, even sketchily. Nevertheless, an attempt will be made to highlight some aspects relevant to the solution of the Cyprus problem.

The solutions to the most important problems have actually been found since long ago, only the political will to implement them in real politics is primarily lacking on the Turkish side. The problem of the form of government was already negotiated in 1977 in the High Level Agreement between Makarios and Denktash: Cyprus was to be a bi-communal and bi-zonal federation. There were to be cantons with different ethnic focuses. For a transitional period, the three freedoms of movement, property and settlement would be restricted. Had there been the political will to find a solution, the Cyprus problem could have been brought to a resolution on this basis. Instead, Denktash first proclaimed a Turkish constituent state of Cyprus and, in 1983, in an act of secession contrary to international law, proclaimed the "Turkish Republic of Northern Cyprus", which to this day is only recognised as a state by Turkey.

According to official statements from Ankara and Northern Nicosia, the medium-term foreign policy aim is to obtain recognition. Although Denktash uses the term "federation", on closer examination it is not difficult to see that he understands it to mean a loose confederation. The South strives for a federal solution with a strong central government, the North wants to keep the future central government as weak as possible. A return to an improved status quo ante seems impossible. The dozens of solutions proposed by the UN, the Council of Europe, the EU, etc., all of which contain the elements of a solution already mentioned, are of no interest to Ankara and the north of the island due to a lack of political will, as UN Secretary General Butros Ghali noted in 1996.

Another central problem is overcoming the deep mistrust on both sides. The negotiations of the last 23 years clearly show that all frameworks, global solutions and confidence-building measures fail because of the lack of trust on both sides. However, recently one occasionally gets the impression that the alleged mistrust is only pretended. The negotiations on the Varoşa-Nicosia International Air Port deal broke down over such a ridiculous detail that one may reasonably doubt whether a step towards a solution is even desired by Denktash.[1] In order to reduce mutual fear, the South proposed on several occasions the total demilitarisation of the island.[2] The North rejected this on the grounds that it would mean a return to the insecure conditions of 1963. The consequence was that the South, in order to protect itself from the strong Turkish military presence, began to arm itself with - primarily defensive - weapons.[3] The north then also modernised its weapons systems. Today, Cyprus is a weapons-rigid place; according to the UN, Northern Cyprus is the most militarised area in the world.[4] It would go without saying that potential Western arms suppliers should exercise restraint in view of the tensions. The USA has done this, for example, by observing a ratio of 7:10 for arms aid to Greece and Turkey since a decision by the US Senate. The Federal Republic has not imposed this self-restraint on itself in the past.

Demilitarisation of the island in no way means the creation of an insecure situation, as is repeatedly argued by the Turkish side. The island's internal security would be ensured by UN police contingents or a reinforced international peacekeeping force, which could be financed by the savings in the republic's defence budget. The reduction of the enormous defence expenditure would allow the creation of a reconstruction fund for the run-down North, which could lead to its economic recovery in the medium term.

Cyprus has had a defence alliance with Greece since 1996. This has not changed the fundamental problem of the military situation: The huge geographical distance between Greece and Cyprus prevents an efficient air defence of Cypriot airspace by the Greek air force, whose planes would need over 30 minutes to appear over the island. In contrast, the flight time of the Turkish Air Force is about five minutes. The Greek planes would have to return to their base after a short time to refuel. A military airport planned near Paphos is of little help, as it would probably be the first target of the Turkish air force in the event of a conflict. It is doubtful whether the Russian anti-aircraft missiles ordered by the Cypriot government could completely prevent this. The situation is no better in the naval sector. Cyprus itself maintains neither air nor naval forces; Greek warships would probably encounter strong enemy action on the march to their area of operations near Cyprus. A deployment of Greek troops beyond the 900-strong contingent stipulated in the guarantee treaty is not permissible under international law and - should there be a secret attempt to send troops to Cyprus after all - would be extremely difficult to manage, since all Greek troops are subject to NATO.

On the other hand, the defence alliance links the Cypriot development with the development in the Aegean, which could have fatal consequences, considering the recent developments in this area (Imia crisis, Gavdos). Ankara believes that this has upset the military balance in the Aegean.[5] The previous Cypriot military doctrine was: stalling resistance until international crisis management by the UN and the USA became effective and the aggression was stopped. However, since it was not quite sure whether this would be effective in

---

1 Heinz A. Richter, "Eine neue Runde im Poker um Zypern: Varoşa versus Nicosia Airport" *THETIS* 1 (1994), pp. 108-18.

2 Thus in a letter from Glafkos Clerides to UN Secretary General Kofi A. Annan on 29 September 1997.

3 The order of S 300 anti-aircraft missiles in Russia does not contradict this; they are defensive weapons to ward off the total air supremacy of the Turkish Air Force in the event of a conflict.

4 S/1994/680.

5 *Cyprus Weekly* (14 November 1997), p. 4.

time, the defence alliance was concluded with Greece, which thus acquired a kind of reinsurance character. Whether this calculation will work out will hopefully never have to be seen. But even so, one gets the impression that this alliance calms the nerves of all Greek and Greek-Cypriot participants, which in turn allows for greater composure in critical situations and could thus have a friendship-saving effect.

There is a demographic problem in Northern Cyprus. At the time of partition in 1974, around 106,000 Turkish Cypriots had lived on the island. In the following years, due to the poor economic situation and political pressure, there was a strong emigration, mainly to Great Britain. According to Turkish Cypriot sources, a total of 70,000 people are said to have left the island.[1] Nevertheless, the number of Turkish Cypriots allegedly increased. The phenomenon can be explained by the settlement of 80,000 Anatolian Turks in Cyprus, which has already almost reached the number of Turkish Cypriots, according to information from Northern Cyprus.[2] Initially, Turkish Cypriots had welcomed the mainland Turks as liberators, but enthusiasm has since cooled considerably. Ankara's policy of changing the demographic composition through voluntary or forced settlement of Anatolian Turks outraged the Turkish Cypriots. Denktash's political course of constant favouritism towards the settlers, who form a large part of his electorate, has led to a process of alienation. Many see the immigrants as occupiers. The confrontation with the Turks of the motherland led many Turkish Cypriots to discover their own Cypriot identity and to realise that they had much more in common with their Greek compatriots than with the "Anatolians". The confrontation with the foreigners led to the fact that in the meantime even a discussion about "Cypriotness" has begun.[3] This discovery led to a growing understanding of the other side among some Cypriots on both sides. Both sides recognise where mistakes were made in the past and what fears the other side must have endured. This new attitude allows a rapprochement between the two communities on a new basis.

There are also new approaches in politics. In addition to Denktash, there are political forces in the north that are steering a different course and striving for a solution. A reasonable, Cypriot solution to the problem would be conceivable with the left-leaning Republican Turkish Party or the Communal Liberation Party of the former mayor of northern Nicosia, Mustafa Akinçi, who for years worked together with his colleague from the southern part of the city, Lellos Dimitriades, in the best possible way (Nicosia Master Plan). However, the path tried by the former chairman of the Republican Turkish Party, Özker Özgür, does not seem to lead to the goal. After electoral successes, Özgür had been prepared to participate in the government with his party and entered into a coalition with the ruling forces. He had to realise that even as deputy prime minister he could not move anything. Decisions were still taken by Denktash or the Turkish embassy. This led him to resign. At the same time, a policy directed against Denktash is also risky to a certain extent. Those who venture too far are punished. In 1996, when the Human Rights Commission of the Council of Europe allowed a complaint from Cyprus about violations of human rights by Ankara, a Turkish Cy-

1 *Zypern Nachrichten* 11:8 (November 1997), p. 2; in contrast, during the years of inter-communal unrest (1963-4), only 7,000 Turkish Cypriots left the island.
2 *Ibidem*, based on information in Sabah.
3 See the contributions by Kudret Akay in *THETIS* 2 und 4.

priot journalist, Kutlu Adali, who was prepared to testify as a witness in Strasbourg, was murdered.[1]

The solution to the overall problem lies with the National Security Council in Ankara, which is dominated by the military. Only when they consider a solution opportune will there be any change in Denktash's intransigence. For the south of the island, EU accession is a kind of life insurance. For the north of Cyprus, EU accession would not only bring economic advantages, but also a solution to the security problem, because human rights are normally respected in EU states. The government of Cyprus has made efforts over the last few years to bring its country on course for EU membership. Cyprus already fulfils all the accession criteria, and it will also be an economic asset for the EU, probably even becoming a net contributor. The only problem is its division. Denktash's threat that he would turn the north into a Turkish province if the Republic of Cyprus were to join unilaterally is not very credible. On the one hand, the north is already almost integrated into Turkey; on the other, Denktash would lose his status as president of an "independent state". Moreover, an annexation of the north of the island would snub the EU to such an extent that the door for Ankara to join the EU would be closed for a very long time.[2] The Turkish policy of non-solution is nearing its end. Cyprus will become an EU member in the not too distant future, making its borders external to the EU and thus inviolable.

Hopefully, certain European politicians will not give in to the demand of Turkish hardliners that EU accession should only take place after a solution and that negotiations should be suspended until a solution is reached. On the other hand, a policy that makes Turkish Cypriots victims of the EU-Turkey dispute should also be avoided. Both Cypriot societies are European societies in their political culture, and Europe should finally take note of this and act accordingly. The Cypriots have placed their hopes in Europe and have also psychologically prepared themselves for accession. Europe should reward them for this with a speedy accession.

---

1 *The Cyprus Weekly* (12 July, 1996), p. 7; (23 August, 1996), p. 1f.

2 The well-known Turkish journalist Ali Birand commented on this in the newspaper Sabah on 11 November 1997: *"If Turkey annexes the TRNC, the EU doors will be closed in Turkey's face and never opened again. Washington-Ankara relations, for their part, will suffer a major blow."* Zitiert nach *Cyprus Weekly* (14 November 1997), p. 4.

Band 60 **Heinz A. Richter,**
Griechenland 1950-1974. Zwischen Demokratie und Diktatur (2013) 600 Seiten, 125 Fotos, Hardcover, gebunden, € 49, ISBN 978-3-447-06908-3

Band 61 **Mihailo Popovic,**
Historische Geographie und Digital Humanities. Eine Fallstudie zum spätbyzantinischen und osmanischen Makedonien (2013) ca. 300 Seiten, 33 Abbildungen, 44 Karten, 8°, hard cover, ISBN 978-3-938646-49-6, € 32.-

Band 62 **Joachim Franz, Rosmarie Günther und Reinhard Stupperich (Hrsg.)**
„Ein Wald von Statuen" Kolloquium zum 20jährigen Bestehen der Antikensaal-Galerie in Mannheim und zur Begründung der Kurpfälzer Abguss-Sammlung vor 300 Jahren 300 Seiten, zahlreiche Abbildungen, Hardcover, gebunden, ISBN 978-3-447-10302-2, € 37.-

Band 63 **Harald Gilbert,**
Das besetzte Kreta 1941-1945 (2015) 404 Seiten, 47 sw und 8 farbige Abbildungen, 1 Landkarte, Hardcover, gebunden, € 49, ISBN 978-3-447-10186-8

Band 64 **Harry Cliadakis** (ed. Heinz Richter)
Fascism in Greece (2014) 147 pages, 34 photos, hard cover, threadbound, ISBN 978-3-447-10188-2, € 39.-

Band 65,1 **Heinz A. Richter**
Krieg im Südosten I, Gallipoli 1915 (2014) 340 Seiten, 120 Fotos, 17 Karten, 1 Faltkarte, gebunden, € 42, ISBN 978-3-447-10118-9

Band 65,2 ***Krieg im Südosten II, Makedonien 1915-1918*** (2014) 250 Seiten, 91 Fotos, 4 Karten, gebunden, € 35, ISBN 978-3-447-10249-0

Band 66 ***Von Mainz nach Kreta im Winter 1942-43. Das Reisetagebuch des "Künstlersoldaten" Rudo Schwarz.*** (2015) 150 Seiten, 91 Seiten mit Reproduktionen des Tagebuchs und von Skizzen, 51 Fotos, Hardcover, gebunden, ISBN 978-3-447-10304-6, € 32.- (ed. Heinz Richter)

Band 67,1 **Heinz A. Richter,** ***Geschichte Griechenlands im 20. Jahrhundert,*** *Band 1: 1900-1939,* (2015) 350 Seiten, 4 Karten, Hardcover, gebunden, 40 Euro, ISBN 978-3-447-10396-5

Band 67,2 **Heinz A. Richter,** ***Geschichte Griechenlands im 20. Jahrhundert,*** *Band 2: 1939-2004,* (2015) 467 Seiten, 9 Karten, Hardcover, gebunden, 49Euro, ISBN 978-3-447-10398-5

Band 68 **Heinz A. Richter** ***Griechenland 1915-1917 im Spiegel russischer Akten*** (2016) 118 Seiten, Hardcover, 28 Euro, 2015 ISBN 978-3-447-10612-2

Band 69 **Heinz A. Richter** ***Griechenland 1945-46. Die britische Intervention*** (2016) 456 Seiten, 39 Fotos, gebunden, 49 Euro, ISBN 978-3-447-10533-0

Band 70 **Heinz A. Richter** (ed.), *Griechenland 1942-43. Erinnerungen von Elisabeth und Konstantinos Logothetopoulos* (2015) 320 Seiten, 3 Abbildungen, Hardcover, 28 Euro, ISBN 978-3-447-10460-9

Band 71 **Johannes Fouquet** und **Lydia Gaitanou**, ***Im Schatten der Alten? Ideal und Lebenswirklichkeit im römischen Griechenland*** (2016) 193 Seiten, zahlreiche Karten und Fotos, gebunden, 40 Euro, ISBN 978-3-447-10450-0

Band 72 **Heinz A. Richter** ***Der griechisch-türkische Krieg 1919-1922*** (2016) 222 Seiten, 132 Fotos, 18 Karten, 1 Faltkarte, gebunden, 30 Euro, ISBN 978-3-447-10656-6

Band 73 **Heinz A. Richter** ***The Greek-Turkish War 1919-1922*** (2016) 211 pages, 132 photos, 18 maps, 1 folded map, hardcover, 30 Euro, ISBN 978-3-447-10671-9

Band 74 **Heinz A. Richter,** ***Mythen und Legenden in der griechischen Zeitgeschichte*** (2016) 116 Seiten, 19,80 Euro, ISBN 978-3-447-10703-7

Band 76 **Heinz A. Richter**, ***Hellas und Zypern in meinem Leben. Erinnerungen eines Zeithistorikers*** (2017), 236 Seiten, 56 Tafeln mit 128 Fotos, 30 Euro, ISBN 978-3-447-10846-1

Band 77 **Heinz A. Richter**, ***Geschichte der griechischen Linken***, 560 Seiten, 99 Fotos, gebunden, 50 Euro, 2017; ISBN 978-3-447-10846-1

Band 78 **Harald Gilbert**, ***Der Krieg in der Ägäis 1943-1944***, 340 Seiten Text, 32 Seiten Fotos, 16-24 Seiten Karten im Text, Hardcover, xx Euro, (2017); ISBN 978-3-447-10913-0

Band 79 **Heinz A. Richter**, ***Geschichte der zypriotischen Linken,*** 248 Seiten, 16 Tafeln mit 47 Fotos, gebunden, 30 Euro, ISBN 978-3-447-10867-6

Band 80 **Heinz A. Richter**, ***Die türkischen Meerengen in der internationalen Politik 1900-1917***, 300 Seiten, 32 Tafeln mit 77 Fotos, 7 Karten, 1 herausnehmbare Faltkarte, gebunden, 40 Euro, ISBN 978-3--447-10915-4

Band 81 **Vaios Kalogrias**, ***Die Sicherheitsbataillone 1943/44. Hitlers griechische Armee***. xxx Seiten, xx Tafeln mit xx Fotos, xx Karten, gebunden, ca. xx Euro, erscheint im Herbst 2019; ISBN 978-3-447-10917-8

Band 82 **Caroline M. Fischer**, ***Das Land der Griechen ... gefunden. Mein Leben im griechischen Alltag seit 1979. Erinnerungen,*** *Gedanken, Impressionen.* xxx Seiten, xx Tafeln mit xx Fotos, xx Karten, gebunden, ca. xx Euro, ISBN 978-3-447-10951-2

Band 83 **H. Richter - S. Dordanas - V. Kalogrias**, ***Ernst von Falkenhausen. Tagebuch des deutschen Militärattachés in Athen 1914 - 1916*** xxx Seiten, xx Tafeln mit xx Fotos, xx Karten, gebunden, ca. xx Euro,; ISBN 978-3-447-10952-9

Band 84 **Heinz A. Richter, *Das Osmanische Reich im Ersten Weltkrieg bis zum Friedensschluss 1924,*** 274 Seiten, 32 Tafeln mit 103 Fotos, 32 Karten, 1 herausnehmbare Faltkarte, gebunden, 40 Euro, ISBN 978-3-447-11038-9

Band 85 **Heinz A. Richter, *The Ottoman Empire in WWI until the Peace in 1923*** 256 pages, 32 plates with over 100 photos, 32 maps, 1 folded map, hard cover, 40 Euro, ISBN 978-3-447-11045-7

Band 86 **Heinz A. Richter, *Die Griechen im Osmanischen Reich 1913-1923. Ihre Verfolgung und Vertreibung* 198** Seiten, 32 Tafeln mit über 60 Fotos, 6 Karten, 1 herausnehmbar Faltkarte, hard cover, 40 Euro, ISBN 978-3-447-11131-7

Band 87 **Heinz A. Richter**, ***The Greeks in the Ottoman Empire 1913-1923. Their Persecution and Expulsion*** 188 pages, 32 plates with over 60 photos, 6 maps, one folded map in the back, hard cover, 40 Euro, ISBN 978-3-447-11150-8

Band 88 **Heinz A. Richter** (ed.), *Aspekte neugriechischer Geschichte* 132 Seiten, viele Fotos, hard cover, 30 Euro, ISBN 978-3-447-11132-4

Band 89 **Heinz A. Richter, *Modern Greek Myths*** 120 pages, hard cover, 19,80 Euro, ISBN 978-3-447--11165-2

Band 90 **Heinz A. Richter**, ***German-Greek Relation 1940-1960 and the Merten Affair*** 108 pages text, 28 photos on 12 pages, hard cover, 20; ISBN 978-3-447-11177-5

Band 91 **Heinz A. Richter, *Greece 1936-1946 Events and People*** 192 pages, numerous photos in the text, hard cover, 35 Euro, ISBN 978-3-447-11241-3

Band 92 **Heinz A. Richter**, **Greece 1947-1967 From Civil War to the Putsch on April 21, 1967** 190 pages, hard cover, 30 Euro,ISBN 978-3-447-11255-0

Band 93 **Heinz A. Richter**, **Operation Mercury the Occupation of Crete in May 1961** ca. 400 pages, hard cover, 45 Euro,ISBN 978-3-447-11323-6

Band 94 **Heinz A. Richter, Griechische Verteidigungsanlagen 1941. Die Metaxas-Linie**, 100 Seiten, 51 Fotos. 19 Karten, gebunden, 30 Euro ISBN 978-3-447-11378-6

Band 95 **Heinz A. Richter, Gallipoli 1915. The War in the Southeast 1** about 270 pages, 121 photos, 17 maps, 1 folded map, hard cover, 45 Euro ISBN 978-3-447-11393-9

Band 96 **Heinz A. Richter, Macedonia 1914-1918. The War in the Southeast 2** about 240 pages, 98 photos, 4 maps, hard cover, 39 Euro ISBN 978-3-447-11422-6

Band 97 **Heinz A. Richter, Greece in World War II** about 440 pages, 45 photos, 17 maps, hard cover, 45 Euro ISBN 978-3-447-11443-3

Band 98 **Eckhard Lisec, Tukish Armed Forces from Early History to Modern Times** about 120 pages, 45 photos, 17 maps, hard cover, 30 Euro ISBN 978-3-447-11443-3

Band 99 **Heinz A. Richter, Greece 1940-1950 The Time of the Civil Wars** about 470 pasges, 64 pages with photos, 20 maps , 1 folded map, hard cover, ISBN 978-3-447-11455-4

Band 100 **Andreas Sakkas**

Band 101 **Heinz A. Richter. Greece 1950-1974 between Democracy and dictatorship.** 479 pages, 48 pages with photos, 10 maps , hard cover, ISBN 978-3-447-11502-5

Band 102 **Heinz A. Richter, History of the Greek Left,** 495 pages, 32 pages with photos, maps,hard cover, ISBN 978-3-447-11526-1

Band 103/1 **Heinz A. Richter, History of Greece in the 20th Century**, vol.1, **1900.1939**,319 pages. 4 maps, hard cover, ISBN 978-3-447.11538-4

Band 103/2 **Heinz A. Richter**, **History of Greece in the 20th Century**, vol. 2 **1939-2004**, 9 maps

Band 104 **Heinz A. Richter, History of the Cypriot Left**, 219 pages, 16 pages with photos, hard cover ISBN 978-3-447-11566-7

Band 105 **Heinz A. Richter, Greek Military Lines of Defence 1941 The Metaxas Line**, 96 pages, 51 photos, 19 maps, 2 folded maps, hard cover, ISBN 978-3-447-11589-6

Band 106 **Heinz A. Richter, The Turkish Straits in International Politics**, 302 pages, 11 maps, 71 photos ISBN ISBN 978-3-447-11591-9